STAIRWAYS
TO
HEAVEN

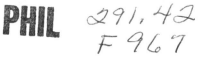

STAIRWAYS TO HEAVEN

Drugs in American Religious History

ROBERT C. FULLER

Westview Press
A Member of the Perseus Books Group

Copyright © 2000 by Westview Press, A Member of the Perseus Books Group

Published in 2000 in the United States of America by Westview Press, 5500 Central Avenue, Boulder, Colorado 80301-2877, and in the United Kingdom by Westview Press, 12 Hid's Copse Road, Cumnor Hill, Oxford OX2 9JJ

Find us on the World Wide Web at www.westviewpress.com

Library of Congress Cataloging-in-Publication Data
Fuller, Robert C., 1952–
    Stairways to heaven : drugs in American religious history / by Robert C. Fuller.
        p.   cm.
    Includes bibliographical references and index.
    ISBN 0-8133-6612-7
    1. Drugs—Religious aspects—History.   2. Drugs—United States—History.   3. United States—Religion.   I. Title.
BL65.D7F85   2000
291.4'2—dc21   99-059998
                                                                                                              CIP

The paper used in this publication meets the requirements of the American National Standard for Permanence of Paper for Printed Library Materials Z39.48-1984.

10   9   8   7   6   5   4   3   2   1

CONTENTS

Preface

Several years ago I published a book titled *Religion and Wine: A Cultural History of Wine Drinking in America*. Whenever I spoke on the topic, people in the audience would invariably ask about how drugs other than alcohol have factored into American religious life. Unfortunately, there hasn't been much written on the topic. This is interesting given that a great deal has been written about the use of drugs in Mediterranean, South American, and Asian religion. Several scholars have examined specific examples of religiously motivated drug use, but no one had yet attempted to pull these diverse materials together into a book-length history of this enduring theme in American religious life.

The subject matter in this book is one of the most fascinating in all of religious history. It is also one of the most controversial. The fact that even a tiny amount of LSD or mescaline can trigger mystical rapture raises challenging questions. What, after all, is an "authentic" religious experience? Is it possible that religious experiences are nothing more than aberrations in our brain chemistry? Or is it possible that the Kingdom of God is truly within us, but awaiting release through whatever means we can discover? Given the widespread cultural support for our government's "war on drugs," how far can we go in tolerating drug use under the banner of religious freedom? And, legal issues aside, how can we go about assessing what may or may not be the legitimate role of mood-altering substances in the development of mature spirituality? These are all issues that have a great deal of scholarly importance. They are also issues that have a great deal of relevance to the personal and public controversies that continue to be debated in our families, legislatures, and courts. For this reason I have tried to write a readable introduction to the topic that academic specialists will find of interest, but that nonspecialists will find enjoyable as well.

The principal thesis of this book is descriptive rather than evaluative in nature. That is, my purpose is to illuminate the many ways in which Americans have used drugs in their efforts both to induce religious ecstasy and to forge religious community. The wide-ranging examples that I have included in my study make it difficult to sustain a narrower argument. Only the most doctrinaire of scholars could impose a single theoretical outlook on the diverse connections between drugs and religion in American history. After all, the kind of interpretation one might have of a mainline Protestant church gathering for coffee after a worship service is quite different than, say, the use of LSD at a 1960s Be-In or the use of tobacco by Native Americans to solemnize an oath. Yet even though I have tried to write a primarily descriptive account of this topic, my narrative does focus attention on the ways in which religious beliefs and rituals have provided contexts for the use of drugs. It is my opinion that the presence of religious beliefs and rituals have—at least in certain contexts—enabled the use of drugs to have a spiritual significance that would otherwise be absent.

I have used the word "drugs" quite loosely throughout this book. For example, I refer to coffee, tobacco, peyote, and wine as drugs. First, this raises the issue that I chose not to refer to these drugs by specifying the presence of specific chemical agents such as caffeine, nicotine, mescaline, or alcohol. It seemed important to highlight the fact that people drink cups of coffee, not caffeine; smoke tobacco mixtures, not nicotine; ingest peyote, not mescaline; sip glasses of wine, not alcohol. Referring to the actual substances we consume as "drugs" is thus motivated in part by my concern with drawing attention to the broader cultural contexts that influence their meaning and significance.

It is also important to realize that many drugs contain dozens of chemical agents whose roles in altering our mental and emotional states are not yet understood. There are, for example, at least nine alkaloids in the button-like top of a peyote plant that exert some influence upon the experiential dimension of a peyote ritual. Although mescaline may have the most prominent psychoactive properties of these, it is by no means the only component of peyote that has enabled this cactus to be revered for its spiritual potential. It seems reasonable, then, to acknowledge both the cultural and pharmacological complexities of drug use by referring to coffee, tobacco, peyote, and wine as drugs.

A second issue related to identifying coffee and wine as drugs is that I have deliberately made no distinction between drugs that can be used legally and those that are currently illegal in the United States. These legal distinctions are arbitrary from a historical point of view and are thus somewhat irrelevant to this story (although the legal status of a drug surely influences the social settings in which it is consumed). We might note, for example, that many Christian churches currently utilize wine in their rituals and have a coffee hour at the end of their worship service. Yet, at other times in history, Christian officials have sought to have both of these substances legally banned. Peyote was used for centuries before predominantly Euro-American legislatures first tried to make its use illegal; now, both state and federal legislatures seem to be arguing that its use for spiritual purposes should be legal for Native Americans but not for other Americans. In short, the story of the relationship between religion and substances that help alter our moods or thoughts far surpasses any one era's legal distinctions.

Several people deserve to be recognized for their help and encouragement. Peoria attorney Robert Fahey dug up mounds of material concerning the legal issues that drug use raises in light of the Constitution's guarantee of the free exercise of religion. His genuine enthusiasm for the intricacies of these legal debates was as valuable as the information he gathered for me. My chairman, Tom Pucelik, and my dean, Claire Etaugh, continue to support my efforts to balance teaching and research. I continue to benefit from the advice and support of my colleagues Douglas Crowe, Kevin Teeven, and Kevin Stein. And, as always, Dave Pardieck listened politely as the project took shape and helped steer me in appropriate directions. Finally, I would like to thank my brother, Tom, to whom this book is dedicated. Tom's doctorate in psychology and his wide-ranging reading interests have enriched our many conversations over the years and have led to numerous new insights into the "religious psyche."

Robert C. Fuller

From the Plant Kingdom to the Kingdom of God

Long before humans first roamed the wilderness of North America, the plant kingdom was steadily laying the foundation for future evolutionary developments. Emerging about 3.2 billion years ago, plants quickly succeeded in covering the earth. The chlorophyll contained in plants enabled them to absorb and store the energy radiating from the sun. With this stored solar energy, plants became the principal fuel for the subsequent evolution of life on earth. That is, plants provided the basic building blocks necessary for the emergence of the animal kingdom. Plants supply animals with energy, vitamins, and minerals. Some plants even perform medicinal functions for the animal kingdom, helping to fight off infection, subdue pain, and stimulate the body's own regenerative processes. In short, plants form the biological substratum without which the animal kingdom could not exist.

In North America alone there are approximately 180,000 species of plants. A few of these display the ability to provide animals with more than energy, minerals, and therapeutic relief. These select plants, the "plants of the gods," exhibit the further ability to provide animals—particularly humans—with the experience of ecstasy.[1] Ecstasy-producing plants contain a number of psychoactive chemical substances. These chemicals act on the central nervous system in such a way as to produce a variety of unusual symptoms. Not all of these symptoms are pleasant. Dizziness, disorientation, and nausea are common. Yet some of these unusual symptoms have a curious attraction to humans. The vision of colorful lights, feelings of enhanced bodily energy, spontaneous laughter, and heightened sensory experience are among the many plant-induced symptoms that humans find pleasurable. Even dizziness and disorientation prove strangely appealing to persons who seek to transcend their common experience of the world.

The use of botanical and chemical substances to produce intoxication is one of the most fascinating behaviors observed throughout the animal kingdom. UCLA professor of neuropsychiatry, Ronald Siegel, makes a convincing case that the quest for intoxication should be considered one of the fundamental drives that motivate animal behavior.[2] Siegel argues that there is a natural force that motivates animals to pursue intoxication, sometimes to the point of overshadowing all other activities in life. Humans are certainly no exception. The drive for ecstatic intoxication is a near universal trait of the human species. Humans have developed quite ingenious methods for maximizing the ecstasy-producing potentials of the plant kingdom. We have also developed quite elaborate cultural explanations for the significance of these intoxicated states, frequently utilizing religious myth and ritual to associate these ecstasies with the gods themselves.

The story of North Americans' pursuit of ecstasy is by no means limited to the quest for simple intoxication. It is also very much a story about the different ways in which American culture has transformed plants and chemicals into entheogens. An entheogen (literally, to generate god or spirit within) is a botanical or chemical substance taken to occasion spiritual or mystical experience.[3] A peculiar property of some plants is the ability to foster an experience of having momentarily transcended our normal range of mental and emotional powers. Given the proper context, certain drugs have been understood to afford humans with a direct experience of a "higher" spiritual reality. In such contexts plants are more than just exhilarating. They also appear to disclose enlightenment; they momentarily narrow the gap between humans and the spiritual powers that are thought to animate our universe. In this sense, the use of drugs is often more about the quest for ecstasy than the quest for intoxication. Ecstasy, after all, means "to stand out or go beyond" one's normal state of being. Certain species of drugs have been valued by humans precisely for their ability to afford this sensation of stepping outside the confines of our physical senses. The quest for ecstasy is thus the quest to penetrate mystery, to make momentary contact with the divine kingdoms thought to surround us. And for this reason, the history of Americans' interest in ecstasy-producing plants is very much a chapter in their continued quest for spiritual understanding.

North America, though not particularly blessed with indigenous species of psychoactive plants, nonetheless has a lengthy history of using drugs to transport humans to the kingdom of the gods. Datura (jimson weed), the red bean or mescal bean, and potent strains of tobacco have historically been the most prevalent of the indigenous psychoactive plants. In some regions (particularly in areas adjacent to drug-rich Mexico), the mescaline-containing peyote cactus and mushrooms containing psilocybin and psilocin have also been included in Americans' treasury of ecstatic elixirs. Over time, a host of new drugs found their way into North American life. Alcohol, marijuana, LSD, coffee, and potent "pure forms" of both mescaline and psilocybin eventually came to supplement the botanical substances indigenous to the territories that now constitute the United States. The human inhabitants of North America, it seems, came to embrace the use of drugs not only for secular amusement but also for inducing sacred reverie. The plant kingdom not only forms the substratum of human existence, but it also provides humans their most vivid glimpses of the kingdom of heaven. The history of religion in the territories that now constitute the United States is, then, partially rooted in the ecstatic experiences first brought about by the plant kingdom's elixirs of ecstasy. The visions induced in these ecstatic flights have illuminated new passageways linking the worlds of plants, humans, and gods. And thus for several thousand years, Americans have ritually ingested sacred drugs in the fervent hope of ascending these stairways to heaven.

Elixirs of Ecstasy

North American attitudes toward elixirs of ecstasy have been shaped by cultural traditions from across the globe. Of the approximately 300,000 species of plants (estimates vary considerably) that make up the world's flora, at least 150 are known to be employed for their intoxicating properties. Nearly every society in world history has regarded at least one of these intoxicating plants as having religious significance. Plants provide humans experiences of ecstasy. That is, they take humans beyond the realm of reason and into states of supernatural awareness. The ecstatic states of consciousness induced by intoxicating plants are regarded by almost every culture as having extraordinary powers. Perhaps the most common power attributed to drug-induced states of ecstasy is that they bestow divinatory abilities, giving individuals access to otherwise hidden information about such matters as the location of lost objects, the identities of criminals, or the foreordained outcome of an anticipated hunt or battle. Clairvoyance, telepathy, and other paranormal mental powers are also frequently associated with the states of mind induced by intoxicating drugs. Many societies believe that ecstatic states give persons access to potent healing powers. And, finally, drug-induced states of ecstasy are also thought to be capable of transporting individuals to the spirit world, allowing them to communicate with ancestors and with divinities who influence human health or economic well-being. It follows that those who possess special knowledge of plants—the shamans and priests—are considered persons of extraordinary spiritual power. An entire community's physical, mental, and material well-being may depend upon the success with which they can ascend their magical stairways to heaven and restore productive relationships between the divine and human realms.

The many cultures that have flourished in what is now the United States have utilized ecstasy-producing botanical substances in their religious ceremonies. As we shall see in Chapter 2, the early inhabitants of North America valued aroused psychic states, attributing them to the active presence of gods or other spiritual powers. The earliest Native American cultures developed elaborate myths to explain the special connection between plants and the kingdom of the gods. Native American religions sought to influence the supernatural realm by using psychoactive plants in their ritual supplications. It was the duty of shamans (individuals who are capable of entering into trances that enable them to communicate with the spirit world) to acquire precise knowledge about sacred plants. The shamans were entrusted with the important cultural task of reducing the mysteries of the plant kingdom to what might be termed a "technology of ecstasy." Sacred plants such as datura, tobacco, and the peyote cactus were humanity's chief means of communing with the spirit world and were for this reason regarded with awe and respect.

North Americans did not, however, develop their attitudes toward entheogens in a cultural vacuum. As successive waves of immigrants came to North America, new cultural traditions emerged for the sacred use of the continent's indigenous elixirs of ecstasy. For example, many of the earliest inhabitants of the Pacific Northwest had migrated from regions of Asia. They brought with them a tradition of ecstatic shamanism that included the ritual use of such intoxicating plants as datura and the fly agaric mushroom. The use of the fly agaric mushroom, for example, had long been associated with

Asian cults of ecstasy.[4] And datura, probably introduced into China from India, had for centuries been associated with divinatory rituals and ecstasy-seeking meditation. There are, of course, many other Asian influences upon North American understandings of botanically induced ecstasy. For example, in more recent years a sizable number of people have emigrated to the United States from India, a nation that has a long history of employing elixirs of ecstasy in its religious rituals. In ancient Vedic times, Hindus utilized the intoxicating beverage soma to trigger ecstatic communion with the gods. Religious ascetics in India have historically relied upon both datura and cannabis to usher themselves into ecstatic trances in which they shed their former worldly identities and are regenerated as enlightened beings. Although it is doubtful that many Indian immigrants have directly introduced Americans to their culture's historic use of ecstasy-producing drugs, segments of the American reading public have been studying books on Hindu mysticism since the late nineteenth century.

The arrival of Africans and persons from the African diaspora communities throughout the Caribbean also brought beliefs and ritual practices that were to become important parts of American religious life. Although Africa is relatively poor in psychoactive plants, native religious traditions nonetheless valued certain elixirs of ecstasy for their ability to enable persons to see God or to communicate with the dead who inhabit the spirit world. In the wet tropical areas of west-central Africa, the ibago plant has been employed for centuries by shamans who seek assistance in communicating with the spirit worlds. In other parts of Africa, marijuana (cannabis), thorn apple (datura), and henbane have similarly been used for purposes of divination, healing, and communicating with the dead. As we shall see in Chapter 5, the Caribbean-based Rastafarians are a ready example of the ways in which African rituals for seeking ecstasy have been transplanted into American religious life.

Mexico and Central America have also contributed heavily to the historical development of religion in the United States. Indeed, much of the Native American use of hallucinogenic mushrooms and peyote was influenced by Mexican traditions. Datura, the mescal bean, *ayahuasca,* and the puffballs known by the Mixtecs as *gi-i-wa* are among the hallucinogens used for centuries by various Mexican societies. Marijuana, or cannabis, has also been regarded as having religious value (and a fair amount of twentieth-century marijuana use in the United States has its origins in the migration of Mexican workers across the Texas border in the 1920s). Of far greater importance to Mexican religious history has been the hallucinogenic mushrooms known by the Aztecs as *teonanacatl* ("divine flesh"). These mushrooms, belonging to the genus Psilocybe, contain the powerful chemical psilocybin. Psilocybin intoxication is characterized by the vision of dazzling arrays of colored lights, often shaped in intricate geometrical patterns. Rituals utilizing these sacred mushrooms have been ceremoniously practiced throughout Mexico and Central America for centuries. The ultimate goal is to diagnose illness, to see through to the spirit world, and to make contact with spiritual powers that will bring healing and worldly success.

The peyote cactus has similarly been revered in Mexico for its vision-giving powers. Although the use of peyote in the territory that is now the United States is fairly recent, peyote has been considered a sacred plant in Mexico for several hundred years. Peyote is a mescaline-containing cactus that is revered for its divinatory and healing powers. Much of what is known about the religious uses of peyote has been learned from the Huichol of northern Mexico.[5] Once a year the Huichol engage in a sacred "peyote hunt." The peyote hunt consists of a pilgrimage under the direction of the tribal shaman, who is thought to be in close contact with the oldest Huichol god, the Peyote-god. The shaman guides the pilgrims on their sacred journey, demanding that they fast, remain celibate, and adhere to the strictest standards of moral purity throughout the trek. When the peyote cactuses are finally found, offerings are made to the gods and preparations are made for a ceremony that takes place over several days and nights. Peyote ceremonies are carefully orchestrated affairs, replete with ritual chanting, dancing, and prayers to the gods and goddesses. The peyote ceremonies have many purposes: healing, divination, and procuring worldly prosperity through the blessings of the gods. But above all, peyote ceremonies facilitate a variation on traditional death-rebirth rites whereby persons can "die" to their former identities and be spiritually reborn. Peyote rituals are characterized by the participants' earnest desire to deepen their moral resolve and to become more spiritually pure. Toward this end the liturgy recited in peyote rituals frequently emphasizes utopian themes, promising participants that a new age is coming when all will be pure and the entire world will be morally regenerated. These traditional uses of peyote—as well as hallucinogenic mushrooms and marijuana—for the pursuit of spiritual goals have factored significantly into American religious life, as we shall see in Chapter 2.

Immigrants from Europe brought still other cultural traditions for utilizing intoxicating substances in their quests for heavenly paradise. As far back as ancient Greece, European cultures recognized the value of ecstasy-producing substances for producing mystical awareness. The wine used in Greek and Roman orgies, the hallucinogenic substances involved with the mystical rites at Eleusis, and the use of various members of the nightshade family by Greek and Roman priests reflect the ancient heritage of utilizing intoxicants for the purpose of triggering religious rapture. Medieval witchcraft similarly sustained a tradition of employing hallucinatory substances for the purpose of undertaking "journeys" to mysterious spiritual worlds. As we shall see in Chapter 4, Judaism and Christianity also bequeathed American religion a tradition of employing wine as vehicle for achieving both sacramental communion with God and communal solidarity with fellow believers. In colonial times, European merchants introduced coffee and the spirited atmosphere of coffeehouses. And, in more recent times, LSD migrated from the laboratories of a Swiss pharmaceutical company to the American religious underground.

All in all, Americans have engaged in a great deal of creative borrowing from their ancestral heritages. Nowhere is this any more evidenced than in the combination of "elixirs of ecstasy" that have provided Americans with religious exhilaration. And although much has been written about the role of hallucinogens in other world cultures, little attention has as yet been given to the various stairways that Americans have climbed in their pursuit of heavenly paradise.

Drugs and Two Sacred Worlds

What makes humans so fascinating is that we are both material and spiritual beings. We go through life alternating between the worldly and the heavenly, the profane and the sacred. In his 1956 classic, *The Sacred and the Profane*, Mircea Eliade explained how "the sacred and profane are two modes of being in the world, two existential situations assumed by humans in the course of history."[6] The profane "situation" is one that focuses exclusively on the material (economic and political) dimensions of life. To be profane is be thoroughly secular, eschewing the validity or importance of any religious outlook on life. It is worth noting in this context that the vast majority of drug-induced states of intoxication are restricted to the profane dimension of human existence. Drugs produce novel sensations that arouse curiosity and excitement. They also frequently bring physical pleasure, providing short episodes of bliss and a retreat from the stresses or strains of social existence. There is, in fact, little question that the economic and political structures of profane existence provide a context for much of the drug use in the United States. For example, a great deal of the consumption of coffee by contemporary Americans is motivated by a desire to be sharper and more productive at work. The consumption of alcohol, on the other hand, is often motivated by the desire to wind down from a day's activities, to reduce stress, and to rejuvenate oneself for the next day's work. In a similar way, patterns of drug use (especially alcohol) also seem to siphon off political dissent, keeping the working classes content with their lives and uninterested in political rebellion. Thus, a great deal of the use of drugs is motivated and maintained by decidedly profane, nonspiritual factors.

In contrast to our participation in the profane structures of existence, humans also live with an awareness of, and desire for, the sacred. The sacred orientation to life acknowledges a divine or holy reality that stands over and against the everyday, commonsense world of experience. Eliade followed Rudolf Otto's classic analysis of the "holy" as a distinct reality that confronts humans as awe-inspiring mystery. The holy has a numinous or mystical quality that appeals to our aesthetic senses.[7] The holy also confronts us as an overwhelming, superior power. To Eliade, "the sacred is equivalent to a power, and in the last analysis, to reality. The sacred is saturated with being."[8] Whoever adopts the sacred mode of being thus lives with an overriding awareness of a Sacred Reality that in some mysterious way surrounds the world of everyday experience. To live religiously is to yearn for special communion with this Sacred Reality. The sacred mode of existence is thus dominated by the quest for ecstasy, the quest for opening ourselves to a deeper communion with this Sacred Reality.

Importantly, there are two distinct ways in which a person can be introduced to a sacred perception of reality.[9] The first of these paths to the sacred has to do with an immediate experience of a Sacred Power. Such an experience is life transforming. It is experienced as an entirely different order of existence "breaking into" our everyday world of experience. The experience of a Sacred Power reorients our values. It also changes our understanding of the causes or forces that operate in the universe and therefore simultaneously changes our understanding of what is "real" and what affects our mental or physical well-being. Personal religious experience thus instantaneously ushers us into a sacred world. The second means of entering into a sacred world is that of living in a religious community. This second sacred world originates in the processes of socialization, comprising experiences in the home, places of worship, and with influential social groups.[10] Religious communities gradually create a variety of mechanisms for socializing persons into a sacred way of life. Myths, rituals, doctrines, and moral teachings are all intended to lead a person gradually into a lifestyle in which he or she finds harmony with a Sacred Reality. A religious community's "way of life" endeavors to transform people's thoughts, emotions, and actions in such a way as to usher them into a felt sense of living in harmony with a Sacred Reality.

The major thesis of this book is that in addition to all the ways in which drugs have factored into the pursuit of profane intoxication, they have also been intimately associated with Americans' desire to participate in the sacred. Certain botanical and chemical substances have, in the American context, been viewed as entheogens (i.e., substances used to occasion spiritual or mystical experience). And, importantly, the spiritual use of such drugs have factored significantly in both the sacred worlds of personal experience and religious community.

There is, perhaps, a tendency to focus on the role that drugs play in eliciting personal religious experiences. Anthropologist Felicitas Goodman has written that the common neurophysical basis of all religious experience is a particular kind of brain "tuning," the religious altered state of consciousness, a trance facilitating contact with an alternate reality.[11] There is, of course, a social basis or context underlying these religious trance states. Cultures have utilized fasting practices, ritual dancing, rhythmic music, and various breathing exercises to provide a specific context in which the resulting ecstasies are understood to have spiritual significance. Not surprisingly, drugs have also proven to be highly effective means for altering an individual's state of consciousness in such a way as to "tune" individuals into an alternate reality. Native American cultures utilized tobacco, datura, and peyote in ritual settings aimed to assist individuals in their vision quest. Nitrous oxide, mescaline, LSD, and marijuana have also been used by Americans eager to gain metaphysical illumination. And, too, coffee and alcohol (especially wine) have been intimately associated with Americans' quest for insight into a higher spiritual order.

The second sacred world is that transmitted to individuals through socialization into a living religious community. Religious communities seek to incorporate members into a distinctive way of life predicated upon their shared religious outlook. Rituals, communal activities, and formal instruction all aim at bonding individuals into an intact community of believers. Elixirs of ecstasy, too, have historically been instrumental in helping religious communities incorporate new members into their sacred visions of the world. For example, the early Israelite community lived in continuous awareness of the awesome presence and power of Yahweh. Over the years Hebrew scripture and moral precepts came to define what distinguishes a life dominated by this awareness of God's power and justice. Annual religious holidays, Sabbath observances, dietary customs, and a myriad of family practices all developed with the intention of inducting each new generation into the Jewish sacred world. No small part in this perpetuation of a living religious community has been the ritual presence of wine. Wine, originally associated with the ecstasies of Mediterranean religious cults, was preserved as an indispensable part of ushering persons into the sacred world of Jewish faith. This is, of course, also true of Christianity, which similarly made the drinking of wine central to its major sacrament. The amounts of wine used in both Judaism and Christianity are sufficiently small to minimize the risk of inducing ecstasy (and its antinomian tendencies). Yet the ritual context nonetheless links the use of wine with a sacred reality and thus facilitates a symbolic (rather than ecstatic) induction into the sacred world of shared beliefs and values.

Peyote, coffee, and marijuana have also been consumed in ritual contexts that help socialize Americans into a set of beliefs and values that constitute a sacred world. The use of peyote on Native American reservations forged communal solidarity over and against the more dominant white culture, while simultaneously affirming a religio-cultural vision that combined native traditions with Christian precepts. The sharing of marijuana by members of the '60s and '70s counterculture not only enabled persons to experience alternate realities but also to bond with fellow spiritual seekers. Coffeehouses provide both physiological exhilaration and important modes of social bonding that have factored significantly in the transmission of various strains of "alternative spirituality" in recent decades. The point here is that drugs are not only associated with the sacred world of private religious experience. When consumed in particular ritual settings, they are also avenues of communal bonding and communal affirmation. Throughout the course of American religious history, drugs of various kinds have repeatedly factored in the process whereby individuals are inducted into the sacred world of a living religious community.

The fact that the use of drugs is connected with both the profane and the sacred spheres of human life alerts us to what might be called the "politics of consciousness." As we noted above, there are strong social and economic factors that influence the patterning of Americans' use of such mood-altering substances as caffeine and alcohol. The nation's fierce commitment to competitive capitalism and its Puritan religious heritage have combined to extol the virtues of efficiency and productivity. Puritan piety, after all, calls for a tight control over our emotions and a single-minded devotion to rational self-control. In this way the Puritan religious outlook helped give rise to the inner-worldly asceticism that Max Weber argues made possible the rise of capitalism as we know it. That is, the Puritan outlook helped discipline consciousness for the relentless pursuit of efficiency and instrumental rationality. As a consequence, the profane dimensions of American culture foster a deep suspicion of nonutilitarian modes of thought or life. A culture that places paramount importance on the repression of spontaneity has no normative place for aesthetic delight, the enjoyment of emotions or sensations for their own intrinsic value. And thus the pursuit of intoxication through the use of botanical or chemical substances has always been viewed with suspicion in the politics of profane American culture. Drug use can be sanctioned as long as it ultimately serves the greater causes of economic efficiency and orderly control (e.g., coffee consumption at the work place, moderate alcohol consumption to unwind and regenerate oneself for the next business day), but not when it interferes with these prime values of our secular culture.

The politics of consciousness is even more pronounced in the sacred sphere of American life. As anthropologist Marlene Dobkin de Rios has shown, entheogens are generally valued to the degree that a society considers firsthand religious experience to be the true way to knowledge.[12] For example, Native American cultures historically recognized that shamans must have the ability to "travel" to the spirit world. It followed, therefore, that Native Americans viewed "elixirs of ecstasy" with awe and acclaim. In fact, many Native American societies encouraged all males to engage in a vision quest, making the ritual use of drugs even more "democratized" and pervasive. In these contexts, the use of drugs is completely congruous with the sacred world endorsed by the culture as a whole. However, not all societies value firsthand religious experience. Many religions restrict access to the sacred to a specific class of officials (whose status is often conferred according to doctrinal and bureaucratic criteria unrelated to their ability to themselves enter into ecstatic religious states). Religious cultures that restrict access to the sacred world of personal experience typically discourage use of entheogens. The use of drugs in such cultural settings is thus often an expression of defiance or rebellion against the reigning religious establishment. The process of religious innovation often focuses upon an individual or individuals who emerge as prophets of a new sacred order. A prophet is an agent of religious change who takes the responsibility for announcing a break in the established normative order. To legitimate this break, the prophet must invoke a source of spiritual authority. Not surprisingly, this authority is often grounded in the prophet's personal experiences of the sacred, experiences in which he or she claims to see, feel, or touch a sacred reality independently of the religious establishment and its ordained officials. As we shall see in Chapters 3 and 5, much of the use of marijuana and LSD in the '60s and '70s fits this pattern. Individuals who found that their spiritual needs were not being met by the existing religious institutions turned to the counterculture for the ideas and experiences that would yield metaphysical illumination. And thus, just as drug-induced mystical states can be used to sustain the existing religious order, they can also be used to legitimate rebellion against this order.

Perceiving God in the Natural Order

The following chapters examine the historical record of the role that drugs have played both in fostering personal religious experience and in helping to create social solidarity among the members of religious communities. It is important, however, that we remind ourselves that a great deal of religion in the United States exists outside of churches, temples, and synagogues. And while some drugs have functioned in the two sacred worlds associated with America's "churched" religions, others have functioned in the service of what might be called "unchurched" religion.

This is particularly true in connection with what religious historians term "nature religion." Nature religion has been a persistent theme in American religious history.[13] It is a form of spirituality that is independent of the doctrines or rituals of institutional religion. Nature religion doesn't define spirituality in terms of church attendance or adherence to any specific creed. Nor does it possess a sacred scripture or claim to have been granted absolute knowledge in the form of revealed truths. Instead, nature religion looks to human experience for intuitive knowledge of God. It is based upon the conviction that God is always and everywhere available to humans, if we but learn to become receptive to the subtle presence of divine spirit in and through the natural order. Whereas the biblical religion of America's churches stresses the transcendence of God, nature religion is based upon experiences of God's immanence. And, importantly, whereas biblical religion teaches that there is a gulf or chasm separating humans from God, nature religion is a form of spirituality that sees the "natural" and "supernatural" as intimately connected orders of life.

The term *nature religion* is applicable whenever a form of spirituality is based upon the belief that "contact" with God can be initiated within nature. What distinguishes nature religion from the revealed religions of Judaism and Christianity, then, is this conviction that every human being can awaken to the presence of a divine power. Religious orthodoxy in both Judaism and Christianity teaches that any contact between the human and divine realms must be initiated by God (or perhaps one of God's angelic messengers). The gulf separating humans from God is traditionally thought to be bridgeable only by divine intervention such as might happen in a biblical miracle or in the delivering of divine revelation. This explains in part why religious institutions are wary of mysticism among its members. The claim to mystical experience by lay members is an implicit challenge to the authority of the ordained clergy who are entrusted with guarding orthodoxy. Mystical experiences imply that these individuals—on their own—have learned to initiate "contact" with the divine. This helps to explain why religious institutions often develop negative attitudes toward ecstasy-producing drugs (even when drug-induced mystical states were prevalent in the early development of this religion). Prohibitions against drugs are, as anthropologist Mary Douglas has demonstrated, frequently motivated by the desire to prevent individuals from having direct access to the divine.[14] Conversely, advocacy of drug use to obtain religious experiences is often an expression of commitment to some version of nature—rather than churched or biblical—religion.

Nature religion, because it affirms that God is already present throughout the natural order, tends to have an aesthetic and often even mystical tone. A particular kind of inner receptivity is required to experience the sacredness of our natural universe. Nature religion thus presupposes our ability to become receptive to dimensions of experience that exist at a deeper level than the physical senses alone can afford. Historian William Clebsch uses the phrase "aesthetic spirituality" to refer to this enduring strand of unchurched American religious life. An aesthetic spirituality, in Clebsch's view, promotes a "consciousness of the beauty of living in harmony with divine things."[15] This consciousness of living in harmony with an immanent divinity can be thought of as existing along a scale or continuum. This scale ranges from simple aesthetic delight in nature's pristine pleasures to ecstatic encounters with divinity. Indeed, some forms of nature religion are decidedly nonecstatic. For example, most wildlife and ecological enthusiasts revere the sacredness of pristine nature on what might be considered a philosophical rather than mystical basis. And, too, many adherents of popular psychologies affirm the sacredness of every person even though they have never been overwhelmed by the awesome and mysterious power that Rudolf Otto associates with experiences of the holy. Viewing nature as "the symbol of spirit" often grows out of calm deliberation. Striving to live in harmony with nature can have religious significance without entailing any overriding desire for ecstatic communion with a more-than-worldly power.

Importantly, however, nature religion has an inherent tendency to quest for more ecstatic forms of mystical experience. Nature religion implies that every human being has the potential to experience a vivid connection with the divine spirit that flows through all things. Thus, when the nineteenth-century philosopher and mystic Ralph Waldo Emerson went alone into nature, he was moved to the mystical realization that the individual human mind can open itself to the influence of a divine power. Emerson wrote that in such moments, "all mean egotism vanishes. I become a transparent eyeball; I am nothing; I see all; the currents of the Universal Being circulate through me; I am part or parcel of God."[16] With these words Emerson voiced what might be called the ecstatic form of nature religion.

Emerson was claiming that there are particular states of consciousness that create a connection between the divine and human realms. When "mean egotism" or the normal mind-set of everyday life is temporarily set aside, we make ourselves receptive to a range of sensations that are ordinarily excluded from awareness. Such nonegoistic states of consciousness enable us to become receptive to what Emerson described as "an influx of Divine Mind into our mind."[17] Mystical ecstasy is thus an imminent possibility of experience. The path to achieving full communion with God is one that leads right through our own minds.

A major premise of nature religion is that a mystical encounter with a divine reality is ever available at the margins of human awareness. In Emerson's words, religious insights "arise to us out of the recesses of consciousness."[18] An aesthetic spirituality is thus inherently drawn to activities that move the mind along the continuum leading to these recesses. Contemplation of nature, artistic creation, and meditation have all been embraced as vehicles for facilitating mystical receptivity. Native American cultures have also appreciated the role that fasting, chanting, dancing, and tortuous ordeals might have in awakening persons to the realm of spirit. The youth counterculture of the '60s and '70s recognized how a fusion of rhythmic music and vibrant lights alters the senses and triggers new forms of perception. Devotees of contemporary coffeehouses are cognizant of how the aesthetic arrangement of visual art and background music establish a certain mood capable of awakening a deeper appreciation of human relationships.

Those who yearn for a closer harmony with nature's sacred depths are attentive to those conditions that permit us easier access to the "recesses of consciousness." And this, of course, is precisely why certain drugs have been a continuous part of American religious history. Tobacco, datura, peyote, LSD, marijuana, wine, and coffee have all been seen as vehicles to direct, personal mystical experience. These elixirs of ecstasy are believed to be mind-manifesting, mind-expanding. They are thought to open up a range of sensations ordinarily relegated to the margins of awareness. And, in so doing, they give persons a communion with nature and a divine reality that is beyond the mind's ordinary reach.

The story of drugs and American religious life is surely a fascinating one. The use of ecstasy-producing drugs both within established churches and in the many unchurched forms of nature religion testifies to our nation's enduring quest for the sacred worlds of experience and community. There is both inspiration and puzzlement in the fact that a few button-like tops from a peyote plant can instantaneously open the doors of the kingdom of God. What does it mean, after all, if such dramatic religious epiphanies can be produced by ingesting various species of the plant kingdom? Are all mystical experiences and all visions of the kingdom of God nothing more than the malfunctioning of our neural chemistry caused by a botanical agent? Or are the advocates of entheogens correct that the kingdom of God is already within us but awaiting to be brought forth from the recesses of our mental nature? Still other questions abound: How philosophically reliable are the insights gained from drug-induced ecstasies? Given the threat that drugs pose to society, can we afford to let individuals procure, distribute, and use them under the banner of religious freedom? Are drug-induced experiences compatible with mature spiritual development?

Clear and definitive answers to these questions are difficult to come by. Yet the questions illuminate the underlying issues raised by Americans' historic quest for ecstatic communion with a power greater than themselves. The history of religion in America is at least in part the story of how persons have sought pathways that might lead from the kingdom of nature to the kingdom of God. And thus this study of Americans' attraction to various elixirs of ecstasy provides important clues about our enduring search for stairways to the heaven of mystical experience.

2

The Native American Heritage

In 1968 Carlos Castenada published *The Teachings of Don Juan: A Yaqui Way of Knowledge*. The book purported to be based upon Castenada's field notes taken during his four years of participant-observer research into Yaqui Indian beliefs and practices. Initially published through a university press, the book seemed destined to sell only a few hundred copies to scholars and research libraries. As it turned out, however, Castenada's book became a phenomenal commercial success and the lead volume in a best-selling series that initially included *A Separate Reality: Further Conversations with Don Juan* (1971) and *Journey to Ixtlan: The Lessons of Don Juan* (1972).[1] These three volumes were later followed by others with titles such as *Tales of Power, The Fire from Within,* and *The Power of Silence.* By the mid-1970s Castenada had sold more than eight million books purporting to introduce American reading audiences to the esoteric wisdom he had learned directly from a Native American "man of knowledge."

What Americans learned from Castenada's books was that Native American culture relied heavily upon hallucinogenic drugs to gain "insight into a world not merely other than our own, but an entirely different order of reality."[2] Castenada explained in detail how his spiritual mentor, Don Juan, used psychoactive plants to open "the doors of perception to a world of 'non-ordinary reality' completely beyond the concepts of western civilization."[3] More specifically, Don Juan was adept at using peyote *(Lophophora williamsii)*, jimson weed *(Datura stramonium)*, and a hallucinogenic mushroom *(Psilocybe mexicana)*. Under Don Juan's tutelage, Castenada also learned to use these drugs to journey beyond the boundaries of normal human perception. His ultimate goal was to learn to "see" reality in a new way, a way that revealed the true nature of our universe.

The story of Castenada's apprenticeship under Don Juan makes for exciting reading. When Castenada was under the influence of these psychoactive drugs, he would journey to a world inhabited with spirit beings appearing in the form of animals or monster-like creatures. These encounters were fraught with drama and intellectual mystery. He might on one occasion be attacked by these spirit creatures. On the next occasion they might query him and instigate a series of philosophical discoveries.

Castenada's drug-fueled journeys into the spirit world gradually enabled him to acquire the ability to "stop the world." "Stopping the world" meant freeing himself from social conditioning. It seems that his experiences with hallucinogenic drugs provided him with new perspectives on how society programs us to think and feel. The ability to enter into alternative mental states helped relativize the cognitive map that society had been instilling in him since birth. In this way Castenada learned to erase his personal history and recreate himself in ways that cast aside the limitations and restrictions that bourgeois culture tries to impose upon us. To be a man of knowledge, then, is to be able to disentangle oneself from social conditioning and to have the power to create one's own reality.

Castenada's readers were fascinated by the accounts of his drug-induced experiences with "states of nonordinary reality." His books were published in an era that witnessed unprecedented interest in non-Western religions, altered states of consciousness, and esoteric philosophies dealing with the hidden powers of the mind. What Castenada did was to bring nostalgia for Native American cultures into this same metaphysical complex. Castenada's journey to become a "man of knowledge" was spiritually inspiring and whetted Americans' interest in both the expansive powers of drugs and the neglected wisdom of Native American culture. With Don Juan's teachings as their most ready example, Americans simply took it for granted that Native American culture was rife with drug-ingesting "men of knowledge," whose experiences might help any of us learn to connect with a separate reality. Native Americans, it seemed, had much to teach about how drugs might be used to obtain mysterious, life-enhancing powers.

Castenada, of course, is hardly to blame for the popular misconception that hallucinogenic drugs have been a dominant theme in American Indian religion. After all, Castenada never suggested that his account of a Yaqui Indian's experiences of "nonordinary reality" represented *the* Indian means of making contact with the spirit world. Nor should his readers be blamed if they made a few unwarranted generalizations from Don Juan's seeming insistence upon using hallucinogenic drugs to make contact with nonordinary reality. The general public knows relatively little about Native American religion. Hollywood images of Indians sitting in a tipi and smoking from a pipe is about as much as most Americans know about Native American rituals. A little exposure to Castenada-type literature is probably sufficient to raise the general impression that those pipes were always filled with hallucinogenic materials. Such, however, has not been the case—past or present. It is true that over the course of Native American history there have been numerous instances in which intoxicating drugs have been employed to enter into ecstatic states. Their use, however, has been far more limited than Castenada's works would lead us to expect. Moreover, even when intoxicating drugs have been used, their influence has been more determined by cultural heritage than by any properties of the drugs themselves. It is important, therefore, that we review a few central themes of Native American religion and the ways in which it bestows sacred status on certain kinds of ecstatic experience.

The Pursuit of Ecstasy in American Indian Religion

It is difficult to make generalizations about Native American religion. The main reason for this is that the terms "Native American religion" and "Native American culture" imply some kind of unity among the thousands of ethnic groups that inhabited North America prior to European settlement. The fact is that these groups were separate and distinct societies. They used hundreds of different languages. They were geographically separated, thus inhabiting quite different climatic regions. Some were hunting and gathering societies, whereas others developed fairly advanced agricultural economies. We are also dealing with traditions that developed over the 15,000 to 20,000 years since these various peoples first arrived on the North American continent. Few statements apply to all of these cultures. There is, therefore, no such thing as *the* Native American religious tradition.

Another difficulty in generalizing about Native American religion is the fact that we have relatively few historical sources of information. Although the history of the people we commonly refer to as "Indians" spans nearly 20,000 years, we have written sources from only the last four hundred. And, unfortunately, the majority of these were written by Christian missionaries and settlers whose accounts are blatantly biased. We do have access to considerable archaeological materials, including numerous artifacts and symbols used in ancient religious rituals. However, because most Indian societies were not literate, there are gaping holes in our understanding of these materials. There is very little that we can confidently conclude about the meaning of the various religious symbols bequeathed to us in archaeological remains.

Fortunately, the past sixty years have produced a number of excellent studies of the rituals and traditions of individual tribes. These works have provided sufficient understanding to permit cautious statements about thematic elements that appeared in one form or another in the vast majority of North American tribal cultures. One of the most respected scholars of religion among the American Indians, Ake Hultkrantz, suggested that

> the Indian religious perspective centers around the supernatural world, populated by gods and spirits but also by human beings, animals, plants, and inanimate objects, for the supernatural breaks through into the everyday world. Its foremost means of expression is supernatural power, at times perceived as a specific, defined potency, at times merely experienced as a psychological reality underlying supernatural occurrences.[4]

Hultkrantz pointed out two important features of American Indian religion: belief in the existence of a supernatural world and belief that this supernatural world expressed itself in various forms of supernatural power. These two beliefs provide a helpful starting point for understanding why most Native American societies valued ecstatic states of consciousness and, in turn, why these societies valued certain rituals that employed drugs for religious purposes.

As Hultkrantz observed, American Indians have traditionally believed in a variety of natural and supernatural powers. Many Native American societies recognized a high god (creator god). Although often conceived as distant or removed from everyday human life, this god was responsible for the breath of life in every creature. Much closer to everyday concern were the multitude of spirits and powers connected with our natural world. The entire natural order was considered to be under the control of numerous spirits and powers. These spirits could cause illness or health, affect the cycle of planting and harvesting, control the weather, or influence the outcome of battles. Although many spirits were understood to be individual entities, there was also a tendency to recognize the existence of a certain impersonal "power" permeating all living things—a sacred power that could be either helpful or harmful to humans depending upon how it was approached. As one scholar of world religions put it, "the attitude of the American Indian toward the forces in nature seems to have been similar to that of modern persons toward electricity. That is, the forces are unseen and may be helpful if handled properly; if they are not handled properly these forces can be extremely dangerous."[5]

In short, Native American peoples traditionally viewed the world as surrounded by unseen spirits and powers whose actions affected their everyday well-being. The ability to establish harmonious relationship and connection with this unseen realm of power was therefore the key to efficacious living. The need for such a relationship or connection emerged in almost every kind of relationship with the surrounding natural order. Thus, for example, nearly every human endeavor required the guidance provided by some form of divination. Native Americans needed to discern the disposition of particular spirits or powers before hunting, going into battle, or entering into an important agreement. The desire to exert control over the weather or to influence agricultural cycles also gave urgency to the quest for establishing special connection with supernatural agents.

One of the most important Native American rituals for heightening one's relationship to spiritual power was the "vision quest." Many Native American cultures believed that important undertakings should be guided by a vision. Deciding to go to war, making warriors brave in battle, changing tribal customs, engaging in important hunts, curing sick friends and relatives, asking favors of the spirits or high god, and bestowing names upon children were some of the activities thought to necessitate the guiding authority of a sacred vision. A principal goal of the vision quest, particularly among the Plains Indians, was procuring a guardian spirit. Among the Plains Indians, visions were thought to serve as a means of cultivating connection with a tutelary spirit who could protect and guide individuals as they confronted the dangers of everyday living.

Visions were especially significant at major rites of passage, such as puberty rituals during which the tribe recognized the transformation of a boy into a full-fledged member of the adult community. From a very young age, a young boy knew that he must eventually undergo a major transformation, which required that he go alone into the wilderness to seek a vision from the spirits. Undertaking this solitary quest for a vision was a physical, emotional, and social ordeal. This ordeal was ritually structured in such a way as to link the individual with the tribe's system of beliefs and meanings. This ritual required several days of fasting. In some societies, minor bodily torture was included to help simulate the "death-rebirth" transformation the young boy was about to undergo. Deprived of food, water, social support, and shelter from the elements, the young man awaited the vision in solitude. If the vision did not come after several such days of asceticism, the initiate might even inflict wounds upon himself to become properly humble before the world of spirits. Finally, the spirits would come, often in the form of animals or mythic figures. The appearance of these spirits was positive proof that his new status had been blessed and empowered by the spirit world, bestowing upon him the status of an adult member of the tribe.

Hultkrantz noted that there were two types of visions: spontaneous and solicited.[6] The spontaneous vision appeared suddenly and unexpectedly (often in a dream). Such visions were most likely to come to the tribal shamans, those individuals with particularly close relationship with the spirit world. Solicited visions were more common. Indians also learned to use various forms of ascetic measures to help induce visions (particularly those related to major rites of passage). Fasting, isolation, and prayer are the principal avenues for pursuing a vision. Sometimes steam baths or different means of mortification or self-torture were employed.

Although the vision quest was ordinarily an individual undertaking, some tribal societies (particularly among those of southern California) sought visions in a collective or societal way. Such vision quests typically utilized dancing, singing, and drumming. The songs used were ordinarily simple, consisting of a few lines repeated over and over again. The effect of hours of song and steady rhythmic beating upon the nervous system gradually induced a reverie conducive to contact with the spirit world.

Drugs were also occasionally employed in Native American vision quests. It should be emphasized, however, that many tribes made little or no use of psychoactive botanical substances to induce visions. Indeed, a great deal of North American religion was not particularly ecstatic. Yet, as we shall examine more fully in the following sections, the historical record indicates that some Native Americans have employed dozens of botanical materials in their quests to make contact with the spirit world. The important point here is that the Native American belief in the supernatural world and supernatural power bestowed great importance upon vision-like states of consciousness in which an individual might experience a particularly close connection with these powers. To this extent, then, Native American cultures created a religious complex that gave sacred meaning to botanical substances capable of assisting individuals in their quest for visionary contact with the spirit world.

Healing was yet another important sphere of life associated with procuring a special connection to the spirit world. Native American cultures traditionally attributed a vast number of diseases to supernatural factors. It was believed that disease could be caused by the breaking of a tribal taboo, soul loss, spirit possession, or various forms of what is known as "object intrusion" (i.e., the belief that either an offended spirit or a malevolent sorcerer had the supernatural ability to transmit a foreign object into a person's body in such a way as to cause illness). The diagnosis and cure of illness had to take into account such religious or supernatural factors. To be sure, Native American medicine recognized literally thousands of botanical remedies for the relief of pain and the stimulation of bodily healing. However, it was also important that the medicine man be able to receive visions from the spirit world and, in most cases, receive guidance from the spirits (who often took the form of an animal, such as a bear or a badger). For example, a medicine man's spirit might give him visions concerning how the ill person's behavior had violated tribal taboo. The medicine man could then use this information to give patients moral instructions concerning how they might bring their behavior into line with tribal custom. In this way, the healer's ecstatic contact with the spirit world could have important consequences both for healing individuals and for preserving social harmony.

In many cases, the tribal medicine man was able to perform his therapeutic duties without entering into any ecstatic trance. In other instances, however, the medicine man needed to possess exceptionally strong connections with helping spirits. This was particularly true in cases where either soul loss or object intrusion was involved in the etiology of the illness. Even in tribal societies that encouraged all individuals to have visions, the medicine man needed to be more religiously and mystically gifted than others. The medicine man had to be able to gain access to, and control, extraordinary supernatural power.

It is for this reason that the medicine man frequently came to dominate the religious life of Native American societies. It is also for this reason that we frequently refer to Native American medicine men by the term *shaman*. The term shaman comes from an Asian (Tungusic) word referring to individuals who, with the help of guardian spirits, attain ecstasy in order to create rapport with the supernatural world on behalf of members of his social group. Shamans help in many ways other than healing. They might, for example, help control the weather, resolve interpersonal disputes, or provide various kinds of divination services.

It is important to note that the terms "medicine man" and "shaman" are not exactly interchangeable even though a great deal of scholarly literature uses them as synonyms.[7] The distinguishing trait of a shaman is his (or in some tribes, her) use of ecstatic devices to enter into psychologically distinct states in which he can mediate between the natural and supernatural worlds. Because medicine men needed to deal with illnesses of supernatural causation, they frequently needed to avail themselves of shamanic practices.[8] However, not all medicine men made recourse to ecstatic states of consciousness. The two terms should thus probably be distinguished. Yet the common practice of using the terms interchangeably is helpful in that it draws attention to the fact that Native American medical and religious life were historically dominated by what might be called the shamanic complex. The concept of shamanism draws attention to the interrelated nature of Native American belief in (1) the supernatural world, which contains spirits and power, (2) the ability of some individuals to use ecstatic techniques to enter into extraordinary states of consciousness that produce contact with the supernatural world, and (3) the further possibility of using the power gained by such contact with the spirit world for the good of the social group.

The noted historian of religion, Mircea Eliade, has argued that "pure shamanism"—especially as it was classically practiced in Siberia—does not make recourse to drugs in the pursuit of these ecstatic trances. Eliade believed that drumming, fasting, praying, and various forms of self-deprivation are the only proper techniques for inducing shamanic trance. Eliade maintained that the use of drugs represents a "vulgarization" of shamanic trance.[9] Narcotic intoxication, he argued, is an "easy way" of imitating shamanic trance, but it fails to duplicate the authentic states reached through the "difficult ways" of classic shamanism. The facts, however, do not support Eliade's contention. Archaeological evidence indicates that the use of various hallucinogenic substances for shamanic activity dates back to antiquity.[10] And although not all Native American shamans used psychoactive botanical substances, the majority did—at least if one includes the ubiquitous presence of tobacco.

The Native American religious heritage, then, centered around the supernatural world that suffuses the world of everyday life. The gods, spirits, and power of this world had great influence over worldly affairs. They controlled everything from health to the weather, from the outcome of a hunt to the degree of harmony present in social relationships. Achieving harmony and felicitous connection with these powers was thus central to Native American religion. And, as we have seen, American Indians held great reverence for certain ecstatic states of consciousness in which this connection was vitally realized. The seeking of a guardian spirit, vision quests, healing rituals, and numerous agricultural ceremonies all required the attainment of an exceptional state of mind that established contact with the invisible spiritual world. In many societies, it fell upon the shaman to perform these ecstatic flights of the soul. Yet, in other tribes and particularly among the Plains Indians who lived in the region ranging from the Rocky Mountains to the eastern woodlands, all males were expected to engage in vision quests and to have personal connections with the spirit world. And thus American Indians were particularly disposed to have great reverence for the botanical substances that would help induce these exceptional states of mind.

The New World "Narcotic Complex"

The cultural importance of drugs in Native American societies is underscored by Harvard botanist Richard Schultes's finding that whereas New World natives knew eighty to a hundred mind-altering drugs, the Old World had only about a half dozen.[11] This statistical anomaly is particularly interesting when we consider that common sense would suggest the reverse to be true. After all, the Old World has far greater landmass than the New World and contains an even wider variety of climates. Moreover, the overall number and diversity of food plants are reasonably balanced between the Old World and the New World. And, too, humans have existed for an incomparably longer period in the Old World than in the New, giving them far greater likelihood to have discovered and identified psychoactive plants.

Anthropologist Weston La Barre has made a compelling argument that this discrepancy in use of psychoactive drugs can be explained in cultural terms.[12] La Barre's thesis was that there were cultural factors that predisposed North Americans to be more interested in identifying intoxicating plants. More specifically, La Barre pointed to what he called a "narcotic complex" underlying Native American cultural systems:

> The striking discrepancy between the Old and New Worlds in the numbers of known psychotropic plants must rest on ethnographic rather than botanical grounds. It is, in fact, the ubiquitous persistence of shamanism in aboriginal hunting peoples of the New World that provides the solution. . . . It is simply that in the Americas the hunting base of shamanism has been better preserved to "ethnographic present" times. . . . It should be noted that ecstatic-visionary shamanism is, so to speak, *culturally programmed for an interest in hallucinogens and other psychotropic drugs.*[13]

Despite the fact that his assumption concerning the persistence of an aboriginal hunting base in North American tribal societies was a bit tenuous, La Barre was undoubtedly correct that certain cultural forces favored the continuing existence of a "narcotic complex" in the New World. Indeed, the religious elements of Native American culture bestowed normative status upon certain extraordinary states of mind. And, in turn, Native Americans sought to enhance these extraordinary states of mind through the use of psychoactive (what La Barre termed psychotropic) drugs.

One way of illustrating the cultural differences between Old World and New World attitudes toward ecstatic states of consciousness is by examining the numerous accounts of Native American culture written by Catholic priests. When Catholic priests, the "official emissaries" of Old World culture, first encountered psychoactive drugs in the Americas, they were certain that they were observing the work of the devil. Their descriptions of drug use in the New World were far more concerned with theological denunciation than empathic understanding. One reason for this is that by the time of Christopher Columbus, European religious life was highly bureaucratized. This brought the attainment of exceptional states of mind under the regulation of the Christian church. Ecstatic states were thought to be restricted only to those under the careful control of the Church, such as those individuals who inhabited monasteries. The common believer participated only symbolically in such visions of heavenly bliss. There were, of course, occasional outbursts of interest in mystical and ecstatic religion. Movements such as the Begards, the Brethren of the Free Spirit, and the "Spiritual" Franciscans all espoused interest in mystical states, but these movements were decidedly heretical and their advocacy of ecstatic states had a decidedly political, rebellious tone.[14] Medieval witches, too, relied upon the ecstatic states induced with ointments containing belladonna, henbane, and mandrake. The fabled witch's broomstick appears to have served as a means of rubbing this ointment over the skin and into the vagina where it could be readily absorbed, often yielding sensations of levitation and flying.[15] Needless to say, such practices were expressions of extreme spiritual unrest and deviance from the cultural norm. And thus with the exception of these countervailing examples, ecstasy was not something to be experienced by the average believer. Church officials were highly suspicious of individuals who claimed to have had direct communion with a "higher" reality and frequently suggested that such claims were in fact the deceitful workings of the devil.

By way of contrast, the Americas were populated by people who embraced very different understandings of how one might find harmony and connection with supernatural power. As La Barre argued, American Indians preserved the shamanic ideology of ancient hunting peoples, whose "epistemological touchstone for reality was direct psychic experience of the forces of nature."[16] This "epistemological touchstone" granted normative cultural status to ecstatic mental states even in those Indian societies that over time grew more agricultural. And, therefore, the use of hallucinogenic plants remained a fundamental part of the cultural complex governing many North American societies.

This is not to suggest routine use of narcotic substances. For example, in many tribal cultures only shamans sought to establish contact with spirit helpers by inducing trance states with the help of music, dancing, prayer, fasting, or drugs. Furthermore, a great deal of shamanism was nonecstatic. Nonetheless, La Barre's thesis is helpful. The Americas were indeed heir to a narcotic complex that valued botanical assistance in achieving union with the supernatural powers that surrounded them. There was, for this reason, ample reliance upon psychoactive drugs such as beer, mushrooms, datura, mescal beans, peyote, and—of course—tobacco.

Intoxicating beverages were commonly used by Native Americans. This, of course, was particularly true in South America, where the beverage *yajé* has been used for centuries to produce profound mystical experiences. Although the exact combination of botanical substances used in preparing *yajé* can vary considerably, the principal ingredient is bark from the jungle vine *Banisteriopsis*, which contains a number of psychoactive elements including harmine.[17] As with many highly narcotic substances, *yajé* frequently gives rise to an initial nausea, accompanied by vomiting. This initially unpleasant stage is soon followed by a euphoria, then by visual hallucinations of colors and animals. In this way *yajé* simulates the kind of death-rebirth experience found in so many religious rituals. The Peruvian name for this jungle vine, *ayahuasca,* means "vine of the souls." Imbibers feel themselves separating from their physical bodies and undergoing a transition to a wholly spiritual form of being. Schultes noted that among Colombian Indians, the drinking of this preparation represents "a return to the maternal womb, the source of all creation; the partakers see all the gods, the first human beings and animals, and understand the establishment of their social order. Those who take *yajé* 'die' only to be reborn in a state of greater wisdom."[18]

Yajé is ceremoniously used in a variety of contexts by South American Indians. It might, for example, be used in rituals intended to reinforce commitment to social morals and customs. In his study of narcotic drugs among the Indians of Colombia, G. Reichel-Dolmatoff showed that the pleasurable and awe-inspiring sensations elicited by *yajé* were ritually channeled in ways that reinforced socially desired behavior. Reichel-Dolmatoff noted that the principal occasions on which *yajé* is consumed

> are the gatherings of people from two or more exogamic units and consist of solemn events accompanied by dances, songs, and recitations. These collective trances, during which the participants are gathered together for one or several days, are religious ceremonies. The interpretation of the hallucinations emphasizes the law of exogamy, and the principal objective of the total experience is to demonstrate the divine origin of the rules regulating social relationships.[19]

Yajé is also consumed by individuals or small groups of men in search of contact with the supernatural sphere. It might, for example, be used for divination purposes such as identifying one's enemies or locating optimal sites for hunting. It is also a valuable tool for the shaman in the curing of disease. *Yajé*, in combination with tobacco and other drugs, is a valuable tool in diagnosing the cause of a disease. Sometimes the patient, too, ingests the drug and describes his visions to the shaman to assist in this diagnosis. Often the shaman will discover that the causes of disease are to be found in moral shortcomings and improper social behavior. In such instances, the shaman might explain that tensions in interpersonal relations are very "weakening" and make the patient prone to attacks from spirit-beings. The shaman and his narcotics, then, become a means of mediating between the behaviors of humans and the behaviors of spirits. His flights to the supernatural sphere make it possible for him to learn how certain human behaviors disrupt one's relationship with the spirit world and, in turn, how one might adjust social conduct in such a way as to restore harmony between the natural and supernatural realms.

The use of yajé and other hallucinogenic substances among Colombian Indians is thoroughly structured by cultural factors. Reichel-Dolmatoff concluded that "narcotic drugs are certainly not used for purely hedonistic reasons; their individual or collective use is always connected with the aim to transcend the bounds of empirical reality and to obtain a glimpse of that 'other world' where the miseries and trials of daily existence may find their remedies."[20] Reichel-Dolmatoff was himself a skeptic concerning the actual existence of this so-called "other world." A psychoanalytically oriented scholar, Reichel-Dolmatoff believes that religious ideas reflect our own psychological fears and desires. Thus, to him, the "other world" contacted by yajé

> is nothing but a projection of the individual mind, activated by the drug. Unconscious mental processes—fears and desires—are brought into focus and are projected upon the shapes and colors of the visions, and the interpretations given to this imagery by the [shaman] refer in all essence to problems of food, sex, disease, and aggression, that is, to problems of physical survival.[21]

Reichel-Dolmatoff raised the difficult issues concerning how outsiders should go about interpreting belief in drug-induced contact with the spiritual world. Are the visions of mystics and shamans little more than aberrations unleashed by disturbances in our neural chemistry? Or are the mystics and shamans correct that we are surrounded by a supernatural sphere and that the entry point to this higher world is right within us, awaiting our recognition? Discussion of these issues is taken up in the final chapter. In the meantime, it is sufficient that we not ignore Reichel-Dolmatoff's main point that drug-induced experiences cannot be fully understood without connecting them with other social and cultural patterns.

Native Americans who inhabited territory that is now part of the United States also used intoxicating beverages.[22] With the exception of the Pueblo, whose highly institutionalized religion appears to have militated against individual experiences of intoxication, nearly all Southwestern tribal societies used some form of intoxicating beverage. The Apache of Arizona and New Mexico often preceded their ceremonial drinking of *tulpi* (a beer made of the maguey plant) with a long fast that enhanced the intoxicating effect of the beverage. Other Apache tribes have used various species of yucca to make an intoxicating beverage, often mixed with the roots of datura. A major function of ceremonial drinking is the forging of social solidarity. When the Papago make fermented liquor from the fruit of the saguaro cactus, "the men dance in a great circle around a fire, following a leader with a rattle, and later the women join them. . . . Thus they dance and sing for two nights, while the medicine men make magic with strings of eagle feathers and sprinkle the dancers with eagle down, which symbolizes clouds. . . . No family may drink its own liquor lest the house burn down, but they drink at other houses, vomit, and go on to visit others and sing songs."[23] Alcoholic beverages, then, have been ritually employed to facilitate certain modes of social bonding. They also have had a number of other ceremonial uses. Alcohol has been used to incite emotion in ceremonies before battle and to celebrate various rites of passage such as puberty rites, wedding rites, or funeral rites. It has also been used in ceremonies surrounding vision quests. For example, the Comanche, Oto, and Tonkawa tribes occasionally mixed peyote and the mescal bean to create an extraordinarily potent drink. This drink, which found its greatest use just prior to the rise of the peyote-using Native American Church, may well have been a "transitional link" between pre- and post-reservation uses of botanical substances in American Indian religion.

Psychoactive mushrooms have also been a part of the Native American narcotic complex. The fly agaric mushroom (*Amanita muscaria*), for example, was undoubtedly used by the Maya of highland Guatemala. They called this mushroom "the lightning mushroom" and related it one of the gods, Rajaw Kakulja or Lord of Lightning. Richard Schultes and Albert Hofmann noted that this same mushroom was ritually used in Asia for centuries. Evidence suggests that use of this mushroom subsequently traveled across the Bering Strait into North America. Schultes and Hofmann reported that indications of the hallucinogenic use of the fly agaric mushroom "have been discovered among the Dogrib Athabascan peoples, who live on the Mackenzie Mountain range in northwestern Canada."[24] Among this tribe, the fly agaric mushroom was used as a sacrament in shamanism, bringing with it experiences of dismemberment, death-rebirth, and meeting with a tutelary spirit. Schultes and Hofmann also pointed out that the religious use of this mushroom as a sacred hallucinogen was discovered in an ancient annual ceremony practiced by the Ojibway Indians who live on the shores of Lake Superior in Michigan. The fly agaric mushroom is indigenous to the upper Midwest and could well have been used in any number of religious and medical ceremonies. Unfortunately, because we have so few records of North American Indian culture, we know very little about the uses of mushrooms in most tribal societies.

When the Spaniards conquered Mexico, they found the natives worshiping their deities with the help of several inebriating mushrooms, most of which belong to the genus *Psilocybe*. One obstacle to knowing more about the religious use of these mushrooms is that the Catholic clergy found them particularly offensive and succeeded in running the cult underground. The Catholic missionaries denounced these pagan rituals as the work of the devil.

Even though we do not have a complete historical record of the uses of mushrooms in Mexico, we know that in more recent times they have been employed in the divinatory and religious rites among the Chinantec, Chatino, Mije, Zapotec, and especially the Mazatec.[25] The modern mushroom ceremony is an all-night affair, often including a curing ritual. The ceremony lasts for hours and is filled with ritual chanting under the general direction of the shaman. Mushrooms are collected in nearby forests at the time of the new moon. After the mushrooms have been briefly placed on the altar of the town's Catholic church, they are ingested by the participants. Chemical studies of these mushrooms reveal that they release varying amounts of the psychoactive ingredients psilocybin and psilocin. Depending on the setting in which they are used and the individual's personal beliefs and expectations, these substances tend to induce an intoxication characterized by colored visions in kaleidoscopic movement, sometimes accompanied by auditory hallucinations and various forms of fantasy. Other alterations include great fluctuations in time perception and emotional changes such as extreme hilarity and difficulty in concentration. As Schultes has explained, the subject "is rendered completely indifferent to his environment, which becomes as unreal to him as his dreamlike state becomes real."[26]

Some variation on this ritual use of *Psilocybe* mushrooms has been in practice south of the Rio Grande for at least two thousand years. It is unclear, however, whether these particular rituals filtered very far into what is now the United States. It might be noted that *Psilocybe mexicana* was the species of mushroom that Don Juan taught Carlos Castenada to smoke in his quest to become a man of knowledge. The smoking (rather than eating) of *Psilocybe* mushrooms stands out as bit of a curiosity in Castenada's writings, as does the apparent use of this mushroom in the contemporary American Southwest.

The use of datura is even more widespread in the Native American narcotic complex. Tribes throughout the Southwest and Northwestern Mexico have relied upon the vision-giving powers of this flowering plant (frequently referred to as jimson weed). In California alone, at least twelve different tribes used datura for prophecy, divination, healing, and attaining visions. Datura was in all probability indigenous to eastern America as well. It seems reasonable therefore to conclude that tribes along the eastern seaboard also made use of datura for religious purposes.

The effects of datura are pronounced, earning the plant a reputation as a dangerous and potent drug.[27] Datura contains a large amount of tropane alkaloids, which are highly toxic and include atropine, hypocyamine, and scopolamine. As the drug takes effect, it produces a sense of weariness and listlessness. A short time later, datura tends to produce visionary experiences such as might be involved in divination procedures, sometimes followed by vivid hallucinations. These symptoms are typically followed by the loss of consciousness and deep sleep. In excessive doses, death or permanent insanity may occur, further contributing to the awesome reverence with which this drug is regarded. The psychoactive potency of all species of datura have prompted people all over the world to view them as plants of the gods.

The uses to which Native Americans have put datura are varied.[28] Among some tribes, such as the Havasupai, datura leaves were eaten only occasionally and for what appears to be the purpose of bringing purely secular pleasure. Many Plains Indian tribes used datura for divination purposes, relying upon its capacity to induce visionary experiences in order to locate deer, reveal the identity of someone who had stolen property, or to locate lost articles. The Pima had a datura song, which was used to bring success in deer hunting as well as to cure certain physical ailments such as vomiting and dizziness. Among many tribes it was used for purposes of sedation during simple operations, when cleaning wounds, or while setting broken bones. The Zuni considered datura to be one of the medicines formerly belonging to the gods and restricted its use to the rain priests. These priests put the powdered root into their eyes to help them commune with the dead and to ask their assistance in coercing the spirits to bring rain. Indians of Virginia used a narcotic medicine called *wysoccan* in their initiatory rites. The active ingredient was probably *Datura stramonium*.[29] The boys were isolated for up to twenty days and given no other food or sustenance other than the datura-laced concoction designed to facilitate their death-rebirth initiation into the tribe. During the ordeal, they were said to "unlive their former lives" and begin their manhood after having lost all memory of ever having been boys.

The Mountain Cahuilla of California were typical of groups who employed datura ritual in their puberty ceremonials.

> Manet (*datura*) was given to boys of 18–20 in a ceremony lasting 3 to 6 days in which other younger boys of 6–10 years were taught clan and "enemy" songs by their fathers. . . . The drinking ceremony or kiksawel took place inside the ceremonial dance house, and women and children were warned away by the manet-dancer's bull roarer. Each boy was given a drink of a decoction of *datura* pounded in a mortar by the clan chief. The men in the enclosure took each boy by the waist, and they all danced around the fire, led by the manet-dancer. The boys remained unconscious in the house all night when the effect of the drug became manifest, and were removed the following afternoon to a secluded canyon where for a week they were taught songs and dances nightly. . . . After an ant-ordeal and a fire-dance, they were regarded as men and full-fledged members of the clan.[30]

The Navajo took datura for its visionary properties, using it as an aid in diagnosis and healing. In addition to using it for its purely intoxicating pleasures, the Navajo also used datura for various magical purposes. For example, Navajo men might have sought revenge upon a female who had scorned them by putting datura on some object connected with her while singing a chant intended to drive her mad.

The Yman tribes believed that the reactions of braves under the influence of datura could foretell their future. They also believed the datura plant could grant them magical power. For example, if a bird sang to a man in a datura trance, it was thought that he magically acquired the power to cure.[31]

The mescal bean is yet another drug associated with the ecstatic element in Native American religious history.[32] The seed of a small tree found in Mexico and the American Southwest, the mescal or red bean is a powerful narcotic. The contents of a single bean are capable of producing nausea, convulsions, hallucinations, and even death by asphyxiation. The nausea-producing effects of the drug fostered its medical use as an emetic. The Iowa Indians, for example, used the bean to clean their systems by inducing vomiting and evacuating the bowel. The mescal bean was also thought to be a powerful fetish. Collected in medicine bundles, mescal beans were believed to bring success in war, hunting buffalo, and horse racing. Warriors often tied the red beans around their belts when they went to war, believing that the beans would protect them against injury. Omaha Indians, for example, rubbed this medicine on their bodies before battle and rubbed it on their bullets to make them more effective.

The principal use of mescal beans, however, was in a tea-like beverage made from ground beans. At least twelve tribes of the Plains and Southwest (Apache, Comanche, Delaware, Iowa, Kansa, Omaha, Oto, Osage, Pawnee, Ponca, Tonkawa, and Wichita) had some form of a mescal bean cult utilizing this intoxicating drink. Music played an important part in these mescal rituals. Drummers and singers took up positions associated with the four cardinal directions and performed throughout the ceremony. Their songs called upon the powers of the spirit world for the purpose of blessings and assistance. At the appointed time, the mescal bean beverage would be consumed. The drug was both a powerful emetic and stimulant, preparing participants for personal renewal and spiritual insight. Participants would pray repeatedly, vomit, and feel the evil being driven from their bodies as they were ceremoniously cleansed. In many tribes, it was thought that the mescal bean also enhanced the curing and divination powers of the tribal shaman. In other tribes, warriors used the mescal bean to enter trances in which they could commune with animal spirits who would instruct them to be brave and promise them protective power in an upcoming battle. The visionary powers of the mescal bean were also used in agricultural rites in which thanks was made to Wakanda (the high god) for vegetable foods and tobacco.

Many elements of the mescal bean cult appeared in the later peyote cult. It is quite possible that the relatively mild and safe hallucinogen, peyote, was eventually substituted for the lethally toxic mescal bean. The singing, drumming, and prayer in the mescal bean ritual all had close parallels in the peyote ritual. Both cults also featured magical performances by shamans who healed and provided divination. In fact, the leader in many Plains Indian peyote rituals wore a necklace made of mescal beans. Thus, although there is no conclusive proof that the peyote cult is a direct descendent of the earlier mescal bean cult, tribes made similar use of these two native plant to purge themselves of defilements and avail themselves of higher powers.

There are at least two other botanical substances integral to the Native American "narcotic complex."[33] Both of these, peyote and tobacco, deserve extended treatment. Although peyote was not in widespread use until the late nineteenth century, it has received sufficient notoriety in recent decades to warrant more complete discussion in the following section. It is, however, tobacco that has figured most centrally in Native American religious life.

There is abundant evidence from both North and South America to demonstrate that "tobacco is *the* supernatural plant *par excellence* of the American Indian, for tobacco was used aboriginally everywhere it would grow in the New World—that is, from middle Canada southward to Patagonia."[34] The tobacco used by Native Americans varied from region to region, as there were at least nine species of *Nicotiana* indigenous to North America alone (although *Nicotiana rustica*—a species much stronger than the *Nicotiana attenuata* used commercially today—was the most widely used).[35] Moreover, tobacco was frequently used in mixtures with other ingredients such as the kinnikinnick used by the Oglala Sioux, which consisted of the dried inner bark of the red alder or red dogwood.[36] In some instances, more powerful substances such as datura might be added to tobacco to prepare a particularly potent smoke. It is, therefore, difficult to be absolutely certain about the botanical and pharmacological properties of Indian tobacco mixtures. We do know that most of the tobacco species employed by American Indians produced strongly intoxicating effects. In all likelihood they contained large amounts of the harmala alkaloids, which can severely alter neural transmission in the visual system and have pronounced hallucinogenic effects. The nicotine in native tobaccos was also a powerful stimulant. It acts through specialized cell formations in the brain and muscle tissues to produce changes in heart rate, alter brain wave patterns, elevate blood pressure, and release hormones affecting the central nervous system.[37] It is thus not surprising that the exhilaration and euphoria caused by native tobacco prompted Native Americans to see it as means of connecting with supernatural power. As Weston La Barre observed, "That tobacco alters the psychic state, however feebly, was enough for the American Indian to believe it had supernatural power and to use it in sacred contexts."[38]

It is important to note that historically Native Americans used tobacco only in sacred, never secular, contexts. Because tobacco was thought to be a gift from the gods and as pleasing to them as it was to humans, it was present in almost every ceremony designed to communicate with the supernatural realm. Florida Indians used tobacco in shamanistic divination, and the Seminoles and Iroquois offered tobacco as an offering to the gods.[39] Paul Radin has shown that the Winnebago tribe poured tobacco over their drums and into their ritual fire when seeking to communicate with spirits. Winnebago warriors also used tobacco when addressing the spirits of those whom they had conquered in battle.[40] Sacred smoking almost always attended the quest for a vision of the guardian spirit. Accompanied by purifying baths, solitude, and nightly vigil, the smoking of tobacco assisted the supplicant in transporting himself beyond the familiar world.

The smoking of tobacco was a nearly universal feature of shamanic ecstasy. For example, tobacco was an important element of curing rituals. Willard Park has described how Paviotso shamans gathered their own tobacco in a secret place far from camp in order to escape the danger of using tobacco that had been in the presence of menstruating women (which would jeopardize the efficacy of the tobacco).[41] This tobacco would be combined with various mixtures of leaves and grasses and stored in a kit with the shaman's pipe, rattle, and other healing paraphernalia. In the curing rite, the shaman sat beside the patient and lit his pipe. After smoking for a few minutes he began to sing, and at the beginning of the sixth song he picked up his rattle and shook it in rhythm with the song. A bit later, the shaman took several more puffs from his pipe and then passed it counterclockwise among those gathered for the curing rite. If anyone refused to smoke, the shaman stopped the performance until that person was coerced into compliance. The pipe was repeatedly circulated in this way about every half hour as long as the curing rite continued, which was often until the next morning. It was the shaman's job to enter into a trance to diagnose the cause of the illness (e.g., soul loss, object intrusion, sorcery, etc.) and then to discern the action necessary to restore proper connection with the spirit world. For this he had to sustain his personal power and therefore continued to utilize his special preparation of tobacco.

The Oglala Sioux performed a curing ritual known as Yuwipi. The essential feature of the Yuwipi rite was wrapping the patient in a blanket or quilt. The ritual of wrapping the patient was undoubtedly connected with the ancient practice of wrapping strings of tobacco. Proper performance of this healing rite required offering "tobacco bundles" to the tutelary spirits needed for diagnosis and cure. During the ritual, these spirits were thought to pick up the essence of the tobacco and later smoke it with other spirits.[42]

Yet another ritual use of tobacco was to solemnize an oath. The significance of these rituals was to summon the potent spiritual power of tobacco and to infuse this power into the bonds established by the oath. Breaking the oath would therefore unleash disastrous consequences upon the guilty party. Among the Woodlands and Plains Indians, chiefs met to smoke the sacred calumet or peace pipe, the rite invoking the power of tobacco upon their sacred oath. The calumet was an elaborately decorated shaft, sometimes as long as four feet. The use of the calumet was shrouded in ritual tradition. Chants and dances were employed to invoke the spirits. The names for this dance and chant were variations of a word meaning "to make a sacred kinship." Performance of these rituals was thus understood to be forging intimate social relationships. Custom dictated that if the calumet was offered and accepted, the act of smoking would make any engagements sacred and inviolable. It was thought that anyone who violated this agreement could never escape just punishment. Citing eighteenth-century sources, Ralph Linton described the ritual:

> If the calumet is offered and accepted it is the custom to smoke in the calumet, and the engagements contracted are held sacred and inviolable. . . . By smoking together in the calumet the contracting parties intend to invoke the sun and the other gods as witnesses of the mutual obligations assumed by the parties, and as a guaranty the one to the other that they shall be fulfilled. This is accomplished by blowing the smoke toward the sky, the four world quarters, and the earth, with a suitable invocation.[43]

The pipe, no less than the tobacco itself, came to be viewed as an instrument of sacred power. The pipe was a symbol of the universe, and more specifically humanity's place in the universe. Its use connected humans with the spirits and with one another. Joseph Epes Brown observes that

> in filling a pipe, all space (represented by the offerings to the powers of the six directions) and all things (represented by the grains of the tobacco) are contracted within a single point (the bowl or heart of the pipe), so that the pipe contains, or really *is* the universe. But since the pipe is the universe, it

is also man, and the one who fills a pipe should identify himself with it, thus not only establishing the center of the universe, but also his own center; he so "expands" that the six directions of space are actually brought within himself. It is by this "expansion" that a man ceases to be a part, a fragment, and become whole or holy; he shatters the illusion of separateness.[44]

Both the pipe and tobacco, then, were considered tools for accessing supernatural power. The pipe served as an amulet, often worn for protection or prosperity. As a symbol of the fundamental unity of humanity, the tobacco pipe was present in virtually every Native American ritual—rituals for purifying the souls of the dead, the Sun Dance, rites of purification, rites for the seeking of a vision, and all rites of passage. It is thus not surprising that the sacred pipe also factors significantly in the peyote cult that grew in popularity in the late nineteenth and early twentieth centuries.

Peyotism and the Native American Church

Prior to 1890, peyote was rarely used north of the Rio Grande. Although peyotism was common in Mexico, only five or six tribes inhabiting lands that are now within the borders of the United States used peyote in religious rituals. Yet, within the next twenty years peyote rituals became a prominent religious activity in an additional thirty tribes, concentrated in the Plains but stretching from the Southwest to Wisconsin. The story of the emergence and rapid spread of peyotism among these tribes constitutes a fascinating chapter in the history of American religion.[45]

When the Spanish conquistadors first arrived in what is now Mexico, they discovered that the native inhabitants worshiped three plants: a mushroom *(Teonanacatl)*; a vine belonging to the morning glory family *(Ololiuqui)*; and a small, spineless cactus *(peyotl* or *Lophophora williamsii)*. The Aztecs referred to the last of these, *peyotl* or peyote, as "the flesh of the gods." This carrot-looking cactus produced small "buttons" that were ceremoniously ingested in either their green or dried state.

Peyote buttons contain at least nine psychoactive alkaloids, some of them strychnine-like in physiological action, the rest morphine-like.[46] First and foremost among these alkaloids is mescaline. Mescaline slows the pulse, gives the sensation of immobility, and produces a variety of visual effects, including visions of geometrical patterns and bright colors. Peyotline and anhaline both have sedative, paralyzing effects, which often induce hypnotic susceptibility, while anhalonidine, anhalonine, lophophorine, and anhalamine together produce a dull pain in the head, nausea, and a generally disrupting influence upon the central nervous system. Ingesting peyote leads to an initial nausea, often accompanied by vomiting.[47] There is also a feeling of general stimulation with the face becoming flushed, the pupils dilated, and general feeling of being "lightheaded." As the intoxication increases, there is a tendency to overestimate time, possibly caused by the rapid flow of ideas and the inability to fix attention. The most distinctive feature of peyote intoxication is visual hallucination, principally of a kaleidoscopic display of color. These colors are constantly in motion, assuming a variety of geometric shapes. Yet another effect of peyote is synesthesia, or the translation of data coming in from one sense into that of another. For example, sounds may be perceived in terms of colors or an individual might either "taste" or "touch" something they are seeing. An individual's overall psychic state may range from hilarity to confusion. Many individuals hallucinate animals that may appear so monstrous as to be frightening or so ridiculous as to be hilarious. For the most part, however, emotions and the overall experience of well-being is controlled by the cultural setting.

It did not take long, of course, for the Spanish priests to begin efforts to ban the use of peyote and to persecute anyone who they found using it. But peyote use has continued up to the present day in many parts of Mexico, most notably among the Huichol. Mexican Indians have primarily used peyote as a medicine. Shamans have used its powers to divine the causes of illness or given it to patients to bring them the "power" necessary to effect a cure. Peyote has also been used to obtain visions for purposes of divination or, when used in a group setting, to induce a trance that facilitates tribal dancing rites.

Among the Huichol, the "peyote hunt" or quest to locate suitable plants is itself a sacred ceremony.[48] This annual pilgrimage is a solemn affair and under the strict direction of an experienced *maráakame,* or shaman, who has special relations with Hikuri, the Peyote-god. Participants prepare for this pilgrimage by engaging in rituals of confession and purification. Throughout their hunt they must be celibate and form a cohesive and classless community. Pilgrims must renounce all ego, pride, resentment, or hostility. The trek to the ancestral regions where peyote is bountiful was traditionally an arduous walk of over two hundred miles (though in more recent times this is often traveled by car). This journey is only in part a geographical one. It is also one that transports the pilgrim through the "geography of the mind" to the opening of the spirit world. Finally, under the *maráakame*'s direction peyote is collected and, in a fire-lit ceremony, ritually ingested. The peyote elicits beautiful lights, vivid colors, and visions of peculiar animals. These visions are themselves without meaning, but rather to be enjoyed for their own aesthetic delight. Only the *maráakame*'s visions are considered meaningful, and he helps interpret this ritual encounter with mysterious, sacred power. The peyote experience is said to effect a total unification at every level, to kindle a communal love, to bond persons to the way of their ancestors, and to give participants a direct experience of a spiritual realm that surrounds the world of everyday life. In this way the Huichol peyote hunt recapitulates archaic rituals of returning to ancestral paradise, to a mythic past of purity and spiritual power. As Barbara Myerhoff explained, the Huichol believe that peyote "evokes the timeless, private, purposeless, aesthetic dimension of the spiritual life, mediating between former and present realities and providing a sense of being one people, despite dramatic changes in their recent history."[49]

The diffusion of peyotism throughout the United States was a complex process with distinct religious, social, and psychological elements.[50] Perhaps the most important factor in this northward migration of peyote rites was the systematic segregation of Indians onto government reservations. By 1890 traditional tribal cultures had come under tremendous strain. Native American tribes had formerly been distinct and even somewhat competitive. When merged together onto reservations, these tribal cultures found themselves stripped of much of their former identities. Their land was gone, the buffalo were gone, their tribal traditions were disrupted. In the place of their lost cultural traditions, white culture offered agriculture (on poor soil) and Christianity. It was in this context of cultural disarray that the Ghost Dance religion emerged and incited widespread enthusiasm. The Ghost Dance religion prophesied the imminent dawn of a golden age of pan-Indian harmony. It emphasized the need for peace between the tribes and fashioned a sense of intertribal unity based upon their shared contempt for white man's civilization. The Ghost Dance religion promised that Indians were about to witness a supernatural and miraculous end to white rule. As it turned out, however, these utopian hopes for the destruction of white society were ultimately dashed. Harsh social and political realities endured. But the Ghost Dance had succeeded in establishing intimate and friendly contacts between tribes. And, as Ruth Shonle has demonstrated, the dissemination of the peyote cult flowed easily along the newly opened channels of friendship. It came up from the south with the promise of great power; in its adaptability to new needs and a new state of cultural life it was far superior to the tribal ceremonies, hampered as they were by age-old traditions; and it was Indian in origin, fitted to the Indian mode of thought.[51]

Between 1890 and 1920, peyotism spread along lines opened up by intertribal visits of kinship members. The ritual use of peyote spread to tribes in Utah, Colorado, Arizona, and New Mexico, although it failed to attract a significant following in California or the states in the Pacific Northwest. Peyotism had its fastest diffusion among the Plains Indians of Oklahoma, Kansas, Nebraska, South Dakota, and Wisconsin. The reason for this differential appeal is undoubtedly due to contrasting cultural backgrounds, particularly in respect to the vision traditions in these tribal regions. Nearly all North American Indians made use of visions. Visions, usually induced by fasting and other ascetic ordeals, were part of puberty rites in which young men gained their guardian spirits or were considered part of shamanic "doctoring." But on the Plains, visions were not confined to puberty. Nor were visions the exclusive property of shamans as in some regions of the United States. Instead, visions were thought to be part of an adult male's ongoing connection with the spirit world and were sought at times of mourning, for hunting, before battles, and for divination purposes. Visions were sufficiently normative for all individuals as to almost preclude any role for shamans. As Ruth Shonle concluded,

the underlying belief in the supernatural origin of visions is important among the factors contributing to the diffusion of peyote. . . . Peyote did not have to win its way into a system of religion which was without visions. Rather it facilitated obtaining visions already sought. It was holy medicine given to the Indian that he might get into immediate touch with the supernatural without the long period of fasting.[52]

Peyotism manifested itself differently depending on the tribal context. In the Southwest, with the Mescalero Apache being the prime instance, peyotism remained fairly close to its Mexican roots. The principal purpose of peyote meetings was for ceremonial doctoring, although—as with all vehicles for gaining connection with supernatural power—it might occasionally be used for divining an enemy's location, predicting the outcome of some undertaking, or finding lost objects.[53] A shamanistic premise underlay the use of peyote among most Southwest tribes. In other words, even though all participants sought rapport with their own powers through the use of peyote, the shaman nonetheless remained in control and directed the (principally healing or divination) uses to which the experience was directed.

The more developed or "Americanized" peyotism first appeared among the Kiowa and Comanche in Oklahoma. The Kiowa-Comanche adaptation of peyotism shifted the focus from the shaman to every participant's quest for power. Doctoring was still an important feature but was subordinated to the more general goal of enabling individuals to seek blessing and prosperity through establishing harmony with supernatural power. The "Americanized" form of peyote ceremony is to this day held for any of a number of reasons. Peyote ceremonies are traditionally held to express gratitude for recovery from illness, to procure a safe return home from a journey, to celebrate the birth of a baby, or to seek instruction and power through a vision. Meetings are also held on Thanksgiving and New Years Day, revealing the growing attempt to merge Native tradition with white cultural patterns. In fact, as Native American culture became increasingly Christianized, Easter and Christmas were added to the calendar for holding peyote ceremonies.

The peyote ceremony is held in a traditional tipi, with the door facing east.[54] Preparation for the ceremony begins with rituals pertaining to the acquisition of the peyote, either by sending individuals to Mexico or, in more recent times, by purchase and delivery through the U.S. Postal Service. Once acquired, the peyote is blessed through prayer and consecrated for use in bringing health to all who will ingest it. Participants ordinarily prepare for the ceremony with observances intended to purify themselves, such as sweat baths. Any member of the peyote cult may rise to the position of ritual leader, known as the "roadman." The roadman is assisted by a drummer, a fireman, and a cedar man. Women assist in erecting the tipi, preparing food, and are sometimes permitted to attend the meeting and eat peyote and pray. The precise order and content of the ceremony varies by tribe and the idiosyncratic preferences of the roadman. The ceremony begins in earnest when the roadman makes a tobacco cigarette and passes it clockwise around the tipi while offering a prayer to the power of the peyote:

> We are just beginning our prayer meeting. We want you to be with us tonight and help us. We want no one to be sick at this meeting from eating peyote. [Then he prays for the person who is sick or whose birthday the

meeting celebrates or for relatives and participants.] If there are any rules connected with you, peyote, that we don't know of, forgive us if we should break them, as we are ignorant.[55]

All then begin to pray silently to the "earth-creator" or "earth-lord." Following these initial prayers, participants begin to eat the dried buttons of the peyote plant, followed by the commencement of drumming and singing. The roadman's initial song, chanted in a high nasal tone, implores "May the gods bless me, help me, and give me power and understanding." Throughout the night more peyote buttons are eaten (whereas most members eat about twelve buttons throughout the night, others may consume as many as thirty) and prayer intensifies. As La Barre observed,

> At intervals older men pray aloud, with affecting sincerity, often with tears running down their cheeks, their voices choked with emotion, and their bodies swaying with earnestness as they gesture and stretch out their arms to invoke the aid of Peyote. The tone is of a poor and pitiful person humbly asking the aid and pity of a great power, and absolutely no shame whatever is felt by anyone when a grown man breaks down into loud sobbing during his prayer.[56]

Ceremonial dancing is also an integral part of peyote rituals, particularly in Mexico and the American Southwest. In the Plains, where dried peyote is more common, quiet meditation, prayer, and visions predominate.

In addition to these more generalized purposes of power-seeking, peyotism is also practiced for its ostensible therapeutic benefits. The "power" obtained during peyote ceremonies is central to Native American understandings of health and curing. Most peyote curing ceremonies (particularly among Plains Indians) are simple compared to traditional shamanic practices of divining and object abstraction. Typically the roadman will offer prayers that petition God to cure individuals who have come in search of healing. These individuals usually ingest peyote themselves in an effort to make personal contact with healing power. Cures of almost every kind have been attributed to the power generated in peyote ceremonies. There is no shortage of anecdotes and personal testimony proclaiming peyote's power to cure everything from pneumonia to cancer, depression to alcoholism.

Perhaps the most intriguing feature of peyotism is its overt emphasis upon preaching and moral instruction. Moral lectures are commonplace. Participants admonish one another to forego vices, particularly in regard to abstaining from alcoholic beverages. This preaching element of the peyote ritual escalated with the continued incorporation of Christian elements into the ceremony. Nowhere is the impress of white Christian culture more conspicuous than in the gradual "Christianization" of peyotism. Even as early as the 1890s, the Bible was being introduced to the liturgical format of the peyote "singing." Prayers once made to the Indian spirits were being redirected to the Christian god. Although traditional elements were continued, their symbolism changed drastically: The fire in the peyote tipi became associated with the Light of Christ; the water drunk at midnight became associated with Christ's alleged midnight birth; the roadman's gestures to the four directions became a way of announcing the birth of Christ to all the world; and the meal eaten in the early morning became a sacrament for all those who are saved in Christ.

In the Christianized version of the peyote ceremony, the roadman reads from the Bible and calls upon the participants to confess their sins and repent. Participants respond to the roadman's exhortations by proclaiming their intention to give up sinning habits and testifying that "All this Jesus has done for me." Christian hymns have come to dominate most peyote ceremonies. Peyote songs express traditional evangelical themes such as "Saviour Jesus is the only Saviour," "I know Jesus now," and "You must be born again." In essence, the Christianized peyote rituals synthesized the religious heritages of Native Americans and Europeans. Peyotism thereby fostered the belief that the Great Spirit and the God of Christianity are one and the same. This Great Spirit created the universe and controls the destiny of every person and all events. The Great Spirit put some of his supernatural power into peyote, which when consumed under proper ritual conditions, can have the same redemptive or sacramental power that other Christians avail themselves of when consuming bread and wine.

Some peyotists have retained the traditional rituals and even see the incorporation of Christian elements as antagonistic to their native ways. Yet, on the whole, the Christianized rituals have dominated twentieth-century American peyotism. To be sure, however, peyotism has deep roots in the "narcotic complex" that existed in Native American culture for centuries before contact with European peoples. As Weston La Barre noted, "despite the apparent and superficial syncretism with Christianity, peyotism is an essentially aboriginal American religion, operating in terms of fundamental Indian concepts about powers, vision and native modes of doctoring."[57]

Peyotism never lacked for critics. The most persistent opposition came from white officials who viewed it as contrary to the goal of assimilating Native Americans into white, middle-class culture.[58] One major line of argument against peyote use was that it was allegedly injurious. Despite the lack of any supporting evidence, peyote was seen to be both physically and morally debilitating. A more important objection to peyotism was a political one. The rapid spread of peyotism reinforced traditional culture and amplified nativistic tendencies among American Indian populations. Both Christian missionaries and officials in the Bureau of Indian Affairs were disturbed by the cultural threat posed by this overt continuation of native tradition (and the pan-Indian solidarity that it both celebrated and fostered). By 1907 BIA officials organized an antipeyotist campaign using legislation originally intended to suppress the flow of liquor on reservations. Making little headway, the officials stepped up their efforts by drafting several antipeyote bills. Congress, however, specifically rejected any prohibition of peyote (before 1922), and so the BIA instead sought the help of the Treasury Department, which finally issued a regulation in 1915 prohibiting the importation of peyote "on the ground that it is an article dangerous to the health of the people of the United States."[59] Although this regulation was rescinded in 1937, Native Americans realized that they would have to find new ways to sidestep white antipeyotism.

As early as 1906, a loosely organized group calling themselves the "Mescal Bean Eaters" began to spread in the region from Oklahoma to Nebraska. Finding continued opposition from BIA officials, who denied all requests for the right to use peyote ritually, the Mescal Bean Eaters changed into the "Union Church" in 1909. Adopting the name "church" accommodated to white culture's notions of propriety as well as time-honored legal precedents for respecting the freedom of religious practice. The Union Church failed to make much headway against the BIA's mounting opposition. The relatively small "Firstborn Church of Christ" founded by Jonathan Koshiway and other members of the Oto tribe in 1914 was yet another unsuccessful attempt to secure legal protection for peyote ceremonies. In 1918, the "Native American Church" was incorporated in Oklahoma and soon developed into an intertribal peyote church that stretched throughout the western and central United States. Subsequently reorganized as the "Native American

Church of the United States" and finally the "Native American Church of North America," this group was largely successful at influencing state courts to respect their legal right to use peyote in religious sacraments.[60]

In 1964 the California Supreme Court held that the approximately 200,000 members of the Native American Church had a First Amendment right to use peyote. The Native American Church was eventually able to obtain religious exemption from drug laws in twenty-seven states before being rejected by the Oregon Supreme Court. In 1990, the United States Supreme Court upheld the Oregon Court's decision and ruled that the First Amendment did not protect the Native American Church's use of peyote. Congress responded by passing the Religious Freedom Restoration Act in 1993 which restored the Native American Church's right to use peyote in its religious rituals. Although the Supreme Court overturned significant sections of the Religious Freedom Restoration Act in a 1997 ruling, federal statues are still in place that specifically permit the Native American Church to use peyote in its religious ceremonies. This exemption from state and federal prohibitions of peyote use does not, however, apply to groups such as The Peyote Way Church of God whose approximately eighty (and largely non-Native American) members pursue personal experiences of the Holy Spirit through the sacramental use of Peyote.[61]

Historical perspective allows us to see how peyote performed religious, social, and cultural functions. Religiously, peyotism made it possible to combine Native American and Christian notions of "spiritual power." Peyotism helped sustain native ritual traditions amidst the encroachments of white Christianity. The peyote cult offered to heal and to protect its members through the worship of a Supreme Being who is for all intents and purposes identical with the God of Christianity. The peyote button—like sacramental bread and wine—provided a material vehicle for availing oneself of regenerating power. Peyote is understood as a "medicine," a "power," a "protector," and a "teacher." And although it is combined with almost as many theologies as it has users, it has almost universally fostered such culturally valued ethical traits as love, hope, charity, ambition, and honesty.[62] In this way peyotism preserved traditional Native American religious perspectives while making them amenable to the Christian faith.

More striking is the way in which a botanical substance such as peyote became implicated in the larger social and cultural changes that marked Native American culture in the early twentieth century.[63] Peyote rituals inherited a great deal of the cultural dynamic underlying the earlier Ghost Dance movement. That is, like the Ghost Dance, peyotism was also an attempt to overcome existing social disorganization by means of a collective rite. Peyotism, like the Ghost Dance, emphasized social solidarity. Yet, whereas the Ghost Dance preached the violent demise of white culture through supernatural intervention, peyotism focused on the regeneration of Native American culture through ritual and ethical behavior. Peyotism was about the strengthening of Native Americans rather than the destruction of white society. Peyote, by giving direct access to supernatural power, emphasized how mental, physical, or ethical wholeness was to be found through techniques associated with the Native American vision tradition. In this way, peyotism made it possible to stand up to environmental pressures to accommodate wholly to white culture. Peyotism implicitly permitted peaceful coexistence with white culture, while preserving the psychological and social boundaries of Native American identity.

The peyote ritual has proven to have both personal and social healing value. The peyote experience provides a rich set of aesthetic experiences. These kindle a sense of inner warmth or inner delight, helping individuals to feel that they are intimately connected with the ultimate source of beauty and truth. Much like the Roman Catholic mass, the peyote rite cultivates an aesthetic approach to divinity, giving participants a sense of interior participation in the source of all goodness. Such spiritual renewal fosters psychological reorganization. This is particularly important given the debilitating conditions faced by so many Native Americans during the decades in which peyotism emerged and spread throughout the reservation system. Although the peyote ceremony fosters reorganization by deepening subjective feelings of delight, it does so in a collective rite. The aesthetic feeling of connection with a higher power is almost universally accompanied by overt moral preaching. Peyotism ultimately exhorts participants to avoid moral vice and to subordinate personal desires to group goals or values. In this way, the physical arousal facilitated by peyote not only kindles a personal sense of well-being but also elicits tendencies to conform to the communal order.

In sum, peyotism has performed a variety of important cultural functions in the late nineteenth and early twentieth centuries. Viewed from almost any perspective, peyote rites have been a vehicle for religious and cultural renewal during a bleak period of Native American history. The rites enable individuals to reorganize their personalities in ways that are both personally and communally healthy. Peyotism validates Indian tradition by fostering individual religious experiences that are directly linked with inherited religious patterns. It does so, furthermore, by heightening the sense of social solidarity among participants. American Indians north of the Rio Grande, then, are therefore no less likely than the Mexican Huichol to find that peyote use "evokes the timeless, private, purposeless, aesthetic dimension of the spiritual life, mediating between former and present realities and providing a sense of being one people, despite dramatic changes in their recent history."[64]

Castenada Revisited

Castenada's accounts of the spiritual use of entheogens were thus misleading. His dramatizations of Don Juan's heavy reliance upon peyote, datura, and psilocybe greatly exaggerated the role that botanicals played in Native American spirituality. Yet despite their questionable scholarly status, Castenada's writings nonetheless struck a resonance with the religious consciousness emerging among American youth in the 1960s and 1970s. The teachings of Don Juan blended seamlessly with the cult of drug-induced ecstasy generated by the writings of Aldous Huxley, Timothy Leary, Allen Ginsberg, Alan Watts, and others. This was a time when a great deal of the educated reading public shared psychologist Abraham Maslow's view that all religions have their origins in the "peak experiences" of certain extraordinary individuals. Peak experiences, Maslow proclaimed, are exceptional states of awareness that indicate that the sacred is available to us in the here and now of everyday life if we but learn to see it. In this view, the primary datum of all religion is the attainment of altered states of consciousness that permit fresh perceptions of reality. Everything else associated with religion, such as rituals and doctrines, is therefore considered peripheral to the true core of authentic religion. A significant number of Americans yearned to strip away the outer trappings of religion and return to the experiential basis from which spiritual authenticity was thought to flow. What Castenada did was to connect the growing nostalgia for Native American wisdom with this wider cultural yearning.

Castenada correctly identified some of the principal drugs associated with Native Americans' pursuit of ritual ecstasy (although his reference to smoking mushrooms is questionable). His "field notes" accurately reflected Native American beliefs concerning how botanical materials might bring us into relationship with tutelary spirits or how they might be used in a mentoring relationship between an initiate and his teacher. But Castenada's accounts are in many respects misleading. First, they mistakenly give the impression that the use of ecstasy-producing botanical substances was far more prevalent than it actually was. Even in the pursuit of visions, most Native Americans relied not upon psychoactive plants but rather upon ascetic measures that included fasting, isolation, prayer, and physical ordeal. Drug use can surely be found throughout North American Indian history, but it was far more peripheral than Castenada's account would lead contemporary readers to believe. Second, and more important, Castenada's accounts sever Native American use of botanical substances from the tribal and ritual contexts that structured them and imbued them with meaning. An important purpose of Native American ceremonies is to reinforce group loyalty and rekindle commitment to tribal mores. A shaman's prestige is a direct function of his ability to use his extraordinary states of consciousness for the benefit of the group. Pipe ceremonies are solemn social occasions that forge solidarity and bind individuals to a moral order. Peyote ceremonies are communal rites whose purpose is initially to provide individuals with aesthetic experiences, but ultimately to lead to a vivid sense of being one people. The value or meaning of Native American ceremonies—including visions—is not to be found in the chemical properties of tobacco, datura, or peyote; it is to be found in the belief systems and ritual practices that invest these ceremonies with cultural significance.

Few Americans ever picked up one of Castenada's books with the intention of learning accurate or detailed information about Native American traditions. Instead, they were after something much more personal. They, too, wished to "stop the world." Castenada's readers were disenchanted with middle-class American culture, including its mainstream religious denominations. They yearned for something more personally exciting and relevant. Many craved religious ecstasy, free of the worldly corruptions they associated with the institutional church. The readers of Castenada's books were participating in a spiritual awakening rooted in an American religious tradition that has included such visionaries as Ralph Waldo Emerson, Walter Whitman, and William James. It was this heritage of American aesthetic spirituality, not the heritage of North American Indians, that influenced how American reading audiences responded to Castenada's writings. And it is to this heritage that we will now turn.

Psychedelics and
Metaphysical Illumination

In contrast to Native American cultures, European Americans saw little connection between drugs and spirituality before the 1950s. This is somewhat surprising given the fact that there was a small but persistent group of British writers who sustained European interest in the spiritual uses of drugs throughout the nineteenth century. As early as 1821 the obscure writer Thomas De Quincey caused a stir among British intellectuals and literati with his extravagant *Confessions of an English Opium-Eater*. De Quincey described how his first experience with opium afforded him a panacea for all his worldly woes. The effect of opium, according to De Quincey, was to "greatly increase the effect of the mind" and to reveal "the abyss of divine enjoyment" at the depths of his own inner spirit.[1] First introduced to the drug through one of the era's many opiate-containing proprietary medicines, De Quincey was soon initiated into ecstasies that were alternately sinister and sublime. His narcotic ecstasies had, curiously enough, a distinctive Oriental coloration, including harrowing encounters with Chinese, Hindu, and Egyptian deities.

De Quincey's opiate-driven flights of the soul meshed almost perfectly with the Romantic Revival that flourished in Europe in the early nineteenth century. Romanticism, after all, championed emotional spontaneity, flights of the imagination, an enhanced awareness of nature, and an affinity for exotic religious myth or symbol. It is thus not surprising that, as Martin Booth observed, "opium, and the liberty of thought it produced, was instrumental in the development of the Romantic ideal."[2] Samuel Taylor Coleridge, for example, began taking the opium-containing medicine known as laudanum as early as eight years old. His *The Rime of the Ancient*

Mariner and *Kubla Khan* evidence his extraordinary literary imagination and his opium-influenced penchant for exotic scenes and imagery. Such other Romantic luminaries as Elizabeth Barrett Browning, John Keats, and Sir Walter Scott all appear to have had laudanum-induced states of reverie at one point or another. It is interesting in this regard to note that scholars still debate whether America's Edgar Allen Poe was addicted to opium as well as alcohol. Although it is possible that Poe was never actually addicted to opium, he was surely familiar enough with its use to incorporate it into several of his stories, and its effect upon his Romantic imagination is open to speculation.

A further connection between drugs and Romantic-leaning spirituality in Britain was the career of Aleister Crowley. Crowley freely mingled Eastern and Western occultism with his own rituals of sexual magic. In 1910 he discovered the value of mescaline for transporting persons to uncharted mental and emotional territories and devised a series of seven rites, which he called the Rites of Eleusis. His *Diary of a Drug Fiend,* published in 1922, helped deepen the connection between drug-induced reverie and the strange worlds depicted in occult spirituality. Although Crowley was personally regarded with suspicion and often even contempt, his investigations of occult beliefs and practices had considerable influence upon many in both Britain and the United States who dabbled in various forms of alternative spirituality. It would seem that there is thus some reason to suspect that the nineteenth-century American bohemian and occult undergrounds had some acquaintance with the spiritual "effects" of drug use. Unfortunately, however, there is little historical material to support much more than conjecture as to just how widespread such a connection between drugs and alternative spirituality might have been.

For the most part, patterns of drug use in the United States developed in almost complete isolation from any religious contexts. The middle decades of the nineteenth century witnessed the steady growth of proprietary medicines containing opiates. As a consequence an increasing number of Americans became victim to iatrogenic addiction. For example, it is estimated that in 1842 there were about 0.72 addicts per 1,000 persons. By 1890, however, that figure had climbed to about 4.59 addicts per 1,000 persons.[3] Most of these were middle-aged white females of the middle or upper class. Their addictions were iatrogenic, that is, arising inadvertently from the use of medicines prescribed to settle their nerves or to treat the symptoms of either menstruation or menopause.

Concern over addiction led to steady efforts to curb the medicinal use of opiate-containing medicines. By the turn of the century there was a noticeable decline in the pool of medical addicts, accompanied by federal legislation such as the Harrison Act of 1914 that both forced physicians to maintain careful records of their prescriptions and paved the way for the legal prosecution of those who prescribed narcotics that perpetuated addiction. The unintended consequence of legislation such as the Harrison Act was to make drug addiction a criminal rather than medical issue, hastening its association with the urban "underworld." As the legal supply of narcotics dried up, addicts (some of whom first learned about opium, as well as morphine and heroin into which it can be transformed, from the opium dens of Chinese immigrants on the West Coast) were forced to turn to the burgeoning black market. And since the black-market prices were considerably higher, many turned to various forms of urban crime and vice to support their habit. Thus, by the early twentieth century, a new profile of drug user had emerged. As Jill Jonnes chronicled, "the portrait of the new American addict that was emerging was of a young man adrift, someone without solid roots or any particular vision of his future."[4] For persons already adrift in the world, drugs provided a distinctive identity, replete with a ready-made community, lifestyle, and vocabulary. In short, in the absence of any religious context, secular forces helped create a burgeoning "drug culture" in the United States that exacerbated rather than healed the ruptures arising in twentieth-century American society.

In the early twentieth century, heroin emerged as the most popular street drug. The typical heroin user was male, and until the 1940s, Caucasians outnumbered blacks.[5] New York was the initial center of illicit drug use, with 90 percent of America's heroin addicts living in the greater metropolitan area. Gradually the use of heroin spread to other eastern seaboard cities, then across the entire nation. When larger numbers of black workers migrated north, drug use (heroin, marijuana, cocaine, and morphine) also became associated with black musicians, whose jazz and blues symbolized an emerging American counterculture anchored in a range of emotions that had no official place in WASP American society. Drugs thus had a natural tendency to be associated with activities that were in some way socially or culturally deviant. And because drug use in the United States was largely relegated to secular contexts, it was rarely connected with overtly religious or spiritual concerns—whether deviant or conformist.

All in all, then, patterns of drug use (with the exception of wine) in the United States developed almost wholly outside of any religious context. Indeed, drug use was largely confined to the periphery of American society, associated with poverty and the absence of an articulate vision of the world. Yet in the late 1800s the seeds of just such a connection between drugs and spirituality were sewn by America's foremost psychologist and philosopher, William James.

A Nitrous-Oxide Awakening

In 1882, William James recounted his personal experience with nitrous oxide gas. James had become interested in the use of nitrous oxide while reviewing a book titled *The Anaesthetic Revelation and the Gist of Philosophy*. The book recounted the amateur philosopher Paul Blood's claim that after breathing nitrous oxide, he had been afforded an "insight of immemorial Mystery." Blood was convinced that he had stumbled upon a pharmaceutical pathway to experiences "in which the genius of being is revealed." The epiphany to which he had been treated disclosed how all is in God and God is in all. The gist of his anesthetica philosophy was thus quite simple: "The kingdom of God is . . . within you; it is the Soul."[6]

James considered himself a thoroughgoing empiricist. This meant that all ideas must be tested by experience. So, with respect to Blood's mystical claims, he decided to experiment for himself. The results were impressive. The intoxication proved so enjoyable that James was moved to "urge others to repeat the experiment, which with pure gas is short and harmless enough." He informed his readers that although the effects will vary from person to person, there is nonetheless a general pattern to the subjective effects of nitrous oxide: "With me, as with every other person of whom I have heard, the keynote of the experience is the tremendously exciting sense of an intense metaphysical illumination."[7]

This "metaphysical illumination" was to become a signal event in James's personal and professional life.[8] For one thing, nitrous oxide had enabled James to view religion from the "inside." From that moment forward he was able to appreciate the mystical experience from the mystic's own standpoint. Perhaps more importantly, however, nitrous oxide provided James with an experiential context for his emerging interest in the philosophical concepts he called "pluralism" and "radical empiricism." By pluralism James meant that there are always alternative points of view and that no one point of view is inherently privileged over others. This was more than a simple statement of philosophical tolerance. Pluralism was instead a full-fledged commitment to the possibility that there is no single, absolute truth. In this sense James was moving beyond the vision of modern science to what is often called the "postmodern" view that focuses on how humans construct their various interpretations of reality. James's radical empiricism was also connected with the metaphysical illumination afforded by his experiment with nitrous oxide. James was convinced that experiences such as his and Blood's deserved to be considered authentic perceptions of reality. He reasoned that what the natural sciences ordinarily mean by empiricism is not fully empirical at all; instead, the natural sciences typically restrict their understanding of experience to the normal waking state of consciousness. A radical empiricism would thus pay attention to the full range of human experience, including the kinds of mystical and religious experiences that occur at the margins of waking consciousness.

The developed fruits of James's metaphysical illumination can be seen in his epochal *The Varieties of Religious Experience*. First published in 1902, the *Varieties* argues that personal, mystical experience is the core of authentic religion. All of the various creeds and rituals associated with the world's organized religions are, in James's view, but secondhand translations of the original experiences from which they arose. James was thus contending that authentic spirituality can be traced back to experiences that provide individuals with the felt conviction (1) that the visible world is part of a more spiritual universe from which it draws its chief significance and (2) that union or harmonious relation with that higher universe is our true end. Importantly, James's understanding of the authentic core of religion was at least partially anchored in his own earlier experiment with nitrous oxide:

> Some years ago I myself made some observations on this aspect of nitrous oxide intoxication, and reported them in print. One conclusion was forced upon my mind at that time, and my impression of its truth has ever since remained unshaken. It is that our normal waking consciousness, rational consciousness as we call it, is but one special type of consciousness, whilst all about it, parted from it by the filmiest of screens, there lie potential forms of consciousness entirely different.[9]

As a psychologist, James knew that our normal waking state of consciousness has tremendous utility in helping us adapt to the physical and social environments. But as a psychologist he also knew that many other states of consciousness (e.g., dreaming, hypnosis, mysticism) exist as well. It struck James that these other states of consciousness must have their own utilities: "We may go through life without suspecting their existence; but apply the requisite stimulus, and at a touch they are there in all their completeness, definite types of mentality which probably somewhere have their field of application and adaptation."[10] Indeed, James concluded that

> The whole drift of my education goes to persuade me that the world of our present consciousness is only one out of many worlds of consciousness that exist, and that those other worlds must contain experiences which have a meaning for our life also; and that although in the main their experiences and those of this world keep discrete, yet the two become continuous at certain points, and higher energies filter in.[11]

James, who was a philosopher as well as a psychologist, maintained that "no account of the universe in its totality can be final which leaves these other forms of consciousness quite disregarded."[12] More than anything else, mystical states of consciousness disclosed humanity's continuity with a universe that is far more spiritually extensive than materialistic science had ever imagined. As James put it, such states "point with reasonable probability to the continuity of our consciousness with a wider spiritual environment from which the ordinary prudential man (who is the only man that scientific psychology, so called, takes cognizance of) is shut off."[13] James's point was that mystical experiences, such as his own nitrous oxide–induced awakening, alter our threshold of sensation in such a way as to make us receptive to a range of sensations that we would ordinarily ignore.

James had, in essence, redefined authentic spirituality so as to make it equivalent to the attainment of certain expanded states of consciousness. As historian William Clebsch has noted, James's psychological rendering of religion succeeded in drawing modern attention to the aesthetic spirituality found in such earlier American writers as Jonathan Edwards and Ralph Waldo Emerson. That is, James had defined spirituality not in terms of church membership or consenting to doctrinal standards but in attaining a certain consciousness of living in harmony with a divine reality. In so doing, James "set the agenda for American religious thought, now fully distinct from theology, in the twentieth century."[14]

James was, of course, more an early creature than the historical creator of this modern religious "agenda." Yet his own journey toward an aesthetic spirituality, a journey whose direction was greatly influenced by his nitrous oxide awakening, prefigured the religious pathway that many other Americans were destined to take as they turned away from churched religion while yet desiring metaphysical illumination. Regardless of just how much causal influence can be attributed to James himself, the "agenda" of equating authentic spirituality with the attainment of expanded states of consciousness has, since the late 1950s, factored significantly in the religious life of many Americans. As Wade Clark Roof demonstrated in his highly regarded study of the Baby Boom generation, experimental drug use often led to fascination with a variety of forms of unchurched spirituality.[15] Roof illustrated this thesis with the example of Mollie, one of the persons whose spiritual journeys featured prominently in his sociological study. Mollie, who began experimenting with drugs in the 1960s, "has been on a spiritual quest ever since. She has explored many of the spiritual and human potential alternatives of the post-sixties period; holistic health, macrobiotics, Zen Buddhism, Native American rituals, New Age in its many versions. She's read a lot about reincarnation and world religions. . . . She's an explorer down many religious paths."[16] It would seem that Mollie, much like William James before her, traveled a path that led from a drug-induced metaphysical illumination to a spiritual outlook that might be characterized by such words as pluralism, postmodernism, and religious eclecticism.

It appears, then, that were was a slumbering potential for drug use among middle-class Americans to become associated with religious concerns. By the 1960s there would be a sufficient core of middle-class Americans who would become culturally and spiritually restless. They would be especially receptive to newly emerging religious prophets who would introduce them to the psychedelic stairways they might ascend in search of exciting metaphysical illuminations.

The Doors of Perception Swing Open

A revolution in middle-class America's metaphysical outlook began on a sunny morning in Los Angeles. It was May 4, 1953, and Humphry Osmond was eager to share three hundred milligrams of mescaline with the British writer and intellectual Aldous Huxley.[17] Osmond was a psychiatrist visiting Los Angeles to attend the annual meeting of the American Psychological Association. He had become interested in how mescaline, the principal psychoactive substance in peyote, might help us understand schizophrenia and other mental disorders. It was Osmond who coined the term psychedelic from the Greek words for "mind" and "to manifest." The term psychedelic had obvious advantages over such other possible nomenclature as "drugs" or "narcotics." Indeed, both mescaline and the newly synthesized substance known as LSD-25 seemed to act less as poisons than as catalysts for revealing the manifold powers of the mind. Osmond was curious about what Huxley might think about mescaline's mind-manifesting capacities.

Of all the minds residing in California in 1953, few could have been more interesting to "manifest" than that of Aldous Huxley. Huxley was an intellectual *par excellence*. Equally versed in the sciences and humanities, Huxley was also a visionary and cultural critic as evidenced in his best-selling *Brave New World*. Huxley was particularly interested in philosophy and religion, having studied Vedanta Hinduism under Swami Prabahananda in the 1940s. Vedanta philosophy had been an important influence upon his well-known *Perennial Philosophy*, which argued that there is a common theme to be found in the mystical literature of all world religions. Huxley's basic thesis in the *Perennial Philosophy* was that underlying the world of sensory appearances is an ineffable, timeless, spiritual reality (referred to by the Hindus as Brahman, the impersonal "One," or by the Buddhists as the Indwelling Buddha-Nature). There can be little question, then, that Huxley brought a fairly sophisticated repertoire of metaphysical categories to his first experience of psychedelic illumination.

Huxley's mescaline experience is well worth recounting. His eloquent description of mescaline-induced ecstasy provides valuable insight into how psychedelic experiences came to be viewed in a particular kind of religious framework. Huxley's writings not only described his own metaphysical illumination but, in turn, provided a vocabulary and interpretive structure that shaped other Americans' experiences with psychedelics for the next several decades. A half hour after swallowing a glass of water containing the dissolved dose of mescaline, Huxley realized that his visual perceptions were intensifying. Colors became brighter and more vivid. Gazing at a glass vase containing three flowers, Huxley began to see things in novel way: "I became aware of a slow dance of golden lights . . . red surfaces . . . bright nodes of energy that vibrated with a continuously changing, patterned life."[18] Huxley believed that the mescaline had somehow allowed him to bypass the filtering functions ordinarily imposed upon experience by our limited physical senses.

He was beholding the universe in its indescribable glory. He recorded that his experience was that of "seeing what Adam had seen on the morning of his creation—the miracle, moment by moment, of naked existence."[19]

When trying to communicate his mescaline-induced epiphany, Huxley recalled a line from William Blake's *Marriage of Heaven and Hell:* "If the doors of perception were cleansed, everything would appear to man as it really is, infinite." Huxley proclaimed that mescaline had cleansed his doors of perception. He found himself staring face to face at the infinite, sacred reality permeating the whole universe. Everything that he beheld radiated the very essence that the mystic Meister Eckhart had called Istigkeit, "isness." This "isness" was in one sense what Plato had called "Being," except that Huxley now realized that Plato had made the grotesque mistake of separating Being from becoming. Plato, apparently, had never been afforded a full cleansing of perception. And for this reason he "could never, poor fool, have seen a bunch of flowers shining with their own inner light."[20] Yet this was precisely what Huxley could now see. Having pierced beneath the world of verbal description, Huxley was immersed instead in "a world where everything shone with Inner Light, and was infinite in its significance."[21]

Huxley was not above poking fun at his own fumbling encounter with the "isness" of Being. Mescaline had transformed such mundane objects as chair legs and a pair of trousers into sources of mystical euphoria. As he put it, cleverly turning the famous line of William Blake, he had seen "eternity in a flower, infinity in four chair legs, and the Absolute in the folds of a pair of flannel trousers."[22] But he also believed that what had transpired through those mescaline-widened doors deserved more serious philosophical reflection.

Huxley proposed a reconsideration of the French philosopher Henri Bergson's concept of Mind at Large. In Bergson's view, each one of us is potentially Mind at Large, meaning that we are potentially capable of perceiving everything that is transpiring anywhere in the universe or knowing everything that has ever happened. However, because we are biological animals, our brains must primarily function in the service of biological survival. To do this our brains must act as reducing valves. That is, they must screen out all of those perceptions and forms of knowledge that are not directly relevant to survival. And thus although humans are potentially capable of infinite awareness, our brains reduce this potentially unlimited flow of consciousness down to a measly trickle.

In Huxley's view, what mescaline does is to impair the efficiency of the cerebral reducing valve. The result is that all kinds of experiences ordinarily screened from awareness become possible. In some cases there may be extrasensory perceptions. Other persons discover a world of visionary beauty. Still others catch a glimpse of the infinite glory and meaningfulness of naked existence.

Huxley did not consider psychedelic experience to be the ultimate purpose of life. He compared mescaline-induced experience to what Catholic theologians call "a gratuitous grace." It shakes us out of the ruts of ordinary perception and allows us to see life as it is apprehended by Mind at Large. And although Huxley did not offer a full theological discourse on the ontological and metaphysical significance of Mind at Large, he did give some broad hints. First, it was clear to him that institutional Christianity had little of importance to say about the Light that radiates through Being. True, certain Christian mystics had slipped past the doors of ordinary perception and gained insight. But by embracing the doctrine of the Fall, Christianity long ago adopted a deprecatory attitude toward nature that jams the doors of perception shut. Christianity, by proclaiming that the Absolute was incarnate only in Christ, makes it difficult to see that the Absolute is actually incarnated in the whole of Being. In contrast, the Romantic visionaries such as Blake, Wordsworth, and Whitman are reliable guides to circumventing the reducing valve of the brain and to glimpsing the "isness" of existence. So, too, are the philosophies of Vedanta Hinduism and Zen Buddhism. In fact, Huxley realized that mescaline had ushered him directly into the realms of Eastern enlightenment. He had studied Eastern philosophies for so many years, realizing that they were alluding to understandings that evade all verbal description. Now he had found his own way of cleansing the doors of perception, paving the way for an experiential realization of how the radiating presence of the "Dharma Body" of the Buddha permeates all living things.

Huxley had long sought his metaphysical illumination. By the gratuitous grace of mescaline he came to have a clear understanding of the abstract truths he had been pursuing in libraries for decades. The situation was very different for Albert Hofmann. Having graduated from the University of Zurich in 1929, the young Hofmann went to work for a Swiss pharmaceutical company by the name of Sandoz. He was assigned to work at Sandoz's pharmaceutical research facility at Basel and was mostly involved with studying alkaloids that might be valuable in obstetrics. His particular research specialty involved ergot alkaloids, which were produced by a fungus that grows on rye. In 1938, Hofmann produced the twenty-fifth substance in a series of lysergic acid derivatives: lysergic acid diethylamide, which he abbreviated LSD-25 for laboratory use. One of Hofmann's colleagues studied the effects of LSD-25 on the uteruses of experimental animals for a time, noting that the animals became restless and exhibited abnormal behavior. The Sandoz research teams went on to investigate other alkaloids until five years later when Hofmann decided to go back and run a new series of tests on the nearly forgotten batch of lysergic acid. On April 19, 1943, he synthesized a new batch of LSD-25 before being interrupted by unusual sensations. Thinking that he might be coming down with an illness, Hofmann decided to go home early. A few days later he sent the following report to his supervisor:

> Last Friday, April 16, 1943, I was forced to interrupt my work in the laboratory in the middle of the afternoon and proceed home, being affected by a remarkable restlessness, combined with a slight dizziness. At home I lay down and sank into a not unpleasant intoxicated-like condition, characterized by an extremely stimulated imagination. In a dream-like state, with eyes closed (I found the daylight to be unpleasantly glaring), I perceived an uninterrupted stream of fantastic pictures, extraordinary shapes with intense, kaleidoscopic play of colors. After some two hours this condition faded away.[23]

Hofmann could not be entirely sure what had caused his extraordinary experience. Suspecting that his fingertips might have absorbed some of the alkaloid substance that he had been working on, he decided to have a further look at LSD-25 on the following Monday. In the late afternoon of Monday, April 19, Hofmann dissolved a minuscule amount (just 250 millionths of a gram) of LSD-25 into a glass of water, gulped it down, and waited to see what would happen. A half hour later, he began to experience some dizziness and visual distortion. He then got on his bicycle and started to ride home. In his book chronicling the social history of LSD, Jay Stevens records that Hofmann had just "pedaled off into a suddenly anarchic universe. In Hofmann's mind this wasn't the familiar boulevard that led home, but a street painted by Salvador Dali, a funhouse roller coaster where the buildings yawned and rippled. But what was even stranger was the sense that although his legs were pumping steadily, he wasn't getting anywhere."[24]

When Hofmann finally got home from what had seemed to be an interminable journey (his assistant who accompanied him on the bicycle trip thought that it had been a rather quick ride), he lay down and awaited assistance from a doctor. The doctor found him physically well, but mentally deranged. Hofmann claimed to be hovering near the ceiling, gazing down at his apparently lifeless body. The kaleidoscopic play of colors that had danced through his head on his first LSD "trip" now eluded him. Instead, he was descending into a veritable hell of fears and anxieties. He became ever more agitated and confused. The face of a neighbor, who tried to help him by offering a glass of milk, turned into a grotesque mask. It occurred to him that he might have triggered a psychosis. The LSD might have caused brain damage, rendering him permanently insane.

By the next day, Hofmann had returned to normal and his mind appeared none the worse for wear. Indeed, he was eager to learn more about this peculiar chemical. Hofmann reasoned that LSD could not be toxic. If LSD produced toxic effects, then it would only give rise to pathological experiences. Hofmann believed that the effects of LSD were, on the whole, quite salutary. True, he actually knew very little about how or why such minuscule quantities of LSD could produce such pronounced effects. But the very fact that the doses of LSD were so minimal struck him as proof that the experiences he was studying would ultimately reveal less about the chemical properties of LSD than about the mind itself. He conjectured that what LSD did was to excite the cross-connections or synapses between billions of brain cells. In this sense, LSD was simply magnifying the brain's innate capacities. He further speculated that LSD would have its greatest application as an adjunct in psychotherapy. Because LSD seemed to facilitate the instantaneous memory of forgotten or repressed experiences, it could significantly speed up the process of self-discovery and thereby shorten the course of psychotherapeutic treatment.

Curiously, however, Hofmann concluded that the greatest significance of LSD was not so much scientific as religious. The accounts of his initial experiences with LSD record nothing that strike the reader as being of an intrinsically religious nature. Yet in late career Hofmann wrote an autobiographical account of his discovery titled *LSD: My Problem Child,* in which he describes this twenty-fifth batch of lysergic acid derivatives as "a sacred drug." He, too, had learned what it is like to have the doors of perception cleansed: "Of greatest significance to me has been the insight that . . . there are many realities, each comprising also a different consciousness of the ego."[25] He was, however, more adept at science than metaphysics. He promptly corrected himself and suggested that perhaps it is not so much that there are multiple realities as there are multiple aspects of *the* reality. He now embellished upon his earlier conjecture that LSD excites brain synapses and proposed that it shifts the "wavelength setting of the receiving 'self.'" Fortuitously, the wavelength to which LSD adjusts our minds makes it possible for us to have a more complete relationship with the surrounding world. LSD could, in short, forge a mystical union between self and world:

> This condition of cosmic consciousness, which under favorable conditions can be evoked by LSD or by another hallucinogen from the group of Mexican sacred drugs, is analogous to spontaneous religious enlightenment, with the *unio mystica*. In both conditions, which often last only for a timeless moment, a reality is experienced that exposes a gleam of the transcendental reality, in which universe and self, sender and receiver, are one.[26]

LSD had given experiential reality to what Hofmann called the "heart of my Christian beliefs." His encounter with a sacred drug had illuminated the very words of Jesus recorded in John 14:20: "At that day ye shall know that I am in my Father, and ye in me, and I in you." Hofmann's metaphysical illumination had not, however, helped him to embrace the institutionalized part of Christianity. He complained that ecclesiastical Christianity espoused a "nature-alienated religiosity" that corrupted the pure insights of the great Christian mystics such as Jakob Boehme, Meister Eckhart, Angelus Silesius, Thomas Traherne, William Blake, and others. For this reason he counseled fellow citizens of "Western industrial societies who are sickened by a one-sided, rational, materialistic world view" to look to Eastern religions such as Zen Buddhism.[27] Here persons will find emphasis upon the metaphysical dimension of the human mind through which we can come to know our unity with God. Hofmann hoped that one day we might learn to use LSD as an adjunct to daily periods of quiet meditation. Used as a material aid to meditation, LSD would reveal itself to be a sacred drug capable of eliciting the condition of cosmic consciousness.

Hofmann's initial reports about LSD were offered to the scientific community and focused principally on issues of interest to pharmaceutical researchers. At first LSD attracted little attention in the scientific community. This was, however, a period in which academic psychology was beginning to make great strides in the study of the brain's neurochemistry. LSD-25 caught the interest of a few of these researchers, particularly those interested in studying the cause and cure of profound mental disorders. By 1965, more than one thousand scientific papers on LSD had been published. Yet for all of this scientific attention, there was almost no consensus about just how or why LSD produces such unusual effects. There was general agreement among researchers on the more simple issues concerning the "phenomenology" of the LSD experience. That is, the verbal reports given by individuals who had undergone a session with LSD contained certain common themes: changes in visual, auditory, tactile, olfactory, gustatory, and kinesthetic perception; changes in experiencing space and time; greatly enhanced awareness of color; changes in body image; enhanced recall or memory; ego dissolution; and magnification of character traits (especially those revealing classic psychoanalytic themes).[28] Attempts to explain just how LSD produces these effects went nowhere. Although various researchers have sought to isolate specific neurochemical changes, there is still no commonly accepted model for just how and why psychedelic drugs alter mental processes.

The scientific community was also at odds over the value or benefit of LSD intoxication. Some studies found that LSD, while mimicking psychosis, had little value to scientific psychotherapy. Others found that the euphoric experiences produced by LSD were of great value in treating both depression and alcohol addiction. Most studies took the middle ground and suggested that the set (i.e., the subject's background, beliefs, attitudes, and expectations of the drug) as well as the setting (i.e., the immediate environment in which the drug is used) probably had more influence upon the "LSD experience" than any properties of the drug itself. The study of the psychological state produced by LSD that appeared in the *Journal of Abnormal Psychology* in 1963 is probably typical in this regard. The psychological researchers, Martin Katz and Irene Waskow, administered LSD to a group of male prison inmates. Using control groups, the researchers found that the subjects exhibited very intense emotions without any apparent outside stimulus. But the character of these emotions varied from mildly euphoric to ambivalent to dysphoric (impaired cognition, jitteriness, and tension). And, importantly, they found no reactions that struck them as of religious importance.[29]

Yet for every study that remained indifferent about the importance of LSD, there seemed to be an equal number that raved about its utopian potential. A good many of these "studies" straddled the boundary between professional and popular. Jane Dunlap's *Exploring Inner Space: Personal Experiences Under LSD-25* (1961) was of particular importance in introducing the general reading public to the psychedelic world. Dunlap (a pseudonym for Adelle Davis, the well-known writer of books on nutrition and health foods) recounted how in 1959 she took 110 micrograms of LSD and came to a stark realization of the limitations of "God-denying scientific materialism." She was at first ushered into a phase of aesthetic delight. Her senses blended together to create the experience of synesthesia: colors seemed to transform into music; music turned into colors. Next came a sequence of vivid hallucinations in which she relived the evolutionary history of our planet. The progressive development of life forms from the age of dinosaurs to the present raced before her mind. Fantastic visions followed one after another. In one instant she might find herself at the library in ancient Alexandria and, in the next, conversing with the Buddha. As the panorama of biological and historical evolution flashed before her mind, she realized that the impulse underlying the whole of creation was nothing short of the universal "urge to reach God." Her initiation into the mysteries of life transformed her total outlook on life: "For a few short but forever unforgettable hours LSD gives one the love of God, the forgiveness of Christ, the humility of St. Francis, the intellect of Einstein, and the compassion of Allah, the All Compassionate."[30]

Dunlap's book was followed by a number of similar entries into the strange new literary world of psychedelic diaries. Alan Watts's *The Joyous Cosmology* appeared in 1962, promising that just one session with LSD was sufficient to transport a person into the psychic region commonly referred to as "cosmic consciousness." His book provided a verbal and visual tour of the world as experienced through cosmic consciousness—a world in which matter dissolves into patterns of energy and which reveals "a cosmology not only unified but also joyous." Constance Newland's *My Self and I* appeared in 1962, offering an exciting account of how LSD could unlock the unconscious forces blocking personal fulfillment. Sidney Cohen, eager to inform readers how LSD occasions "superlative knowing," published *The Beyond Within: The LSD Story* in 1965. By 1964 there was even a journal, titled *Psychedelic Review*, devoted to publishing all things mind-manifesting.

It appears that by the early 1960s there was a sizable reading audience eager to learn about alternate realities. The newly emerging literature on LSD ushered them through the doors of perception into a realm of metaphysical excitement. Although it remained on ambiguous ground in the scientific community, LSD was seized upon as the royal road to ecstasy by a growing sector of popular American culture.

Prophet of a New Spiritual Consciousness

The year 1960 turned out to be a critical one in the social history of psychedelics in the United States. Prior to this time, LSD—while legal—was for the most part confined to the laboratories of a handful of pharmaceutical and psychological researchers. Yet larger social forces were at work that were destined to implicate LSD in a major cultural revolution. The transformation of LSD from laboratory alkaloid to cultural icon is a fascinating story in American history. And like most good stories, this one centers around a main character of mythic proportions. In the summer of 1960, Timothy Leary took a vacation to Mexico before beginning his new job at Harvard's Center for the Study of Personality. A Berkeley psychologist, Frank Barron, had told Tim about the psilocybin mushrooms (*teonanacatl*, the "flesh of the gods") that had played such an important role in classic shamanism. Leary, who later described himself as someone who had never met a drug he didn't like, purchased a few of these sacred mushrooms and gave them a try. "The journey lasted a little over four hours," he wrote. "Like almost everyone who had the veil drawn, I came back a changed man."[31]

When Leary assumed his duties that fall at Harvard he found that he had little interest in the relatively boring field of personality assessment. Statistical analyses of questionnaire responses paled by comparison to the wonders unleashed by the psilocybin, mescaline, and LSD he was experimenting with on a nearly daily basis. Leary and his colleague Richard Alpert shifted their research interests in a way that allowed them to turn their favorite hobby into a full-time occupation. Within months they had managed to become the directors of what they christened the Harvard Psychedelic Drug Research Project. During the next four years, Leary and Alpert managed to "arrange transcendent experiences" for over 1,000 persons. Their subjects included students, writers, artists, convicts, and sixty-nine members of the clergy. Also notable for their participation in Leary's investigations were Aldous Huxley, Allen Ginsberg, Alan Watts, and Huston Smith. Although Leary was the most charismatic prophet of the psychedelic gospel, these latter individuals were among the most able apostles.

Leary and Alpert focused principally on studying the ways in which "set" and "setting" influenced the nature of an LSD trip.

Their studies indicated that when the setting was supportive but not explicitly spiritual, between 40 and 75 percent of their test subjects nonetheless reported life-changing religious experiences. Yet when the set and setting emphasized spiritual themes, up to 90 percent reported having mystical or illuminating experiences.

Leary was only an advisor and experimental subject in the most famous of these studies on psychedelic spirituality. In the spring of 1962, a graduate student in the Philosophy of Religion program at Harvard Divinity School approached Leary about an exciting project. Walter Pahnke was an M.D. and a minister. He now wanted to earn a degree in religion by conducting an empirical test of the categories scholars use to describe the mystical experience. Pahnke enlisted the help of twenty theology students who gathered on Good Friday at Boston University's Marsh Chapel. The test was a controlled, double-blind experiment in which he divided the twenty subjects into five groups of four students each. Ninety minutes before the Good Friday service began, Pahnke administered identical capsules to each subject. Half of the capsules contained thirty milligrams of psilocybin. The other half contained two hundred milligrams of a vitamin that causes feelings of warmth and tingling but has no effect on the mind. The subjects then attended a two-and-a-half-hour religious service consisting of organ music, prayers, and personal meditation. The subjects were later interviewed and asked to fill out a 147-item questionnaire designed to measure phenomena related to a typology of mystical consciousness. Of note is the fact that nine of the ten students who had taken the psilocybin reported having religious experiences, while only one of the subjects who had been given a placebo reported any such sensations.[32] Pahnke maintained that psychedelics extinguish the "empirical ego" and assist individuals in transcending the subject-object dichotomy of ordinary rational consciousness. His study concluded that LSD occasions every major characteristic of "authentic" mystical experience (e.g., sense of unity, transcendence of space and time, alleged ineffability, paradoxicality, and subsequent elevation of mood). One of Panhnke's group leaders, Walter Clark, surmised that the miracle of Marsh Chapel was "the most cogent single piece of evidence that psychedelic chemicals do, under certain circumstances, release profound religious experience."[33]

Leary and Alpert believed that discoveries such as these were about to usher in a new era in human spiritual consciousness. They believed that they were on the verge of reducing centuries of theological abstractions down to a simple chemical formula. Their studies indicated that if the proper training and setting could be provided, nearly everyone was capable of achieving a sense of mystical oneness with God. Yet much to their surprise and dismay, the world did not run to embrace the implications of their research. Scorn, not praise, met their psychedelic gospel. Part of this disapproval was theological. Already scholars were contending that the "nature mysticism" engendered by LSD was not true or authentic mysticism. However, the central objection to Leary's seemingly indiscriminate advocacy of psychedelics was concern over widespread licentiousness, particularly among youth. The use of LSD was spreading across the country. Easily synthesized in makeshift chemistry labs (and legal until late 1966), the availability of LSD and other psychedelics escalated while the price continued to drop. Chemical euphoria was instantly accessible to the emerging "hippie" culture. Leary frequently warned against misuse and hoped that psychedelics would be restricted to the philosophical elite. But if his words cautioned discretion, his overall demeanor and actions fostered chemical promiscuity. Harvard had made Leary and Alpert pledge not to use undergraduate students in their "research." They never complied. Reports of ribald partying and sexual dalliance in Leary's office swept across campus. Harvard officials had no recourse but to remove both Leary and Alpert from the faculty and shut down their center for psychedelic research.

For a short time, Leary became a rebel without an expense account. His colleague, Richard Alpert, later ventured to India, where he took up the practice of yoga meditation and changed his name to Ram Dass. Alpert had found that the psychedelic experience ultimately led nowhere. Now, in the transformed incarnation of Ram Dass, he continued to believe that psychedelics were of value in helping a person break out of their restricted consciousness. But Ram Dass maintained that such an awakening is only the beginning of an authentic spiritual life. Thus while never renouncing the possibility that drugs might introduce persons to spiritual dimensions of reality, Alpert shifted the focus of his countercultural ministry to Hindu-style meditation and spiritual discipline.[34]

Leary, however, was more determined than ever to advance the cause of psychedelics. Believing that he could generate sufficient income from his writings, speaking fees and donations, Leary organized the International Federation for Internal Freedom (IFIF) in 1963 for the purpose of continuing his psychedelic research. After being expelled from the organization's original headquarters in Zihuatanejo, Mexico, Leary was offered the use of an estate located in Millbrook, New York. The Millbrook estate provided the perfect setting in which to engage in outlandish behaviors that ranged from serious research to bacchanalian debauchery. For about four years Millbrook was a monastery, school, research laboratory, religious commune, and opium den all rolled into one. The sixty-four-room manor was home not only to the IFIF (subsequently renamed the League for Spiritual Discovery, and finally the Castalia Foundation in reference to the monastery in Hermann Hesse's *The Glass-Bead Game*) but also to a constantly revolving door of visitors who came for drugs, sex, and stimulating conversation. Leary even turned Millbrook into a weekend getaway for those with discretionary income to spend on "consciousness-expanding" retreats. All the while Leary was taking notes on his and others' experiences in an attempt to create a map of the previously unexplored regions of the mind.

Leary and others were increasingly persuaded that LSD was giving Westerners access to regions of the mind that practitioners of Eastern meditation systems had known for centuries. For this reason he hoped that Eastern texts might be of great value in his attempt to create a cartography of inner space. Leary first adapted the verses of the *Tao Te Ching* in a book he called *Psychedelic Prayers*. Then, in 1962, he, Ralph Metzner, and Richard Alpert created a psychedelic variation on the Buddhist scholar W. Y. Evans-Wentz's translation of *The Tibetan Book of the Dead*. *The Tibetan Book of the Dead* is an ancient Buddhist meditation manual that purports to explain the realties (termed *bardos*) into which one travels following physical death. It was originally designed to be read to those near death in order to prepare them for the next stage of their metaphysical journey. Leary, Metzner, and Alpert titled their version *The Psychedelic Experience*. They were convinced that the dissolution of the ego afforded by LSD permitted entry into the same realms of consciousness described in Buddhist metaphysics. *The Psychedelic Experience* blended the esoteric terminology of Eastern mystical thought with buzzwords then current in popular American psychology. In this way the Millbrook pundits helped steer their readers to the insight that psychedelic research had at last uncovered the fundamental truths uniting East and West. This volume eventually went through sixteen editions and was translated into seven languages, giving it a long-lasting influence upon subsequent understandings of the realities disclosed by a psychedelic adventure.

Catastrophes had a way of following Leary. His obvious wit and the constant twinkle in his eyes endeared him to many. But his theatrical excess and cavalier ways frightened others. Drugs were beginning to destroy the lives of a good many young people, and Leary was an obvious target for blame. Leary himself had been arrested in 1965 for possessing marijuana as he attempted to cross the Mexican border. Despite his argument that marijuana had a legitimate religious use and thus the arrest violated his First Amendment rights, he was convicted by a Texas jury. The conviction was eventually overturned, but in the meantime Millbrook was itself raided by G. Gordon Liddy (who was destined to become a symbol and spokesperson for conservative American culture when the Watergate scandal thrust him into national prominence). Liddy, then the assistant district attorney of Dutchess County, led a small troop of law enforcement officials in a midnight raid with the hopes of finding Leary with his pants down and his head turned on. Just what was going on at Millbrook when the police came busting through the doors is still a matter of dispute. Ironically, Liddy and Leary eventually reunited as friends and colleagues on the college lecture circuit and turned their conflicting accounts of the event into entertaining repartee. One thing was clear, however: Government toleration of psychedelics was nearing an end. By 1967 California made the manufacture or possession of LSD illegal. Leary's never-ending attacks upon "the system" were drawing a response. And in 1970, Leary was again convicted of drug possession and sentenced to a minimum security prison in San Luis Obispo. Leary managed to escape from prison and live in exile outside the United States for several years before being caught and returned to prison. Finally released in 1976, Leary continued to promote the psychedelic cause until his death in 1996 (his ashes were sent up in a satellite to orbit earth, which seemed a somewhat apt transition from navigating inner space to orbiting outer space).

Following his 1970 arrest, Leary never quite regained the peculiar role he had achieved in advocating a new, drug-enhanced spirituality. Yet by this time he had already succeeded in spreading his psychedelic gospel throughout the country. The Haight-Ashbury district of San Francisco had surfaced as the Vatican of the Acid Church as early as 1965, giving the psychedelic cause a geographical and symbolic foothold in the terrain of a newly emerging segment of American culture. No one ever quite rivaled Timothy Leary as the High Priest of America's new spiritual consciousness; he and his apostles had spread the psychedelic gospel far and wide.

Turning On

Leary was well suited for his role as self-appointed spokesperson for the growing hippie movement. The word hippie, probably derived from the forties and fifties jazz terms hep and hepcat, suggests a desire to be "with it."[35] And if any one in the United States was possessed by the conviction that he knew what it meant to be "with it," it was Tim Leary. Furthermore, Leary was able to condense his message into a crisp, catchy slogan: "Turn on, tune in, and drop out." Leary's slogan was multivalent, carrying different messages to different people in different settings. In this way it helped piece together the disparate elements of the sixties counterculture. Leary's genius was to synthesize otherwise contrary impulses into a mantra of common aspiration.

Turning on was the fun part. Psilocybin, mescaline, LSD, methedrine, and later STP were the "major hallucinogens" of the hippie movement. Marijuana and alcohol were its "minor hallucinogens." Although the official rhetoric was that these substances were simply *upaya* (the Sanskrit term for "skillful means," which Ram Dass used to explain the value of psychedelics for opening consciousness past the restrictive ego), most users were probably content with the emotional rush. Even Millbrook usually resembled an opium den or upscale fraternity party more than a research facility. Jay Stevens offered the apt description of as "a house party of unparalleled dimensions."[36] The weekend marathons of drugs and sex at Millbrook set the tone for what turning on was all about to a good many who dabbled in the sixties and seventies hippie counterculture. Leary chided the Puritan or antipleasure strain in American culture. He argued that the hedonistic pursuit of pleasure is a basic human right, perhaps even a moral duty. Leary's point was that we should take full advantage of the pharmaceutical breakthroughs that will allow us to "design one's life for pleasure through chemical turn-ons and turn-offs."[37]

Sense and sensuality are natural sacraments in Leary's view. Turning on, then, is a form of nature religion. Much as earlier Americans such as Henry David Thoreau or John Muir had turned attention to the sacredness of forests, Leary was turning attention to the sacred sensations to be found in our own natural constitution. What Leary discovered was that God is infused in every life-generating emotion, including sexual desire: "I was awed and confused by the sexual power [of turning on]. It was too easy. I was too much an Irish Catholic, too prudish to deal with it. Too Western Christian to realize that God and Sex are one, that God for a man is woman, that the direct path to God is through the divine union of male-female."[38]

Turning on also meant more than hedonistic pleasure. It had to do with ecstasy, with expanding consciousness. As the Episcopal priest turned psychedelic messiah, Alan Watts, wrote, "ecstasy is a legitimate human need—as essential for mental and physical health as proper nutrition, vitamins, rest, and recreation."[39] Leary went even further, likening himself to a religious prophet, a revolutionary seer whose message concerning spiritual ecstasy was slightly ahead of his time. He insisted that psychedelics open up the metaphysical vistas glimpsed by Moses, Mohammed, Blake, Boehme, Shankara, and St. John of the Cross. In his psychedelic gospel, experience and message were one and the same: "Listen! Wake up! You are God! You have the Divine plan engraved in cellular script within you. Listen! Take this sacrament! You'll see! You'll get the revelation! It will change your life! You'll be reborn!"[40]

Tuning In

Tuning in had a slightly more esoteric ring to it. The mid- to late sixties was also the time of the human potential movement. Figures such as Abraham Maslow and Fritz Perls were among the many "third force" or humanistic psychologists whose writings attracted a broad following. Humanistic psychologists were proposing an extremely optimistic view of human nature based largely on the view that the unconscious mind has unlimited energies that can be tapped for self-realization. Many human potential writers saw psychedelics as a way of tuning in to the "higher" energies of the unconscious.

Those who studied the psychedelic experience went out of their way to draw attention to the remarkable personal growth observed in their research subjects. For example, Sidney Cohen extolled LSD for stimulating "super-conscious bursts" of knowing.[41] Robert Mogar, summarizing the current status of LSD research in 1965, suggested that the principal use of LSD in the future would be to serve as a catalyst for rapid personal growth.[42] When R. E. Masters and Jean Houston wrote their oft-cited *The Varieties of Psychedelic Experience* in 1966, they took it for granted that "psychedelic (mind-manifesting) drugs afford the best access yet to the contents and processes of the human mind."[43] In their professional opinion, psychedelics pointed the way to the next step in human evolution. The work being done in this field was destined "to result in eventually pushing human consciousness beyond its present limitations and on towards capacities not yet realized and perhaps undreamed of."[44] Not to be overlooked was their bold hint that among these "undreamed of capacities" are the abilities for telepathy, ESP, and other paranormal phenomena. Masters and Houston, like a good many other apostles of the psychedelic message, could not resist making broad hints that psychedelic research was on the verge of documenting humanity's unexplored potentials for extrasensory perception.

Tuning in had other connotations, too. Psychedelic researchers were not interested in limiting their work to the development of a new psychological model of the human mind. When Albert Hofmann suggested that LSD adjusted the "wavelength" setting of the receiving self, he was arguing that our ordinary consciousness fails to apprehend all that there is to reality. Almost all psychedelic researchers agreed. It was argued that psychedelics do not distort reality but disclose dimensions or levels of existence that are otherwise screened by the rational ego. Psychedelics didn't just help us tune into previously untapped levels of our own mind; they also helped us tune into previously unrecognized dimensions or levels of reality.

Tuning in, then, sought to do more than enhance the kinds of mental processes that psychology already dealt with. Leary's psychology aimed at ecstasy, not normalcy. His own experience with LSD had all the hallmarks of a shaman's death-rebirth initiatory rite. It followed "that the religious-ontological nature of the psychedelic experience was obvious to me, and any secular discussion about psychedelic drugs—creativity, psychiatric treatment, etc.— seemed irrelevant."[45] What was relevant was helping persons to tune into the Kingdom of God residing deep within themselves.

Psychedelic researchers faced a major difficulty in pressing LSD sessions into the service of religious metaphysics. The data didn't completely justify their metaphysical claims. Few subjects actually had experiences that substantiated the hybrid of Eastern mysticism and Western occultism nurtured by the likes of Leary, Huxley, Watts, and Smith. Only about 3 percent of Alpert's and Leary's subjects ever "tuned in" to such metaphysical realities.[46] Masters and Houston put the figure at about 5 percent.[47] Psychedelic researchers were convinced, however, that these relatively small percentages could be accounted for. It was argued that subjects who failed to have an appropriate mystical experience might have brought the wrong set (personality, belief structure) to the session. Others might not have been afforded the right kind of supportive setting. Yet another possibility was that the dose might not have been high enough or the subject just clung too rigidly to his or her ego rather than letting the experience unfold on its own.

By 1966 Masters and Houston provided a neat typology for explaining such discrepancies between experimental findings and the claims that the researchers wanted to make on behalf of their newly found stairways to metaphysical illumination. They contended that there are four distinct levels of psychedelic experience. Each is successively "deeper" than its predecessor. Not every person moves easily through all levels, however, any more than every person can rapidly progress through the levels of musical or athletic performance. All of their subjects who used LSD were able to attain the first level, the level of enhanced sensory awareness. At this level of experience, subjects report seeing colors more intensely, sensing an extraordinary beauty residing in things, and witness an endless flow of dancing geometrical forms. Masters and Houston noted that many, but not all, subjects were able to progress to the second level of psychedelic experience, which they referred to as the recollective-analytic. At this level, subjects become acutely aware of their mental and emotional processes. Memories of past events surface, and insight is gained into the psychological effect they have had. The third level, attained by even fewer subjects, is the symbolic level. Here the subject experiences primal, universal, and recurring themes of human experience. This level affords insight into the rites of passage, initiations, and other archetypal experiences we all go through. Masters and Houston called the fourth, and deepest, level the integral level. The integral level is mystical in nature. It affords individuals a vivid sensation of being "one" with the deepest level of reality. Unfortunately, only 11 of their 206 subjects had reached the deep integral level. Those who did described a feeling of oneness with God. Masters and Houston note that their subjects' descriptions of God do not exactly match conventional religious language. Rather than describing God in biblical terms, they utilized words more reminiscent of Paul Tillich's definition of God as the Ground of Being. As Masters and Houston explained, "When we examine those psychedelic experiences which seem to be authentically religious, we find that during the session the subject has been *able to reach the deep integral level* wherein lies the possibility of confrontation with a Presence variously described as God, Spirit, Ground of Being, Mysterium, Noumen, Essence, and Ultimate or Fundamental Reality."[48]

Another and more elaborate version of this typology was advocated by Stanislav Grof. Grof began conducting research into psychedelic drugs in his native Czechoslovakia in 1956. In 1967 he came to the United States and resumed his investigations at the Research Unit of Spring Grove State Hospital in Baltimore, Maryland. By 1973 Grof had conducted over 2,500 psychedelic sessions (each lasting a minimum of five hours), giving him the largest data base of any researcher in the field. His subjects were drawn from various groups, including terminally ill patients, severe psychoneurotics, alcoholic patients, graduate students, nurses, psychologists, artists, and theologians. Grof, too, proposed that there are four major levels of psychedelic experience.[49] He labeled the first level "abstract and aesthetic experiences." The second level was "psychodynamic experiences," which he claimed so closely manifested the kinds of psychosexual dynamics that Freud described that this level of psychedelic experience might be seen as an empirical confirmation of Freud's hypotheses. The third level varied somewhat from Masters and Houston's symbolic level. Grof called this the "perinatal" level, since his subjects frequently relived the trauma of birth and uterine existence. Jungian archetypes, death/rebirth imagery, and even visions of wrathful deities accompany these spontaneous impressions of perinatal existence. He wrote, "Everyone who has *reached these levels* develops convincing insights into the utmost relevance of the spiritual and religious dimensions in the universal scheme of things."[50] Grof termed the final level that of "transpersonal experiences." Those of his subjects who reached the deepest level spontaneously exhibited a variety of experiences that suggested that their conscious functioning was no longer restricted to the sensory plane or to the restrictive activities of the socially constructed ego. Subjects found themselves reliving earlier moments in the earth's evolutionary history, having instances of clairvoyance or precognition, enjoying out-of-body experiences, or conversing with suprahuman spiritual entities.

Grof's model, like that constructed by Masters and Houston, appealed to many. A major part of the spiritual awakening of the sixties and seventies was the excitement of "discovery." People were discovering new aspects of themselves. They were discovering new worldviews that told of other realms or levels of existence awaiting our exploration. Psychedelics contributed to the excitement of this discovery process. Even for those who didn't take them, psychedelics seemed to lend experimental confirmation to the kinds of metaphysical claims being made by those attracted to Eastern religions, the Western occult traditions, and the new human potential psychologies. That is, the results of psychedelic research were understood to have substantiated the claim that there are whole new worlds awaiting to be discovered right within ourselves. Tuning in, then, was the key to enlightenment.

Perhaps no one's life was more affected by tuning in than Huston Smith's. Smith was a professor of philosophy at MIT when he first learned about Timothy Leary's investigations. On New Year's Day, 1961, Smith visited Leary's home and accepted his host's kind invitation to try some mescaline. Smith's philosophical outlook on life was never the same. It was but a moment before he realized what Bergson had meant about the brain's role as a reducing agent. Free of the ego's restrictions, Smith now saw deeply into the mysteries of the cosmos. Perhaps most striking was his insight into "the metaphysical theory known as emanationism, in which, beginning with the clear, unbroken and infinite light of God or the Void, the light then breaks into forms and decreases in intensity as it diffuses through descending degrees of reality."[51] Smith's psychedelic illumination enabled him to see that Light was in all, all was in Light. All levels of existence are connected with one another. He further realized that the "power" of being flows continuously from higher levels to lower ones. It followed that the key to genuine spirituality is learning to become receptive to this spiritual inflow.

Smith became increasingly fascinated with what he called the common vision of the world's religions—the vision of this emanationist cosmology. His lectures, workshops, and prolific publications all promoted the "perennial philosophy" that he was quite literally turned on to while visiting Timothy Leary. In *Forgotten Truth: The Common Vision of the World's Religion,* the book that most clearly summarizes his own worldview, Smith appended a brief essay titled "The Psychedelic Evidence."[52] Smith held that the data collected by Stanislav Grof provided empirical evidence supporting the claims of the perennial philosophy: The self exists on many levels; the levels of self (or consciousness) correspond to levels of the cosmos that are ordinarily obscured from human view; enlightenment is reached by finding a means of circumventing the ego and having a direct experience of the deeper levels of the cosmos.

Even Huston Smith acknowledged that such metaphysical illuminations are probably not for the masses. The uninitiated must rely on the exoteric teachings of institutional religion. But for the initiated, the one who has turned on and tuned in, the esoteric teachings of the perennial philosophy were now being understood as objects of direct, immediate perception.

Dropping Out

Dropping out also had multiple meanings. Some were political. Others were social. And still others were religious. When Aldous Huxley first opened the doors of perception in 1953, most Americans were too busy building a brave new world to step back and evaluate it. The postwar economy was booming. The good life was there for the taking. Supermarkets, affordable automobiles, and an expanding freeway system symbolized a nation in hot pursuit of material paradise. The terms of economic, social, and technological progress were all well defined. It was only up to individuals to conform to those terms and then work for the success that would be theirs. Only a few middle-class Americans seemed interested in questioning, let alone dropping out of, the American way of life.

By the mid-1960s things had obviously changed. Pockets of discontent couldn't be overlooked or contained at the periphery. Racial unrest broke out from Harlem to Watts. But the biggest source of discontent was to be found in America's youth. Although seemingly poised to inherit an economic paradise, college-age youth seemed restless, yearning for something that was somehow more authentic, freer, more pure. In his *The Making of a Counter Culture,* Theodore Roszak emphasized the importance of the period's antitechnology sentiment.[53] People were balking at regimentation, the loss of individuality in a world of mass merchandising. There was something more at work, however. This was an age of what religious historian Robert Ellwood called a "New Romanticism."[54] The cultural mood swung toward a celebration of childhood, an endorsement of individuality, and an embracing of the "new epistemology" of the supernatural, as found in ESP, astrology, and Eastern meditation. As Ellwood aptly put it, the 1960s witnessed a dramatic cultural shift away from modernism to postmodernism. And the psychedelic movement was both a contributing cause and a symptomatic effect of this cultural shift.

What Ellwood refers to as modernism was the intellectual and cultural expression of rationalistic science. Intellectually, modernism affirms the existence of single, universal truths that can be discerned through disciplined rational inquiry. Psychologically, modernism posits the unity of the self, asserting the existence of a true or essential self lurking behind the various identities that society imposes on us. And culturally, modernism assumes the inevitability of material progress. In contrast, postmodernism embraces relativism and what physicists call the uncertainty principle. Although postmodernism means different things to different people, it is commonly understood as a philosophical outlook that distrusts the subject-object dichotomy of conventional rationality. It is skeptical of universal, general truths and finds value instead in multiple perspectives and conversations. And if modernism emphasizes the "distance senses," such as viewing, reading, or hearing, postmodernism embraces the "proximity senses" of touching, tasting, or—in the words of the sixties—just happening. Postmodernism sees the self as plural, capable of being many identities without any conflict or necessary incompatibility.

The use of psychedelics turned the logic behind modernism upside down. The point here is not that psychedelics were alone responsible for the major ideological reorientations of the sixties and early seventies. Many arrived at new philosophical outlooks without ever using mind-altering substances; and many who did use psychedelics never changed their fundamental way of viewing life. But the use of psychedelics, in conjunction with exposure to the philosophical themes of the era's youth culture, provided tens—maybe hundreds—of thousands of Americans with an experiential template for arriving at a new spiritual outlook that might be characterized by such words as pluralism, postmodernism, and religious eclecticism.

Psychedelic experiences were thought to have exploded the pretensions of rationalistic science to understand the totality of existence. As James would have put it, they proved that normal rational consciousness is but one special type of consciousness. They also brought the proximity senses to the forefront of experience and discovery. Under the influence of mind-manifesting drugs, what is felt or experienced is valued more than rational abstractions. Psychedelic experience focused upon immediate bodily sensations. It seemed to show that the universe was no one, single thing but rather altered with changes in subjectivity and awareness. At a cultural or intellectual level, then, psychedelics challenged the modern intellectual paradigm.[55] At a personal level, the use of psychedelics initiated persons into a new stance toward the world; the psychedelic trip was a rite of passage into a distinct counterculture. For thousands of Americans, the use of psychedelic drugs was thus the first step toward dropping out of a worldview that had framed middle-class American life for decades.

Dropping out became a slogan for the era's reappraisal of middle-class values. It meant attempting to stand back and undo one's social conditioning, to reassess the value of almost everything that fifties America assumed it fully understood: the relative importance of such things as a job, sex, conformity, material acquisition, technology, and church. Jay Stevens suggested that drugs provided the emerging counterculture with a "deconditioning agent." In a matter of seconds, psychedelics quite literally dismantled the whole cognitive repertoire that society had programmed into individuals. And although the dismantling was only temporary, it gave vivid insight into how arbitrary our "normal waking state" actually is. In their foreword to Alan Watts's psychedelic masterpiece *The Joyous Cosmology*, Timothy Leary and Richard Alpert argued that the freedom to use drugs in order to liberate our minds from the tyranny of social conditioning is a basic American freedom: "Thus appears the fifth freedom—freedom from the learned, cultural mind. The freedom to expand one's consciousness beyond artifactual cultural knowledge. The freedom to move from constant preoccupation with the verbal games—the social games, the game of self—to the joyous unity of what exists beyond."[56]

It is interesting in this context to remember that learning how to "stop the world" was the principal theme of Carlos Castenada's works. Readers turned to Castenada's books hoping to learn how they might disentangle themselves from—and evolve beyond—the seemingly oppressive nature of middle-class society. The allure of Don Juan's teachings was that some combination of psychedelics and Native American wisdom might prove helpful in the quest of "stopping" the power of social conditioning. A surprising number of Americans wanted to learn how they might peel away the layers of socialization and somehow uncover other layers of consciousness that were more pristine, genuine, and teeming with creative potential.

Aldous Huxley devoted a great deal of attention to how psychedelics give new perspectives on the relationship between the individual and culture. In an article appearing in *Playboy*, Huxley maintained that drugs give access to "culturally uncontaminated" levels of thought.[57] Huxley's point was that drugs can bypass the utilitarian thought processes that strip reality of its sacredness. In this way drugs can help recapture an awareness of the divine ground of all being. To be sure, most of this philosophical reasoning was lost on a good many of the entrants into hippie life. Instead, most of the era's youth probably turned to drugs for the emotional thrills. What drugs most allowed them to do was to drop out of the world defined by parental and school authorities. Indeed, Marlene Dobkin de Rios has discerned that one of the most common themes of drug use across world cultures is their implicit and explicit challenge to authority. By prompting individuals to feel that a true, experientially based authority can be found within, drugs make institutional authorities—secular and religious—appear irrelevant.[58]

Dropping out became ever more fashionable as the 1960s progressed. Clothing trends, hair length, music, and everyday jargon all reflected the implicit admiration of the hippie movement. By 1967 there may have been as many as 200,000 full-time hippies across the United States, let alone the multiples of that number who adopted elements of the hippie lifestyle.[59] Wherever they resided or whatever the degree of their affiliation with the movement, they all knew that the counterculture had a geographical center: the Haight-Ashbury district of San Francisco. The Haight-Ashbury district is a section of San Francisco that butts up against Golden Gate Park. Its handsome Victorian homes and proximity to the park had made it a favorite hangout for students and youthful drifters. But in the mid–sixties the Haight-Ashbury district became the Mecca of all things counterculture, including the heavy use of drugs. Upwards of 15,000 young men and women rented space in the adjacent houses and created what Warren Hinkle described as "a tribal, love-seeking, free-swinging, acid-based type of society."[60] In those years it was a favorite haunt of the famed author, Ken Kesey. Kesey, who had traveled the nation in a multicolored bus with his cavalier cohort known as the Merry Pranksters, became a self-appointed emissary of the psychedelic experience. Kesey had been "into" acid since 1960 and delighted in promulgating the psychedelic cause by staging public happenings he called "Acid Tests."

Haight-Ashbury developed to the point where it appeared that dropping out might be a self-sustaining way of life.[61] Coffee shops such as the Blue Unicorn and I/Thou popped up, with chessboards, sewing kits, secondhand clothes boxes, and space for social and intellectual gathering. Later, the Psychedelic Shop opened to sell metaphysical books, incense, marijuana paraphernalia, paisley fabrics, and Indian art. The quintessential expression of Haight-Ashbury's drop-out lifestyle, however, was the so-called "Be-In." Pre-dating Woodstock by a few years, the first Be-In at Haight-Ashbury was part rock concert, part political rally, part art fair, and part orgy. Top rock groups such as Quicksilver and the Grateful Dead performed. Between sets Timothy Leary, Gary Snyder, Allen Ginsberg, and Alan Watts wholeheartedly encouraged their followers to experiment with alternative lifestyles ranging from the most esoteric of Eastern mystical practices to the daily use of mind-expanding drugs. And everywhere could be had the latest batch of LSD synthesized by famed Bay-area "chemist" Owsley Stanley. These Be-Ins were also referred to as "gatherings of the tribes." And gather they did. Particularly important was the way in which Be-Ins gathered together both the more politically active and the more spiritual wings of the counterculture. As Charles Perry has chronicled, the expressed purpose of these gatherings or Be-Ins was to show that "the hippies and radicals were one, their common aim being to drop out of 'games and institutions that oppress and dehumanize' . . . and to create communities where 'new values and new human relations can grow.'"[62]

Dropping out was also an act of religious affirmation. Several short-lived churches emerged that made drugs the center of their otherwise amorphous theologies. The Shiva Fellowship Church, the Psychedelic Venus Church, the Fellowship of the Clear Light, the American Council of Internal Divinity, and the Psychedelic Peace Fellowship were among the groups hoping to legitimize the religious elements of the psychedelic experience.[63] In the late 1990s, Gordon Melton could find evidence that only about a half dozen of these "dope-related churches" were still functioning, with a combined membership estimated to be under six hundred persons.[64]

It is difficult to assess the sincerity of the motives that prompted persons to affiliate with these "dope churches." For some it was no doubt a matter of momentary impulse. The rhetoric of spiritual discovery lent an aura of respectability to the random hedonism that often characterized the hippie movement. Yet others were surely serious about their quests for ecstasy. A retired physician by the name of John Aiken formed the Church of the Awakening in 1963, advocating the use of drugs "as an aid in meditation." Art Kleps, a friend and associate of Timothy Leary, organized the Neo-American Church that mixed cynicism, satire, and the hope of using drugs with the full legal protection of the First Amendment. Timothy Leary reorganized his International Federation for Internal Freedom under the nomenclature of the League for Spiritual Discovery. In his own words, "We're not a religion in the sense of the Methodist church seeking new adherents. We're a religion in the basic primeval sense of a tribe living together and centered around shared spiritual goals. . . . In our religion the temple is the human body, the shrine is the home, and the congregation is a small group of family members and friends."[65] Leary failed to add that his League for Spiritual Discovery (LSD) might also provide a smoke screen under which persons could use drugs without government prosecution.

Most persons connected with the hippie movement never really elevated drugs to the point where they were themselves the object of religion. Instead, drugs were heralded as catalysts or "skillful means" for obtaining religious experience. Psychedelics were said to be vehicles to spiritual authenticity, not authenticity in and of themselves. But one thing was for sure. As vehicles, psychedelics were traveling in a direction opposite of the churches in which the hippie generation had been raised.

The mostly white, middle-class youth who were attracted to the counterculture came from fairly staid religious backgrounds. A significant percentage of the hippie movement had attended college. There they had been exposed to secularizing influences that made it impossible to embrace Sunday-school teachings in any straightforward way. Evolutionary biology, analytic philosophy, and the perspectives on either cultural conditioning or cultural relativism taught by the social sciences had their toll on individuals' allegiance to their parents' churches. Even more critical were the increasingly popular courses in academic departments of religion. Modern scholarship on the Bible provided students with irrefutable perspectives on the human—and hence culturally tainted—authorship of the scriptures they had formerly thought to be delivered from the mouth of God. Courses in comparative religion became the most popular courses on campuses across the nation. Exposure to Hinduism, Buddhism, and Taoism intrigued a new generation who demanded a more experiential approach to religion. In his book on *The Hippies and American Values*, Timothy Miller summarized the counterculture's religious outlook by noting that

> the hippies tended to take unusual (by traditional American standards) approaches to religion, often emphasizing Eastern spiritual teachings, and they were often syncretistic, pursuing a sort of religiosity that combined elements ranging from Hindu mysticism to Neopaganism to Ouija boards. It's a fair guess that most hippies would not have been very welcome in most churches; for their part, the hippies were not interested in getting active in any conventional religious body.[66]

It is thus easy to see why a significant number of Baby Boomers looked to the apostles of the psychedelic revolution for spiritual direction. Alan Watts, Huston Smith, Allen Ginsberg, and Richard Alpert/Ram Dass were homegrown gurus.

Watts was the embodiment of metaphysical illumination. A former Episcopal priest, Watts had been introduced at an early age to Theosophy and other metaphysical vocabularies that mingled Hindu Vedantism with Western occult traditions. His knowledge of Taoism and Zen Buddhism further set him apart as a guide to the mysterious yet uncharted spiritual territories that American reading audiences were eager to explore. When Watts converted to psychedelic enlightenment, he gave the movement its most gifted writer.

Huston Smith, meanwhile, was the movement's closest link to academic respectability. Smith was one of the few psychedelic pundits who was able to retain his academic stature. Writing in calm and understated fashion, it was Smith who did the most to get a fair hearing for the claim that drugs have religious significance.

Ginsberg, on the other hand, was quite possibly the most outrageous of the group; and that's a significant claim in a list that includes Timothy Leary. Ginsberg's connections with the literary and artistic communities preserved the psychedelic movement's ties with the Beat generation that preceded it. Up until his death in 1997, Ginsberg continued to promulgate Eastern perspectives through his own theatrical lecture/Be-Ins.

Ram Dass, meanwhile, was a living symbol that West can go East and return as a self-actualized sage. His message was that we must learn to go beyond conceptual structures. And although he has acknowledged that he still takes drugs from time to time, Ram Dass has dedicated his life to showing others a number of spiritual practices that can make ecstasy a sustained reality rather than a one-shot experience.

Watts, Smith, Ginsberg, and Ram Dass were all more capable religious thinkers than Leary. Whereas Leary encouraged persons to drop out, the others provided at least some broad hints about where persons might drop "in." All four turned Americans' attention to Asian mysticism and the perennial philosophy long connected with the Western occult tradition.

It was Leary, however, who made the clearest case for not needing to be attached to any kind of formal religion at all. A real religious experience, according to Leary, is "the ecstatic, incontrovertibly certain, subjective discovery of answers to four basic spiritual questions."[67] The four basic spiritual questions, according to Leary, are the Power Question ("What is the ultimate power of the universe?"), the Life Question ("What is life? Why and where did it start?"), the Human Destiny Question ("Whence did humans come and where are we going?"), and the Ego Question ("What am I? What is my place in the grander plan?"). In Leary's view, everything outside of these questions—rituals, dogmas, liturgical practices—is completely divorced from spirituality and is best seen as caught up in the corruptions of human institutions. The implication is that true spirituality is inward and personal. The "outer" aspects of religion are separable from true spirituality. Authentic spirituality, therefore, necessitates dropping out of institutional religion. This logic, whether expressly stated or not, permeated the psychedelic literature. A sizable number of Baby Boomers followed the logic to its conclusion and drifted away from the churches. And most never came back.[68] This is not to say, however, that they had turned their backs upon religion altogether. Instead, they had arrived at an alternative, and more personally compelling, spiritual awakening.

Ecstasy and Spiritual Awakening

By the early 1960s it became abundantly clear that a significant ideological revolution was beginning to take shape in American religious and cultural life. Literally millions felt they were searching for something more than they were finding in the established churches. Their intellectual curiosity made it difficult to settle for a one-size-fits-all form of mainline religion. Many also hungered for the spiritual excitement that comes from personal religious experience. This spiritual restlessness gave rise to what historian William McLoughlin termed the "fourth great awakening" in American religious life. By "awakening" McLoughlin means a significant moment in a nation's religious life in which a great many people undergo an alteration and revitalization in their religious thoughts or feelings. In McLoughlin's terms, awakenings "are periods of cultural revitalization that begin in a general crisis of beliefs and values and extend over a period of a generation or so, during which time a profound reorientation in beliefs and values takes place."[69] Such reorientations had happened three previous times in American life: one just prior to the Revolutionary War, a second during rapid western expansion in the early nineteenth century, and a third during rapid urbanization in the late nineteenth and early twentieth centuries. Each of these, however, had happened largely within the established, consensus churches. And each was dominated by the ascetic pole of religion, culminating in the subordination of the intellect and will to biblical authority.

Unlike previous awakenings of American spirituality, however, the awakening that began in the early 1960s occurred largely among those opting for an unchurched or alternative form of spirituality. Robert Ellwood has suggested that the major themes of this reorientation were (1) a shift from mainline to nonconformist religion, (2) a rediscovery of natural rather than revealed religion, (3) a new appreciation for Eastern religious thought, and (4) a new Romanticism that accords spiritual importance to certain nonrational modes of thought and perception.[70] In general, this represented a shift from seeking God in the church to seeking God in the depths of nature (including the depths of our own psychological nature). The spiritual awakening of the sixties was committed to the belief that the sacred is already implanted in the human heart and the natural world. The essence of personal spirituality, in this view, is to seek out new avenues for discovering the point of connection with this immanent divinity. American authors such as Emerson, Whitman, and James surely provided clues. So, too, did the mystical writings of Hinduism and Buddhism. And not to be overlooked were the kinds of metaphysical illumination made possible with the help of mind-manifesting drugs.

Psychedelics were, without doubt, one of most important factors in the spread of spiritual change in the 1960s and early 1970s. Members of the Baby Boom generation used these substances in settings that implicitly connected them with the very themes Ellwood discerns in the spiritual unrest of the 1960s: the shift from mainline to nonconformist religion, the rediscovery of natural religion, a new appreciation for Eastern thought, and a new Romanticism. Drugs induced an experiential ecstasy that lent an aura of mystical authority to the changes taking place in many Americans' orientation to religious issues. This was true not only for those who ingested drugs but also for a good many of those who never used them at all.

For those who used them, psychedelics provided an experience-based rite of passage to the "new Romanticism." As we noted earlier, they elicited an emotional ecstasy based not on the "distance senses" of reading and hearing but rather on the "proximity senses" of touch, taste, and bodily sensation. Psychedelics provided new configurations of the world based not upon reflective reason but upon dream-like free association and idiosyncratic impressions. Psychedelics deconstructed the world of waking rationality and temporarily transported the initiate into a whole new mode of thinking and feeling. This new mode was charged with excitement, mystery, and intrigue. And although this new mode of awareness gave rise to insights that were ineffable upon return to the normal waking state, it nonetheless left the lasting impression that the world is surrounded by a higher order of Being. In this way the use of psychedelics—and the literature describing this use—meshed perfectly with the era's growing interest in writers such as Robert Heinlein, Hermann Hesse, Mircea Eliade, Carl Jung, and Joseph Campbell. All reinforced American reading audiences' desire to imagine new ways of thinking about themselves and their relationship to nonvisible realities.

Drug use was also a springboard to fascination with extraordinary states of consciousness. Aldous Huxley, Timothy Leary, Richard Alpert, Alan Watts, Huston Smith, and Allen Ginsberg were perhaps the closest thing to shamans that middle-class America has ever known. With the help of psychedelics, they made ecstatic flights into other metaphysical dimensions. And when they returned, they were prepared to instruct others concerning the kinds of thoughts and actions that would best align individuals with a higher, spiritual reality. In an article on "Psychedelics and Religious Experience," Alan Watts reported that "I myself have experimented with five of the principal psychedelics: LSD-25, mescaline, psilocybin, DMT, and cannabis. I have done so, as William James tried nitrous oxide, to see if they could help me in identifying what might be called the 'essential' or 'active' ingredients of the mystical experience."[71] His experiments proved most successful. They yielded a variety of insights that were crammed into several best-selling books and hundreds of lectures on college campuses. We can only assume that such proselytizing by the likes of Watts, Smith, Ginsberg, and Leary prompted others to explore the essential and active ingredients of the mystical experience for themselves.

This fascination with extraordinary states of consciousness in turn led to interest in Eastern religions, whose meditation practices struck Americans as perfectly suited to their own new spiritual convictions. Psychedelics were understood to be cleansing the very doors of perception opened through Hindu and Buddhist meditation systems. The role of psychedelics was so important to the growth of Americans' interest in Eastern religions that in the fall of 1996 a major Buddhist journal devoted an entire issue to the topic. One American-born practitioner of Buddhism noted that "many who took LSD, mushrooms, and other psychedelics, often along with reading from *The Tibetan Book of the Dead* or some Zen texts, had the gates of wisdom opened to a certain extent." Opening these gates gave them vivid insight into the fact that "their limited consciousness was only one plane and that there were a thousand new things to discover about the mind."[72]

For thousands of Americans, then, psychedelics and interest in Eastern religious practices went hand in hand. The statistics are staggering. A recent poll of over 1,300 Americans engaged in Buddhist practice showed that 83 percent had taken psychedelics.[73] Some, of course, had eventually decided that the two were incompatible. But 59 percent responded that psychedelics and Buddhism do mix, and 71 percent believed that psychedelics can provide a glimpse of the reality to which Buddhist practice points. Ram Dass, a.k.a. Richard Alpert, was interviewed in this issue and admitted that he still took drugs as a supplement to his other spiritual practices. He offered that "from my point of view, Buddhism is the closest to the psychedelic experience, at least in terms of LSD. LSD catapults you beyond conceptual structures. It extricates you. It overrides your habit of identifying with thought and puts you in a nonconceptual mode very fast."[74]

Drug-induced states of consciousness appealed to many Baby Boomers who yearned for an experientially based spirituality. As one researcher put it, psychedelics serve "as a kind of phase through which we pass when we're trying to become more truly who we are, more authentic, and more genuine."[75] The ecstatic nature of drug-induced states of consciousness lent charisma or authority to the claims made by psychedelic pundits. In this sense they provided a higher authority that legitimated the transition from "consensus" to "alternative" religion. Cultural anthropologist Marlene Dobkin de Rios pointed out that to the extent that firsthand experience is considered the true way to knowledge, drugs will be considered with awe and respect: "In those societies where plant hallucinogens play a central role, one learns that the drug user believes that he or she can see, feel, touch, and experience the unknown."[76] The various social settings in which Baby Boom Americans used drugs tended to foster precisely this conviction that drugs are one means of seeing, feeling, and experiencing a metaphysical reality. There was, of course, a concurrent tendency for these persons to view established religious institutions as a secondhand or less authentic form of spirituality. And thus the use of psychedelics helped accelerate a shift away from mainline to nonconformist religion among those Baby Boomers who were most caught up in the "ideological revolution" of the sixties and seventies.

The psychedelic movement also influenced the spirituality of millions who never used drugs at all. Psychedelics were a cultural icon; they symbolized an orientation to the world that was embraced by those who never even saw a mushroom or tab of LSD. The books and public lectures by the major gurus of the psychedelic revolution spread their message to almost every bookstore and college campus in the nation. Rock music, too, carried the major themes of this movement into American life and thought. The multisensory nature of the psychedelic experience was replicated on album covers, in lyrics, and in the light shows that accompanied live concerts. Rock concerts were their own Be-Ins. And as Woodstock proved, they had a powerful influence in transmitting both the best and worst elements of the counterculture's philosophy. It shocked no one to learn that Paul McCartney, John Lennon, and George Harrison of the Beatles had all tried LSD. Their albums, particularly "Sgt. Pepper's Lonely Hearts Club Band," increasingly communicated the exotic and alluring qualities of an altered state of mind. And when they became interested in Hinduism and Eastern metaphysics, the world was almost obligingly forced to recognize this as a normative spiritual quest.

Even those pursuing a scholarly approach to understanding religion were forced to consider the possibility that drugs constituted a legitimate and genuine path to metaphysical illumination. The highly respected scholar Huston Smith, for example, argued that psychedelics provide an "empirical metaphysics." Smith argued that the extensive data collected by Leary, Masters and Houston, and Grof provided impressive evidence in favor of a worldview that proclaims humanity's inner connection to a wider spiritual universe. In this way Smith, Watts, Leary, and others whose writings often found their way into college courses helped create a bridge linking academe, the use of psychedelics, and the counterculture's advocacy of such themes as individuality, nonrational modes of thinking, multisensory experiences, and the inner divinity of every person.

One example of the connection between the use of psychedelics and the larger awakening occurring within American religious life was the way in which psychedelic experiences helped put new understandings of God into popular circulation. Psychedelic literature hastened the period's trend away from identifying God solely in biblical terms and instead defining God in more monistic and even pantheistic ways. For instance, Alan Watts claimed that psychologists were "studying peculiar states of consciousness in which the individual discovers himself to be one continuous process with God, with the universe, with the Ground of Being, or whatever name he may use by cultural conditioning or personal preference for the ultimate reality."[77] Huston Smith, meanwhile, claimed that LSD research substantiated a very different view of God than is found in the Bible. As he put it, "the God who is almost invariably encountered [while under the influence of psychedelics] is so removed from anthropomorphism as to elicit, often, the pronoun 'it.'"[78] A theological student writing in the mid-1960s witnessed that under the influence of LSD he, as an individual, "ceased to exist, becoming immersed in the ground of Being, in Brahman, in God, in 'nothingness,' in Ultimate Reality."[79] The religious experiences connected with the use of psychedelics were thus powerful testimony to the era's yearning for a religious vocabulary grounded in our own personal existence and experience. And, again, even many who never used psychedelics were confirmed by these accounts in the legitimacy of their growing interest in new and unchurched forms of spirituality.

All in all, then, psychedelics led a good many Americans down the road toward a more Romantic, postmodern, and unchurched form of spiritual thinking. Even among those who didn't use them, psychedelics were a symbol of the metaphysical illumination available to all who venture past the narrow confines of consensus religion. They demonstrated in the most vivid of ways that normal waking consciousness is but one special type of consciousness, parted by the filmiest of screens from unsuspected other worlds of Being. Psychedelics opened the doors separating these otherwise discrete worlds of consciousness, allowing passage back and forth. The ecstatic adventure was nothing short of a metaphysical illumination. And that illumination provided the key symbols and metaphors for a great deal of the unchurched spirituality that has flourished in the late twentieth century.

Wine and the Varieties of American Religious Life

Innovation and diversity have been the hallmarks of American religious history. This is due in part to the provisions of the First Amendment regarding the free exercise of religion. The First Amendment strictly prohibits the government from establishing a religious institution, thereby assuring religious groups that they will compete for members on a level playing field. More importantly, the First Amendment also stipulates that an individual's right to the free exercise of religion is one of the most fundamental principles of the nation's legal system. These constitutional provisions have had a long-lasting influence on the nation's religious life. They created a competitive religious environment that encourages experimentation and pluralism. There are, for example, currently over 2,000 different religious groups in the United States. To survive in America's free-market religious system, each and every one of these religious groups must be successful at performing two essential tasks: providing both potential and current members with some form of religious experience and fostering a sense of communal belonging. It is also important for each group to execute these tasks in a distinctive way. That is, groups must differentiate themselves from one another. They must provide an experience of the sacred and foster group cohesion in a manner that distinguishes them from competitor organizations and thereby create a unique style of spirituality.

The fact that American religious groups "compete" in an open spiritual marketplace encourages them to be keenly concerned with forming and preserving distinct identities. Religious groups are only able to endure over time by devising strategies for fostering members' sense of affiliation with the group's particular form of spirituality. To this extent religious groups in the United States are continually engaged in what social scientists call "boundary-setting" behaviors. They must delineate their distinctive style of spirituality in such a way as to foster group cohesion and to enable members to distinguish between in-group and out-group membership.[1]

The use of wine has contributed significantly to the innovation and diversity of American religious life. Drinking wine in communal settings helps induce experiences of well-being and emotional expansiveness. It can also encourage novel intellectual constructions. And, too, sharing wine readily promotes a sense of social solidarity. For these reasons wine consumption is a natural ally of religious communities. And, as the historical record reveals, wine has played an important role in the various activities by which religious groups have emerged, forged a unique identity, and maintained their distinctive boundaries over the course of American religious life.[2] More than any other mind- or mood-altering substance, the use (and in some cases, the nonuse) of wine has factored prominently in American religious groups' efforts to help members experience a felt-sense of the sacred as well as their efforts to create occasions that foster a sense of solidarity or group loyalty. Thus attention to the distinctive patterns of wine use among American religious groups provides a novel perspective on the dynamic historical process underlying American religious diversity.

The Biblical Heritage

The Bible is a winey book. After all, wine was not a luxury in the Mediterranean culture of biblical times; it was a staple of everyday life. It was drunk by all classes and all ages. The Book of Genesis tells us that the cultivation of grapes and the making of wine goes all the way back to Noah. After the Flood had receded and the inhabitants of the Ark had disembarked, Noah became "the first tiller of the soil. He planted a vineyard; and he drank of the wine, and became drunk" (Gen. 9:20). We might parenthetically note that this biblical passage struck the American scholar and inventor, Benjamin Franklin, as having practical moral import. Franklin rhymed that from Noah's example "plainly we find, That Water's good neither for Body nor Mind; That Virtue and Safety in Wine-bibbing's found, While all that drink Water deserve to be drown'd."[3]

Franklin's musings notwithstanding, Hebrew scripture clearly extols wine as a sign of God's blessing upon humanity (Gen. 27:28;

Deut. 7:13; Amos 9:14). An exceptional harvest leading to an abundance of wine was interpreted as a harbinger of the Messianic Age (Amos 9:13; Joel 3:18; Zech. 9:17). What the Bible most commends about wine is precisely its ability to alter moods and to raise a person's spirits. The "gladdening of the heart" that wine created was not only thought to be morally acceptable but was positively recommended (2 Sam. 13:28; Esther 1:10; Ps. 104:15; Eccles. 9:7 and 10:19; Zech. 9:15 and 10:7).

Early Christianity, steeped in Jewish life and thought, also embraced wine as an integral part of both religious and family celebrations. This is clearly indicated, for example, in the account of the wedding at Cana where Jesus is attributed with his first public miracle: the turning of water into wine so that plentiful amounts would be available for the celebration of an important event. Franklin, incidentally, quipped that Jesus' use of divine powers to transform water into wine was intended to show us that wine is "a constant proof that God loves us, and loves to see us happy."[4] The early Christian community's positive attitude toward wine is also reflected in Paul's advice to "take a little wine for your stomach's sake" (1 Tim. 5:23). Paul's counsel, especially when combined with scriptural passages that explicitly extol the power of wine to "gladden the heart," makes it clear that the authors of the Bible were lauding the spiritual merits of wine (not unfermented grape juice as some temperance-oriented ministers have claimed in the nineteenth and twentieth centuries), inclusive of its alcohol-specific properties. To be sure, several biblical passages specifically condemn drunkenness (Rom. 13:13; 1 Cor. 5:11; 1 Cor. 6:10; Gal. 5:21; Eph. 5:18; and 1 Pet. 4:3). Paul in particular criticizes drunkenness because of its association with a life focused on self rather than either God or one's neighbors. Yet, with the exception of drunkenness, New Testament authors were generally consistent with earlier biblical authors in supporting the moderate use of wine as a means of altering moods and as an important ingredient in religious and family celebrations.

The early history of Christianity was closely connected with the ways in which Christians sought to differentiate themselves both theologically and ritually from Judaism. They did this, at least in part, by making innovations in the way that wine was used for religious worship. Wine had been used for centuries by ancient Israelite priests for the purpose of consecrating the altar before offering worship. And, of course, wine was present at the major ceremonies intended to forge family and communal solidarity. Such religiously significant occasions as the family's Sabbath meal, the Seder meal during Passover, weddings, and the celebration of a *bris,* or circumcision, were all celebrated with the beverage of wine. Jesus was certainly an heir to this tradition. John Dominic Crossan has suggested that the sharing of food and wine was at the very heart of Jesus' ministry. Crossan demonstrated how Jesus used the commensal practices of sharing food and wine to forge community and empower individuals toward an ethic of radical love.[5] Wine was not only a symbol but also a means of producing a community that lived with a sense of the fusion of the sacred and secular.

Wine was not only important to early Christianity's communal bonding, but it also emerged as the focus of the distinctive ritual practices through which Christians carved their separate religious identity. Christian tradition records that Jesus celebrated his last meal, a Seder dinner that is intimately connected with the ritual use of wine, with his closest disciples on the night before he died. Paul explains in 1 Corinthians that during this meal Jesus took a cup of wine and pronounced that "This cup is the new covenant in my blood." Jesus is then said to have commanded his followers to "do this in remembrance of me," and to this day Christians continue to break bread and drink wine to keep alive the memory of Jesus and to anticipate the arrival of a new Messianic Age. This ceremony, perhaps even more than baptism, differentiated Christianity from its Jewish origins and was thus critical to the construction of the earliest boundaries that distinguished Christian from Jewish identity.

It is also interesting how Christians were able to incorporate the age-old use of wine to stimulate religious emotion, while yet keeping these emotions clearly controlled and focused on specific theological themes. This is in contrast to other Mediterranean religious traditions that exploited wine's capacity to induce ecstasy. Ancient Egyptians, for example, honored the god Hathor with a monthly "Day of Intoxication." Several ancient Persian religions built upon a legend recounting how wine had originated from the sacrificial blood of a primordial bull. Each year's crushing of grapes thereby reenacted this sacrificial slaughter and was followed by ceremonies in which wine was consumed to bestow the bull's strength, energy, and vital force upon those who consumed it. Ancient Greek religion honored Dionysus, god of wine, who was hailed as the giver of all good gifts to humanity. Dionysus was said to offer ecstasy, spiritual vision, and wild intoxication to his devotees. As one historian noted, "the Dionysian worshipper at the height of his ecstasy was one with his god. Divinity had entered into him."[6] Christianity was able to build creatively upon these neighboring traditions. It, too, held that one who drinks the sacrificial blood of Christ will come to share in his vital force. And although Christianity's use of wine was surely intended to invoke images of ecstasy and spiritual vision, it soon ritualized the drinking of wine in such a way as to subordinate intoxication to the act of willful affirmation of liturgy or creed.

Throughout history Christians have arrived at very different interpretations of what the Eucharist or Lord's Supper actually entails. These differing interpretations have been implicated in the various forms of boundary setting through which separate Christian denominations have emerged and developed distinctive identities. We might focus, for example, on the Roman Catholic theory of transubstantiation. The doctrine of transubstantiation (from a Latin term for "change in substance") makes use of the distinction that Aristotle made between the substance of a thing (its essence) and its accidents (its appearance, taste, etc.). Medieval theologians used this logical distinction to argue that the accidents of the wine (i.e., its sight, taste, aroma, etc.) remain the same, but that priests possess the ordained power to change its substance into the actual blood of Christ. It is for this reason that leaders of the Protestant Reformation modified the traditional view of transubstantiation. This issue is complex, and entails a number of interrelated theological and ecclesial issues.[7] However, the Reformers' new conception of the Lord's Supper had the practical implication of undercutting the Roman Catholic position that its ordained priests—and only its ordained priests—were empowered to perform the actions needed to make Christ's forgiving presence available to human beings. Protestant groups continued to use wine in its central act of worship but changed its interpretation of what the wine actually signified. Few members of Catholicism or Protestantism actually understood the theological subtleties involved in the disputes between transubstantiation and consubstantiation. But they knew that their different groups viewed and used wine in different ways. And thus something as simple as the use of wine in religious ritual was a concrete symbol of the theological and ritual boundaries separating the major branches of Western Christianity.

Wine and Affiliation with Mainstream Denominations

The early history of wine and religion in the United States is not in the scope of this chapter. However, I might note that the Puritan settlers of New England utilized alcohol both for religious and recreational purposes. As Emil Oberholzer observed in his study of Puritan Congregationalism in early Massachusetts, "the Puritan who shuddered at the very sight (or thought) of a glass of beer or wine, not to mention hard liquor, did not live in colonial Massachusetts."[8] "Grape juice Protestants" became a phenomenon only in the nineteenth century, for reasons that are discussed in the next section. For their part, Catholics also fostered the connection between spirituality and wine. As Catholic priests extended the Mission Trail up the coast of California, they planted grapes and instigated wine production in the area adjacent to each of the newly established missions.

Over the course of American history, a certain cluster of Protestant organizations came to form the mainstream or consensus form of religion in the United States. Presbyterians, Episcopalians, Congregationalists, Baptists, Disciples of Christ, Methodists, and Lutherans are probably the best-known examples of mainstream American religious denominations. By the middle of the twentieth century, both Roman Catholicism and Judaism had also gained sufficient social and cultural stability to be considered mainstream religious denominations as well. The word denomination is being used here to refer to those religious groups that have attained institutional stability and have sustained a similar form of spirituality over the course of several generations. From a sociological standpoint, the distinguishing characteristic of a denomination is that its members are fully acculturated into the larger American social and cultural system. Thus to the extent that the most theologically conservative Baptists and all Orthodox Jews are self-consciously committed to standing "over and against" much of popular American culture, they must also be considered as standing outside mainstream American religion.

In a religiously pluralistic society such as the United States, religious groups must of necessity employ certain boundary-setting tactics to create and sustain their distinctive identities. That is, religious groups demarcate their distinctive position along a theological and ritual continuum by their distinctive forms of religious instruction, sermons, church-sponsored social activities, liturgy, and use of public relations or advertising. Mainstream religious groups, however, encourage forms of religious living that create minimal boundary conflict. Because their members are all acculturated into the same larger American cultural system, they tend to see themselves as capable of peaceful coexistence with other religious groups. And importantly, they tend to define themselves (again with the exception of many Baptist groups and Orthodox Judaism) in ways that make it possible for their members to focus more on their points of similarity with other groups rather than on their differences.

Wine has been an integral part of these denominational traditions. All have demonstrated their continuity with biblical traditions by including wine in their distinctive patterns of worship. This is, of course, particularly true of the most ritual-oriented of these denominations: Episcopalians, Catholics, and Lutherans. Yet even the least ritualistic of these groups has at least historically recognized wine as having a special sacramental and symbolic ability to unite their members with the saving grace of God. The use of wine in the Eucharist or Lord's Supper escalates the participant's sense of expectancy. Even though the actual amount of alcohol involved in these rituals is small, the wine is nonetheless fraught with mystery, since for centuries it has been regarded as capable of magical transformation. The set and setting thus combine to enable wine to produce a mild euphoria and sense of participation in a transcendent spiritual reality.

American Judaism stands out as the clearest example of how wine has factored into the life of religious denominations. Religious communities, as we have already noted, face the dual task of providing members with a felt sense of the sacred and a felt sense of communal belonging. For thousands of years wine has been part of the Jewish heritage, serving these dual needs of the community and thereby enabling Judaism to create and sustain its own unique religious boundaries. Judaism, of course, was a relatively late arrival on American shores. Even by 1825, there were only a half-dozen active congregations in the United States; by the time of the Civil War, there were perhaps only fifty. By the late nineteenth century, the American Jewish population had grown to approximately 250,000. It was the liberal, or Reform, branch of Judaism that first emerged as the most dominant Jewish denomination in the United States. Reform Judaism, as with liberal religion generally, seeks to accommodate biblical faith to the modern cultural setting. It follows that Reform Judaism views traditional Jewish dietary laws as largely irrelevant to faith in the modern world. Reform Judaism views the kosher dietary laws described in the Talmud as the product of rabbinical reasoning in a bygone era and as having no real importance in our own time. Because it is not particularly concerned with setting rigid cultural or theological boundaries, Reform Judaism is also not particularly concerned with whether its members use only kosher foods or wines.

Between 1880 and 1935 as many as 2.5 million Jews immigrated to the United States. The majority of these immigrants were more likely to affiliate with Conservative or Orthodox synagogues, thereby altering the complexion of American Judaism. Orthodox Jews and, to a lesser extent, Conservative Jews are very concerned with living as a separate, holy people. A part of their desire to set boundaries that distance themselves from the wider culture is their concern with strict adherence to kosher dietary laws. For these groups, particular attention to the religious purity of wine is integral to their efforts to sustain a lifestyle that is self-consciously removed from mainstream cultural patterns (and from Reform Judaism, which fails to maintain complete separation from secular culture).

Although differences exist, all three denominations of American Judaism place great importance upon the hallowing life through religious observances. And critical to this hallowing activity is the ritual use of wine. Wine has been considered a symbol of joy in Jewish culture since ancient times. Wine is always present when something in life is to be celebrated or a memory is to be cherished. The classical Jewish toast before drinking a glass of wine is the simple phrase "To life!"[9] This short prayer expresses the Jewish reverence for the sanctity of human life and reveals why wine is present as a major symbol of sanctification in the family's Sabbath meal, at the Seder meal during Passover, at a *bris*—or circumcision ceremony—and at weddings.[10]

Beginning at sundown on Friday evening, the Sabbath symbolizes Jewish belief in the divine origin of all of life's blessings. The Sabbath observance traditionally begins in the home with an evening meal. The entire family gathers to give thanks to God and to draw attention to God's presence in their lives. The male head of the household then holds a glass of wine in his hands and offers the *kiddush,* or Sabbath prayer of sanctification. The kiddush is intended to make the occasion a festive one. After the prayer is recited, wine is shared and consumed by everyone in attendance, including the children. The kiddush and ritual sharing of wine are intended to help fulfill the biblical commandment to remember the Sabbath and to sanctify it. They are also intended to draw attention to the role of the father as a spiritual guide to his children. The festivity of the weekly Sabbath brings a ritual structure to the fabric of family life and kindles family cohesion in a world in which Jews are a religious and ethnic minority.

The Seder meal during Passover is perhaps Judaism's most important ritual for preserving its distinct cultural history. The meal, served on the first night of Passover, is always a festive one in which family and friends gather for a rich retelling of Judaism's most sacred stories. A strict requirement of the meal is that there be enough wine to fill each person's cup four times (with the cup containing at least 3.3 ounces). A separate cup is set out for the prophet Elijah, symbolizing hope for the Messianic Age.

The circumcision ceremony, or *bris,* is likewise a hallowed occasion. The traditional blessing over the wine is said when the eight-day-old boy's name is announced. A piece of cotton is then dipped into the wine and put between the infant boy's lips so that he will relax and have the benefit of this natural anesthetic. When the circumcision is completed, the wine is also brought to the mother so that she may drink from it and recite the blessings herself. Innumerable toasts are made along the lines of "may you have pleasure in your children and your children's children, and in their children." The event signifies the important fact that God is increasing the number of his chosen people. The bris, in turn, is an outward testimony that Jews are fulfilling their part of the covenant with God. Robert Bales's study of the significance of wine in Jewish rituals notes that during a bris, "the cup of wine may be considered a visible symbol and seal of the completed act of union. . . . On this symbolic level there appears to be at least a partial identification of the moral community with its norms with Jehovah and His Commandments, with the wine serving as the concrete symbol of both."[11]

Weddings are another ceremony commemorating the prosperity and joy God bestows upon His creation. The drinking of wine throughout the service sanctifies the marriage and signals that the bride and groom have entered into a new stage in their covenant both with God and with their religious community. During the ceremony the rabbi blesses a cup of wine and hands it to the bride and groom, who each take a sip before passing it on to the closest relatives. It is also customary for the groom to break a wine glass by crushing it on the floor with his feet. Although any number of explanations of the significance of this act have been proposed, its origins and initial meaning are unknown.

Judaism has been using wine to commemorate these rites of passage for over two thousand years. The cumulative effect of this ritualization of wine drinking has, as Robert Bales observed, rendered wine

symbolic of the *sacred source of moral authority,* God and the commandments of God, the law, the moral community and those who stand for it, such as the father; the act of drinking has the ritual significance of *creating, manifesting, or renewing a union* between the individual and the source of moral authority; . . . [every pious Jew] associates the act of drinking (consciously or not) with these profoundly moving ideas and sentiments regarding the sacred and his relationship to it, because of the intimate integration of the meaningful act with the earliest processes of socialization, the rites de passage, the weekly and yearly cycle of religious events, and the relationships of individuals with the family.[12]

Traditionally any wines used for these ceremonies must be "kosher." Jewish dietary laws, called *kashruth,* originated at least in part as a cultural minority's means of maintaining an identity as a "separate" culture, even while existing in predominantly non-Jewish societies. It is important in this regard to note that the cultural anthropologist Mary Douglas has demonstrated the great extent to which a religious group's beliefs about purity and impurity invariably represent an extreme concern with protecting its social boundaries.[13] The concern with the moral or religious purity of food reflects an underlying concern that members not affiliate too closely with outsiders. This would seem to be particularly true of American Judaism's attitudes toward wine. Reform Judaism, for example, considers any wine that meets government health regulations to be acceptable for religious observance. This is in perfect keeping with Reform Judaism's relative lack of any concern with maintaining rigid social or intellectual boundaries. Reform Jews are not only permitted but encouraged to participate freely and openly with the broader currents of American life. Many Conservative (or Traditionalist) Jews also consider all wine to be kosher and do not believe that any rabbinical certification is necessary to consider a wine pure for either everyday or Sabbath consumption.[14] Yet, most Conservative Jews use only certified kosher wines for Passover. In this sense Conservative Judaism's attitudes toward wine mirror its sense of balancing efforts to preserve some sense of separate social and religious identity with some accommodation to mainstream American cultural life. Orthodox Judaism insists that only certified kosher wines ever be consumed. And, of course, it is this branch Judaism that is most concerned with maintaining its separate heritage over and against the trends of modern life.

The laws governing the certification of wine as kosher reflect the dynamics of maintaining a religious community's unique moral and social identity. First, kosher wine must be made under the strict supervision of a rabbi, and a Sabbath-observant Jew must take responsibility for handling the wine at each stage of its production. A winery operating according to kosher requirements must use separate crushers, tanks, and bottling machinery to ensure that the wine remains hygienic and pure from the picking of the grapes to the final bottling. Wine that has been properly supervised displays the rabbi's *hechsher* seal on the label.

The major principle underlying the rabbinical supervision is that it is traditionally considered forbidden for a Jew to drink wine made or handled by a non-Jew. In ancient times this proscription safeguarded Jews from using wine made by heathens. Since it was believed that heathens made wine for the purpose of offering libations to their idols, the leaders of the ancient Jewish community prohibited any use of heathens' wine or even any Jewish-produced wines that heathens had handled. This prohibition is still maintained among Orthodox and some Conservative Jews, but perhaps with additional motives. In more modern times this prohibition has been maintained "in order to prevent the kind of social conviviality, usually associated with the drinking of wine, which leads to intermarriage of a Jew with a non-Jew."[15]

The use of wine to symbolize the sacred and to forge social solidarity in Judaism is undoubtedly richer and more prominent than in other American religious denominations. Nonetheless, it illustrates the ways in which this mood-altering drug helps established religious denominations to both create and maintain their distinctive identities while minimizing boundary conflict with other religious groups.

From Use to Nonuse:
The Deliberate Movement
Away from the Mainstream

Presbyterianism, Congregationalism, Roman Catholicism, Episcopalianism, and Reform Judaism are all excellent examples of mainstream denominations in that they have no objection to their members' participation in the wider scope of American cultural life. Baptists and Methodists, meanwhile, have always stood at the fringes of the mainstream. Since the mid-nineteenth century, these two groups have been wary of the secular society that surrounds them. This is even more true of the holiness and Pentecostal groups (e.g., Seventh-Day Adventists, Assemblies of God, Church of God, Church of the Nazarene), which emerged in the late nineteenth and early twentieth centuries with the express purpose of saving souls from the wretched world in which they lived. Theological and social concerns have prompted these groups to be much more concerned with boundary setting than most mainstream denominations. And, as we shall see, their deliberate turn from the use to the nonuse of wine was a major component of their efforts to set themselves apart from a world of sinful distractions.

Methodists and Baptists are heirs to the "ascetic" style of Protestant Christianity. They view religious faith as requiring an ardent commitment to self-discipline and self-denial. Human nature tends toward sin and must therefore be carefully restrained. Because of humanity's inherent inclination toward moral vice, religion must be about more than receiving the initial gift of forgiveness. Religion also entails a commitment to leading a life of ongoing moral perfection (known as sanctification). John Wesley, the founder of Methodism, dedicated his life to developing a methodical approach to sin-free living. In Wesley's view, this required a turn away from the secular world and its sinful amusements (e.g., dancing, card playing).

Wesley attempted to establish clearly demarcated boundaries within which Christians must live if they wished to devote themselves to the process of sanctification. In one of his major works on moral perfection, *The General Rules of the United Societies,* Wesley included long discussions of food, drink, and exercise. Among his admonitions was a warning against the consumption of distilled spirits. During the eighteenth and nineteenth centuries, most Methodists saw no difficulty with the consumption of beer or wine. But as the temperance movement gained momentum in the late 1800s, Methodists were among the vanguard of those calling for total abstinence. By the turn of the century, Methodists were known for their ardent prohibitionism, and they worked diligently to secure the passage of constitutional amendments at both the state and national levels to prohibit the sale and transportation of alcoholic beverages.

Baptists flourished on the ever-expanding western frontiers. Most of their members, therefore, had little choice but to consider alcohol a necessary part of their diet and an important medicinal aid. Yet, as the nineteenth century progressed, Baptists increasingly found themselves in rapidly growing cities and towns. Soon Baptists, too, became associated with the temperance movement. Like other ascetic-leaning Protestant groups, Baptists have tended to supplement their moral and religious objections to the consumption of alcohol with both medical and social arguments. Believing that alcohol is bad for health and disastrous to family life, Baptists have steadfastly preached against the use of alcohol in all its forms. It should be noted, however, that Baptists have a democratic and decentralized polity, and thus each believer has the right to come to his or her own opinion on such matters. One study showed that 48 percent of Southern Baptists drink alcohol despite strong pressure from the pulpit and denominational authorities.[16]

The Baptists and Methodists (along with the holiness and Pentecostal denominations that have displayed such great vitality in the past few decades) differentiated themselves from other Protestant denominations through their unrelenting emphasis on evangelical theology. Evangelicalism emphasizes the importance of faith (i.e., correct belief) over religious or moral works in securing salvation. Evangelical groups see salvation as dependent upon an individual's conscious, willed decision to accept Jesus as one's personal Savior. Emotionalism is a strong element in evangelical religion but mainly is a factor intended to culminate in a distinct conversion experience. These faiths have, in fact, spread throughout the American population principally by using revivalistic methods to elicit powerful human emotions and simultaneously direct those emotions toward structured religious conversion. Yet, from a theological point of view, these evangelical denominations affirm that emotions themselves cannot bring one to salvation any more than moral or religious works. It is only the grace of Christ received through faith that brings salvation. Evangelical faiths are consequently wary of alcohol because of its ability to release the wrong emotions or to distract the emotions from being properly centered on what ought to be their true object (i.e., Christ).

It is also important to note that American evangelical groups, while emphasizing that works are not the means of salvation, nonetheless proclaim that a disciplined obedience to the moral law must necessarily follow, or result from, salvation. These groups consequently emphasize moral discipline and encourage the subordination of most emotions (particularly those associated with worldly pleasures) to the moral will. Because alcohol releases emotions potentially at variance with a completely self-disciplined body and character, it is to be avoided; consumption of alcohol is viewed as inconsistent with the actions of a person who has been regenerated by the saving grace of Christ.

The boundary-setting maneuvers that caused Protestant groups such as the Baptists and Methodists to shun wine were not solely theological in nature. The shift to a call for total abstinence also had pronounced sociological dimensions. First, a good many members of these groups suspected a hidden danger in wine, given its long association with upper-class intellectuals who were prone to liberal philosophical and religious ideas. Just as kosher restrictions on wine are partially intended to mitigate contact with "cultural outsiders," some evangelical groups' demands for total abstinence are an attempt to isolate its members from corrupting influences. Second, immigration patterns intensified the need for WASP groups to set boundaries that clearly distinguished between insiders and outsiders. Many of the newly arriving immigrants were poor and ill-educated and lived in the squalor of urban ghettos. The drinking of whiskey, gin, and malted beverages among these immigrants became a symbol of their inability to assimilate into the established WASP cultural order. Religious and ethnic prejudice fueled the fire of evangelical Protestants' moral indignation at the immigrants' lifestyles. The fact that even fellow Anglo-Saxon Protestants also acted this way under the influence of "demon rum" led to the identification of alcohol as an evil that threatened to pull down the nation's moral integrity.

Total abstinence from alcohol—including wine, the privileged beverage of the Bible and Christian sacraments—was thus a direct consequence of the boundary-setting behaviors at the turn of the twentieth century. Theological and sociological factors continue to affect the use and nonuse of alcohol by American religious groups in their efforts to maintain distinctive boundaries.

Wine and Sectarian Innovation

The course of American religious history has witnessed the emergence of a number of innovative groups that have in some fundamental way deviated from the mainstream denominations. The term sect, in contrast to the term denomination, is frequently used to signify religious groups that self-consciously differentiate themselves from the more established or socially dominant traditions. In his highly regarded *A Religious History of the American People*, Sydney Ahlstrom uses the term sect to draw attention to the shared characteristics of religious innovation over the course of American history.[17] According to Ahlstrom, the term sect is used to identify a movement in the early stages of formation. A sect is a group, usually small at the outset, that secedes from a more stable, culturally dominant religious group. Sects introduce innovative changes that appeal to individuals who find that the more established denominations no longer meet their religious needs. Sects are typically founded by an individual who possesses an extraordinarily influential personality. This leader's personality is often critical to the group's early success in gaining converts. Also, whereas a denominational affiliation is often inherited at birth from one's parents' religious heritage, sectarian membership is more likely to be the product of a conscious decision by an adult. Sectarian groups must therefore provide experiences that facilitate affiliation and communal affirmation among its new members. In sum, the term sect draws attention to the characteristics of a religious group that has not yet existed for a sufficiently long period of time to have fully entered the cultural mainstream.

The use of wine among many American religious sects sheds additional light on the dynamics of religious innovation. For example, the use of wine highlights the role that altered states of consciousness play in triggering such prototypical religious feelings as awe, surrender, delight, or ecstasy. Scientific research on the effects of alcohol consumption also leads us to believe that use of wine fosters modes of social interaction that are rare in everyday behavior.[18] In his cross-cultural study of alcohol use, Donald Horton found that alcohol facilitates what he called "social jollification," that is, spontaneous forms of social interaction that permit individuals to step outside their socially defined roles and to relate to one another in less artificial ways.[19] The consumption of alcohol can also reduce feelings of tension, guilt, anxiety, and frustration. By using wine in the context of a supportive religious community, then, sectarian groups are often able to meet persons' emotional and religious needs far more effectively than can established denominations.

Wine drinking can also embolden individuals to adopt new ideas. Selden Bacon's well-known studies of alcohol consumption reveal how inebriation fosters what he termed a "variation in ideas."[20] The altered state of consciousness created by alcohol intoxication restructures our customary modes of perception and reflection. Wine use, then, can incite our intellectual faculties and hasten the process whereby we adopt novel conceptions about ourselves and the world we live in. In these ways, wine use can be instrumental for inducting individuals' into a new religious community. Wine consumption produces an exhilaration and enhanced sociability that makes us temporarily feel like new men and women. In this way the social settings in which wine is shared entice persons to cross over religious and social boundaries toward a new religious identity. Of course, the very antinomian effects of wine drinking that help create the ecstatic ethos of a newly emerging religious group can, over time, also make it potentially dangerous to the maintenance of a group's internal structures of authority.

American religious history contains a good many examples of experimental religious groups that utilized wine in their efforts to provide members with "social jollification," aesthetic delight, and mystical revitalization. The Amana colonies in Iowa provide a ready example. The Amana colonies were founded by German immigrants belonging to a religious sect called the Community of True Inspiration. Their identity as "inspirationalists" stemmed from their belief that the community's leaders could directly receive divine inspiration in the same manner as the biblical prophets. The claim to divine inspiration predictably led to a certain amount of ostracism in their original homeland of Germany, prompting a modest number of them to journey to the United States in the mid-1800s. After their arrival in Amana ("remain true"), Iowa, in 1854, they were able to sustain a communitarian society for three generations before the Great Depression forced them to adopt capitalism.[21]

The Amana colonies embraced an austere life. These determined souls endured the economic and social hardships that come from a self-imposed separation from the surrounding world. Their physical separation enabled them to dedicate themselves fully to a life of humility, faithfulness, and love of Christ. Indeed, their austere life was intended to purify them and transform them into "instruments" or "inspired oracles" of holy spirit. Work hours were long, and the tasks were often physically demanding. The community gradually evolved a pattern for punctuating their work schedules with meals prepared in a large community kitchen. The sharing of food and wine rejuvenated workers and sustained community spirit. For this reason, all facets of food preparation were important to the Amana colonies' religious life. From the gathering of ingredients to the cleaning of dishes, food production was an important focal point of conversation and social interaction. Part and parcel of this sharing of bread was the sharing of wine, which was dispensed from the communal kitchen at both lunch and dinner. With each of the seven villages in the Amana colonies producing more than 6,000 gallons of wine annually, there was enough not only to stock the community kitchens but also to allocate at least thirty gallons of wine to each family to supplement their personal supplies.

Wine drinking imparted a sense of camaraderie and festivity to the work schedule. Each farmworker was given two wine breaks each day. Crew bosses would stop by and pick up the daily ration and be certain that every worker received no less than two ounces of wine at both their morning and afternoon breaks. Some tasks earned additional wine rations. For example, one of the most important duties that all males had to perform on a rotating basis was that of looking out on the watchtower for intruders and fires. The watchtower duty was of such vital importance to the community that the colonists found innovative ways of transforming its potential drudgery into an enjoyable activity. Neighbors routinely stopped by with baskets of food especially prepared by the community kitchen, including generous portions of steak and slices of pie or cake and, of course, an extra ration of wine. It was common for others to volunteer to accompany the man on duty, hoping to see the night watch once again turn into a festive party. Card playing, ordinarily frowned upon in this pious community, would often begin, and thus, on an almost daily basis, small groups of men would come together to share food, wine, and one another's company, all in the spirit of helping one another perform an otherwise tedious chore.

The Amana church used wine only once a year. Wine was reserved for the annual communion service called the Liebesmahl, or Love Feast. In this pageant-like communion, members of the colony sat in small groups, each of which had its own communal wine goblet. The officiating elder gave the signal for each person to have a turn drinking from the goblet in a distinct hierarchical order determined by age, marital status, number of children, and so forth. The wine goblet would be continually refilled as it went from person to person, since a good many were "inclined to swallow rather than taking the customary sip."[22]

In addition to the community wine used at meals and for the Liebesmahl, nearly every family in Amana made its own "Hinterlistiger Wein," which roughly translates to "made-on-the-sly." Each family made its own generous supply of wine from black currants, elderberries, wild grapes, or rhubarb. The family wine was used at weddings, given as gifts, or enjoyed in the evenings or on Sundays. Sunday "wine samplings" were, in fact, an informal ritual that contributed a great deal to the fabric of Amana social life. Right after the Sunday worship service, the men of each Amana village would disappear, reconvening at the prearranged site of the week's tasting. All dressed up in their Sunday suits and ties, the men brought some of their own homemade wine to share with others in a friendly tasting competition. Each wine was savored and critically discussed. Sunday was their one day off from the hard work of the community, and their wine samplings gave them time to engage in easy, mellow conversation to refresh themselves for the coming week.

The Amana colonies' use of wine to affirm their communal commitments and to encourage their "inspirational" form of piety almost perfectly illustrates anthropologist Mary Douglas's contention that "the meaning of a meal is found in a system of repeated analogies."[23] There was a mutually reinforcing relationship between the ways in which wine was associated with religious worship, community meals, and informal social gatherings. In this way the meaning of consuming wine in any one context was simultaneously infused with symbolic meanings that wine had in other contexts. The consumption of wine was thus embedded in a much wider system of "analogies" that accentuated its symbolic role in (1) mediating between the individual and the community, (2) mediating between the mundane and the extraordinary, and (3) mediating between the secular and the sacred. And, as Douglas also noted, "Each meal is a structured social event which structures others in its own image."[24] The Amana colonies, similar to many other American communal groups, consumed wine in ways that structured social interaction that bore the obvious imprint of religious devotion and communal solidarity.[25]

Perhaps the single most interesting example of the role wine can play in the dynamics of sectarian religion is to be found in the early history of the Mormons, or Church of Jesus Christ of Latter-day Saints. The Latter-day Saints emerged in the 1820s in Palmyra, New York, when Joseph Smith was visited by God and Jesus, who commissioned him to set himself apart from rival denominations and to prepare himself to become a seer and prophet. It was their intention that Joseph would soon gather the righteous remnant to await the return of Christ and to establish a new order of things on earth. A few years later the Angel Moroni visited Joseph and led him to a local hillside where he uncovered the long-buried scripture titled the *Book of Mormon*. The *Book of Mormon* contained the lost teachings of Jesus, which he had delivered in a special ministry among the tribes of ancient North America. These teachings, which supplemented those of the Old and New Testaments, were said to complete God's revelation to humanity and to constitute the full gospel necessary for achieving the highest levels of exaltation in the afterlife. The highly charismatic Joseph Smith excited his growing number of followers with the conviction that they alone possessed the full, restored gospel of Jesus Christ. The Latter-day Saints' zealous adherence to their new faith somewhat predictably struck their contemporaries as fanatical. The Mormons' early practice of polygamy attracted further scorn, and the group increasingly found itself the object of ridicule and bigotry.

As persecution mounted, the Mormons were forced to move westward. First they gathered all their belongings and ventured to Kirtland, Ohio, then to Independence, Missouri, and finally to Nauvoo, Illinois. It was during the Nauvoo years that Joseph Smith was eventually murdered by a crowd of angry citizens who resented the Mormons' growing presence in their region. Brigham Young succeeded Joseph Smith as leader of the main Mormon community, and he led the Latter-day Saints to their new kingdom in Salt Lake City, Utah. What is of interest is that throughout this saga the Latter-day Saints found that wine helped them bond together in a communal society of "glad hearts" that possessed the internal cohesion to withstand persecution from the outside. Equally of interest is the process whereby the use of wine was gradually suppressed. As a central structure of authority emerged within the fledgling church, continued use of wine proved disruptive of institutional stability and was thus finally curtailed.

The *Book of Mormon* fully sanctions the use of wine as a sacramental substance and as a natural pleasure provided to us by God. For example, in one passage Jesus commanded his North American followers, the Nephites, to "take of the wine of the cup and drink of it" in honor of their Lord (III Nephi 18:8). Joseph Smith was given subsequent revelations from God that in certain respects modified the strong endorsement that wine received in the *Book of Mormon* itself. On one occasion Joseph Smith was alarmed to discover that he had run out of the wine that he was going to use to conduct the church's sacraments. A heavenly messenger met him as he set about in search of a new supply of wine and assured him that the sacrament could be performed even without any wine. The *Doctrine and Covenants* records that Jesus Christ then sent Joseph a revelation instructing him as follows: "For behold, I say unto you, that it mattereth not what ye shall eat or what ye shall drink when ye partake of the sacrament, if it so be that ye do it with an eye single to my glory."[26] Joseph was at this time also worried that some of his enemies might try to poison his wine. It was thus a relief to learn from Jesus that "wherefore, a commandment I give unto you, that you shall not purchase wine neither strong drink of your enemies. Wherefore, you shall partake of none except it is made new among you."[27] He immediately added, "Behold, this is wisdom in me;

wherefore, marvel not, for the hour cometh that I will drink of the fruit of the vine with you on the earth and with Moroni, whom I sent unto you to reveal the Book of Mormon, containing the fullness of my everlasting gospel."[28]

As the Mormons moved to Kirtland, the use of wine continued. It was used to provide "social jollification" and, at least on occasions, as a means of performing the church's principal sacrament. However, in Kirtland the Mormons found a sizable number of the local citizenry who were banding together to support temperance in the region and to try to shut down the area's distilleries, which supplied the region with cheap whiskey. It was at this time that Joseph received the revelation that is commonly referred to as the Word of Wisdom. In February of 1833 it was revealed to him "that inasmuch as any man drinketh wine or strong drink among you, behold it is not good, neither meet in the sight of your Father, only in assembling yourselves together to offer up your sacraments before him, And, behold, this should be wine, yea, pure wine of the grape of the vine, of your own make."[29] With this revelation, the Mormons were officially on record as in support of the temperance cause.

A key phrase included in Word of Wisdom, however, was that its advice was offered "not by commandment or constraint." Neither Joseph Smith nor many other nineteenth-century Latter-day Saints interpreted these cautionary words to be a strict demand for total abstinence in the way that contemporary Mormons do (on September 9, 1951, in a general conference session it was decided that the true intent of the Word of Wisdom was to support total abstinence from alcohol). Thus, on the occasion of a double wedding in 1836, the Mormon Prophet recorded in his journal: "We then partook of some refreshments, and our hearts were made glad with the fruit of the vine. This is according to the pattern set by our Savior Himself, and we feel disposed to patronize all the institutions of heaven."[30] At another marriage the Prophet was presented with "three servers of glasses filled with wine, to bless." He recorded that "it fell to my lot to attend to this duty which I cheerfully discharged. It was then passed round in order, then the cake in the same order; suffice it to say, our hearts were made glad while partaking of the bounty of earth, which was presented, until we had taken our fill; and joy filled every bosom."[31] On yet another occasion, Smith's records indicate that he took his mother and Aunt Clarissa in a carriage to nearby Painesville, Ohio, where they "produced a bottle of wine, broke bread, ate and drank, and parted after the ancient order with the blessing of God."[32]

LaMar Petersen has contended that in the Kirtland, Independence, and Nauvoo years, the Mormons drank fairly large amounts of wine. Caution must be exercised in assessing Petersen's allegations. An ex-Mormon, Petersen's account undoubtedly vents personal resentments. Yet Petersen maintains that even though Joseph Smith was seldom seen intoxicated in public, he drank quite intemperately both in his own home and in the barroom in the back of his store in Nauvoo.[33] It is unclear whether his charge concerning Joseph Smith's penchant for excessive drinking is true. Petersen is, however, on solid historical ground when he draws attention to the fact that a good many Mormons enjoyed wine during the sect's early years. In a world that otherwise presented them with much hard work, scarce resources, and bitter persecution, wine served to bring the early Mormon community together for conversation and merriment. Petersen cites one source that recounts how the Latter-day Saints

> were in the habit of having what they called feasts. . . . They generally had two pails of wine. . . . We had a tincup and when the audience was convened and a speech made then with a cup in each pail they passed around the pails, the women on one side of the house and the men on the other, and we had as much wine as we wanted. Then we had a hymn and sometimes prayer. Then the wine would be passed around again, and then we would have cakes and wine. . . . After the cakes and wine had been passed it was the season then to speak with tongues and I spoke with the rest.[34]

The Mormon feasts provided new members with a personal experience of religious ecstasy. For thousands of years, wine has been used to produced that altered state of consciousness in which persons feel the inflow of some energizing spiritual force. It is apparent from the account above that wine fostered Mormons' sense of living on the boundary between this world and a dawning new spiritual order. And in this way, the religious enthusiasm so central to the early stages in the formation of a new religious sect was transmitted to the widening group of converts.

In addition to its role in inducing religious euphoria, wine was also an important means by which Mormons forged a sense of warmth and intimacy within the gathered flock. One of Joseph Smith's bodyguards, Oliver Huntington, recorded a typical Mormon outdoor sacrament meeting in 1838: "The people came together in the morning without their breakfast to the bowery on the Public Square where there was prepared a plenty of good bread and a barrel of wine. The bread and wine was blessed, every person ate and drank wine as they wanted all day, when they wanted. They sat and talked and walked and conversed upon heavenly and spiritual things as they felt like."[35]

Wine and dancing parties were common in the early years, especially at the Masonic hall built in Nauvoo. One Mormon's diary recounts that a week before the dedication of the Nauvoo temple, a party erupted spontaneously even as the final carpentry and painting work was being done: "It was voted that Bro. Angel go and inform the Trustees that the hands were ready to drink the Barrell of Wine which had been reserved for them." A few nights later a group of workers and their wives met in the attic and "had a feast of cakes, pies, wine &c, where we enjoyed ourselves with prayer, preaching, administering for healing, blessing children, and music and Dancing until near Midnight."[36] And although such revelry would be anathema to modern Mormons, it was an integral part of the communal life of the fledgling faith.

After the death of the Prophet, Brigham Young led the majority of the Mormons to Salt Lake City, where hard economic times continued. In order to enhance their economic self-sufficiency, Young sent some Mormon colonists from Salt Lake to a region in southern Utah known as Dixie, where they were directed to raise cotton, sugar, grapes, and other "useful articles." Young appointed an experienced wine maker from Germany, John Naegle, to direct the Dixie wine industry. Young also saw to it that vines of the Mission grape, a wine press, and a brandy distillery were brought from California. Over the next thirty years, several thousand gallons were manufactured to be used as medicine, as sacramental wine, and to be sold to non-Mormons as a source of additional revenue. The new Prophet advised, "First, by lightly pressing, make a white wine. Then give a heavier pressing and make a colored wine. Then barrel up this wine, and if my counsel is taken, this wine will not be drunk here, but will be exported, and thus increase the fund."[37] Unfortunately, the Dixie Mormons were sufficiently far away from Young that they did not heed his advice too strictly, and they ended up consuming a great deal of their own wine. In 1900, three years after wine was last used in the sacrament, church officials ordered the Dixie wine operation to be discontinued.[38] From that time on, total abstinence became the official means of adhering to the Word of Wisdom.

It cannot be known for certain just why the Latter-day Saints gradually adopted their total ban on alcoholic beverages. Several factors played a role, and it is nearly impossible now to reconstruct precisely what significance to assign each of them. First would be the church's millennial expectancy and the accompanying desire of the Mormons to be morally pure before their Lord. Abstinence from alcohol was part of their larger concern with perfecting their moral lives in anticipation of Final Judgment. As we noted earlier, conservative religious groups tend to be wary of alcohol, since it releases pleasure-oriented emotions and thereby prevents the emotions from being properly focused on what ought to be their true object. A second factor was undoubtedly economic. The Latter-day Saints had precious little in the way of surplus capital. Buying alcohol from "outside" traders drained their economy of sorely needed cash and thus enforcement of the Word of Wisdom was in part motivated by the economic need for self-sufficiency.[39] A third reason pertained to the dynamics of boundary setting. The Mormons gradually adopted strategies that accentuated the ways in which they were different from existing religious groups. Abstinence was one of many strategies that signaled Mormons' desire to be separate. Thus Mormons' eventual concern with abstinence, much like Orthodox Judaism's concern with kosher dietary practices, became one of the many ways they developed to help community members clearly distinguish between insiders and outsiders.[40] As a corollary to this important point, it would also seem that the emotional contagion and inner ecstasy associated with past Mormon use of wine was no longer functional for their community. Very early in their experience, the Mormons benefited from wine's "gladdening of the heart" and the attendant sense of egalitarianism. As the faith gradually generated its own internal lines of authority, wine consumption became a potential liability. Wine intoxication gave rise to a relaxing of normal standards of decorum and even created conflict over who in the community were the appropriate recipients of ecstasy and revelation. As the anthropologist Victor Turner has pointed out, the emergence of nearly all religions is attended by the widespread experiences of ecstasy and communal bonding (what he calls "spontaneous communitas"). But over time, religious institutions routinize these emotions in their rituals and doctrine.[41] At this point, the spontaneous eruption of these emotions in nonordained persons threatens institutional authority. Wine, as we have seen, readily occasions "variations in ideas" and venturing beyond established opinions. Hence, over time, its use could become inconsistent with the demands of a closed theological canon. It is possible, then, that the enforcement of the Word of Wisdom was in part motivated by the need to curtail the wine-driven ecstasy that had formerly enabled Mormons to speak in tongues and receive spiritual prophecy.

Religious Enthusiasm and Cult Formation

The term cult, like sect, is used to identify groups that are in the early stages of their formation. Newly emerging religious groups are frequently led by a charismatic individual who claims special rapport with the supernatural world. He or she is also likely to be characterized by an intense religious enthusiasm. Members believe that they are participating in the unveiling of significant truths unknown by the population as a whole. The key factor in appending the label "cult" rather than "denomination" or "sect" to a religious group is simply that its religious interests and practices are very different than those of the socially established religious organizations. Thus, whereas the major denominations and sects in the United States all espouse some connection with the Judeo-Christian tradition, what we call cults are groups whose religious interests lie outside those of Western churched religion. In some cases, a small Christian or Jewish group can be considered a cult if it emphasizes variant doctrines or lifestyle codes to the point where mainstream culture finds their religiosity to be bizarre or fanatic. For the most part, however, the term cult is used to draw attention to newly emerging religious groups that promote highly innovative understandings of what it means to become spiritually awakened.

A fascinating example of how religious enthusiasm can generate a cult community is the Brotherhood of the New Life founded by the famed spiritualist medium, Thomas Lake Harris. Harris, whom the noted American philosopher and psychologist William James referred to as the "best known American mystic" in his *The Varieties of Religious Experience,* formed a religious organization that was very similar to what is today known as "New Age" religion.[42]

Thomas Lake Harris was an English-born minister in the liberal Universalist Church until his introduction to the mystical philosophy of Emmanuel Swedenborg. Swedenborg had been a scientist before undergoing a series of mystical experiences that convinced him of the existence of unseen spiritual worlds. Angelic beings appeared to Swedenborg and gave him inspiring messages about every human being's capacity to become receptive to the inflow of spiritual energies and divine guidance. Harris's own mystical experiences prompted him to believe that he was a successor to this inspirational spirituality and set about organizing a new religious group committed to bringing every individual to a direct, experiential awareness of "the Divinity within." Harris maintained that true religion is less a matter of church attendance or adherence to Bible doctrines than it is about opening oneself up to a direct inflow of divine spirit. In his words, "to believe in God is but to believe that the spirit which we feel flowing into ourselves flows from an Infinite Existing Source."[43] Harris advocated a form of spiritualism. A part of this spiritualism entailed making contact with the spirits of departed human beings. Yet Harris taught that the core of true spiritualism is entering into mystical states that enable persons to become receptive to spiritual influence. The true purpose of spiritualism, he proclaimed, was to experience "the spirit of Christ, which descends to be immanent in the heart."[44]

As a mystic, Harris was adept at entering into entranced states of consciousness in which he claimed that disembodied spirits would use him as a medium through which to deliver sermons and sundry moral or religious advice. He began to gather a following of persons eager to become a part of this charismatic dispensation from the spirit world. Harris first founded a series of colonies for the Brotherhood of the New Life in Mountain Cove, West Virginia, in Wassaic, New York, in Amenia, New York, in Brocton, New York, and finally in Santa Rosa, California. In each of the Wassaic, Amenia, and Brocton locations, Harris assigned his disciples the task of growing grapes and producing wines. As Harris put it, the major commercial activity of the Brotherhood of New Life was to be "the manufacture and sale of pure, native wine, made especially for medicinal purposes."[45] The Brocton winery, for example, was set up to manufacture about 15,000 gallons annually and included a massive wine cellar to store an equal amount. When he moved the base of his operations to Santa Rosa, Harris's winery produced as much as 70,000 gallons per year and his wines were among the very best produced in the United States.

The real importance of wine for the Brotherhood of New Life was, however, not commercial. For Harris, wine was a sacramental substance that could directly communicate divine spirit to those who properly consumed it. The Brotherhood's theology rested squarely on the premise that we all have the inward capacity to open up to, and avail ourselves of, an "influx of divine Breath." Harris, as guided by his angelic tutors, explained to his followers that God is continuously emanating a sacred energy that flows into and infuses the natural order, and that spirituality has to do with learning to commune with, and be filled by, this revitalizing spiritual power.

It was in this connection that wines held such a vital place in the Brotherhood faith. Harris's mystic vision revealed to him that his wines had divine and miraculous powers. Harris claimed that his wines were in some special way "infused with the divine aura, potentialized in the joy spirit."[46] These wines released their "finer electro-vinous spirit" directly into our bodies, thereby opening individuals to an inflow of the creative breath of God. Because Brotherhood wines were infused with the divine aura, it was claimed that they could not produce alcoholic intoxication or in any way harm those who consumed them. A contemporary noted that the Brotherhood sold these wines "for the refreshment of passing travelers": "It was not merely material food and drink that were given out to them by those consecrated hands; for every glass of wine and helping of solid food to each passing traveler carried with it into the world through him an incipient ability to organic openness to the pure Breath of God."[47]

As mentioned earlier, Harris eventually moved his community from Brocton, New York, to just north of Santa Rosa in the Sonoma Valley of California. During these years, Harris apparently began to give new emphasis to his doctrines concerning the sexual nature of God. The practical consequence of this conception of God was the teaching that every man and woman has a celestial counterpart. Harris taught that it is part of our spiritual duty to seek out our celestial counterparts and join with them both in sexual union and in eternal marriage. We will never know just what role wine played in Harris's search of celestial sexual union, but his numerous efforts to locate his celestially chosen mate led to a series of scandals. By the early 1890s, rumors and lawsuits surfaced charging Harris with wielding dictatorial power over his disciples, appropriating their personal wealth for his private use, and encouraging illicit sexual relations among colony members. Amidst these charges he abruptly left the country for England, only to return to the United States in the last years of his life. The Brotherhood winery Harris founded at Brocton was purchased by a pair of wine merchants from New York and, although subsequently merged with another winery in Washingtonville, is currently the oldest active winery in the United States. The Santa Rosa winery came under the direction of Harris's Japanese disciple Kanaye Nagasawa, who managed the winery until his death in 1934.

A second religious group that falls under the broad designation of "cult" also merits attention for its extraordinary association of wine with the pursuit of an expanded spiritual consciousness. The group, known as Summum, is one of several new religious groups that are commonly referred to as New Age religions. Much of what is today called New Age religion is little more than the resurfacing of ideas that appeared in the nineteenth century in such metaphysical movements as Swedenborgianism, mesmerism, Theosophy, and the kind of spiritualism advocated by Thomas Lake Harris. These groups all believed that the physical universe is enveloped by other, invisible spiritual dimensions. They also believed that each of us is capable of cultivating certain mystical states of consciousness that enable us to become especially receptive to the wisdom and spiritual power flowing from these higher dimensions of the universe. Thus such patently New Age interests as trance channeling, crystal healing, and meditation are not so much new religious interests as renewed enthusiasm for exploring spiritual mysteries outside of the established churches.

It should be noted that most New Age enthusiasts abhor alcoholic intoxication as a harmful pollution of body, mind, and spirit. Yet, many New Agers do drink moderate amounts of wine. The light and "natural" properties of wine render it consistent with the New Age interest in opening up to the spiritual dimensions of nature. It is in this context that we can appreciate Summum's fascination for the use of wine in developing our mystical potentials.

Mr. Claude Nowell was an elder in the Mormon Church and living in Salt Lake City when, in 1974, he began to notice a "ringing" in his ears.[48] Every day when he came home from work and began to relax in his den he would once again experience this intense, but peaceful, ringing. About one year later, Mr. Nowell turned his attention away from all outside noise and focused intently on the ringing sound. He reports that when he opened his eyes he was standing next to an enormous pyramid and surrounded by a strange-looking group of individuals who looked similar to humans, yet had light blue skin and wore no clothes. These individuals led him to a large crystal shaft that was radiating an invisible energy and wisdom. In some mystic way, an entire set of "higher truths" was transmitted directly to the recesses of Nowell's mind. He explains that this was not a case of "channeling" whereby a disembodied spirit delivers a complete message to an entranced human. Instead, the crystal shaft transmitted only the seeds or template of this wisdom into his unconscious mind. It was left to Nowell to work out an understanding or articulation of these deeply implanted concepts on his own.

Since that first encounter in 1975, Claude Nowell has visited with these extraterrestrial beings more than fifty times. These beings, whom he refers to as Summa Individuals, have identified themselves as souls who evolved out of ancient Atlantis and have mastered the secrets of the universe (which are recorded in and can be communicated by their mystical crystals). The Summa Individuals are dedicated to working with all humans who are ready to subordinate their egos and take up the labor of spiritual evolution. Claude Nowell has worked with the Summa Individuals for over twenty years, and his continued spiritual growth is reflected in the fact that he now goes by the name of Summum Bonum Amen Ra.

Summum Bonum Amen Ra has constructed a religious center outside of Salt Lake City to assist others in their spiritual growth. Much of the spiritual path advocated by Summum has to do with meditation exercises aimed at expanding personal consciousness and with studying the teachings that come down from ancient Atlantis and ancient Egypt through the Summa Individuals.[49] One major teaching concerns the "rediscovery" of the unique liquids used by ancient civilizations to convey spiritual power and information to those who ingest them. Summum publications refer to the soma beverage used to bring enlightenment to ancient Hindu sages and to the "nectars of the gods" referred to in the hieroglyphs of ancient Egypt:

> These liquids, the nectar Publications, old messengers of communication, were tools of the Initiates. Since then, thousands of years have passed, and in 1975 evolved Atlantean Initiates [the Summa Individuals who appeared to Nowell] re-established Summum, a society among whose many purposes was to begin recreation of those same nectars. Referred to as publication because of the information they contain, these nectars are provided by the Summum for the benefit of this planet and the inhabitancy thereof.[50]

To make these wines, referred to as "nectar publication," Nowell built a three-story pyramid that rests on large quartz crystals and is precisely aligned on a north-south axis. Within this pyramid—the womb of creation as Summum refers to it—several large stainless steel vats are used to make consciousness-expanding wine. Summum wine is made only at astrologically precise times. Grape juice and other "essences of nature" are placed in the vats along with one teaspoon of powdered crystal rock for every 1,500 gallons. For a period of twenty-seven days, Summum initiates gather around these vats for meditation practices designed to project their acquired spiritual energies and wisdom into the fermenting "nectars." They believe that the powdered crystal suspended in the liquid acts as a receptor and capacitor of the energies they telepathically transmit into the wine. The powdered crystal is then able to transfer these energies to the subatomic particles in the liquid.

The nectars are then bottled and stored in the pyramid, intensifying the energy and information that are contained within them. Although the state of Utah prohibits the sale of wine except through licensed state liquor stores, Summum accepts donations in return for bottles of one of several different nectars that they have produced to date (they plan eventually to produce twenty-seven different spiritual nectars). The nectars are intended to be used in conjunction with meditation. Drinking a small amount of nectar prior to meditation makes it possible for a person's life force to dissolve the crystals suspended in the wine and thereby release its energies into the alcohol. The alcohol in turn carries the "resonations" through the bloodstream into the brain where the stored wisdom is released and gradually assimilated into the individual's consciousness. It is recommended that new initiates use small amounts of the nectar twice daily, morning and evening, followed by meditation. In this way the ecstatic properties of these wines enable the new initiate to ascend in consciousness until the Summum Bonum—the Supreme Good—permeates their very being.

Wine and the Dynamics of Religious Affiliation

The vast majority of Americans with religious affiliations belong to a denominational tradition that has historically viewed wine as integral to its religious identity. Mainstream denominations such as Roman Catholicism, Episcopalianism, Lutheranism, Congregationalism, Presbyterianism, and all three branches of Judaism revere the power of wine both to invoke an awareness of the sacred and to build human community. What is interesting is that the further a group is from being part of this mainstream tradition, the more likely it is to take a more dramatic stand for—or against—the use of wine for these religious tasks.

Attitudes toward wine have thus been one of the ways in which American religious groups have established and maintained their distinctive identities. There are, in fact, at least three different ways in which the use of wine has helped contribute to the innovation and diversity that characterizes American religious history. First, wine's inherent capacity to foster what Donald Horton calls experiences of "social jollification" has clearly contributed to the communal affirmation that is basic to all religious communities. We saw this, for example, in how Judaism connects various personal and family moments with a transcendent standard of meaning by hallowing life with the presence of wine. This was even more pronounced in the Amana colonies and in the early years of the Latter-day Saints when the day-to-day survival of these countervailing religious communities depended upon their sense of social solidarity. In the words of Joseph Smith, the Mormons' "hearts were made glad" by partaking of the earth's bounty and "joy filled every bosom." The slight inebriation brought about by wine use opens up novel and quite egalitarian modes of social interaction. In this way, wine fosters a more open display of warmth and affection than is ordinarily displayed in everyday living. The more a religious group varies from the mainstream, the more important it is for the group to have the sense of communal love and enthusiasm generated by the sharing of wine.

Second, the mental changes induced by wine drinking favor the kind of "variation in ideas" that is often necessary to embolden individuals to strike out in theological directions that veer from the established churches. The enjoyment of wine while being engaged in lively discussions of religion and philosophy was important to affiliation with both the Amana and Latter-day Saint communal societies. For example, recall Oliver Huntington's diary entry that explained how "every person ate bread and drank wine as they wanted all day, when they wanted. They sat and talked and walked and conversed upon heavenly and spiritual things as they felt like." The extent to which "the finer electro-vinous spirit" or the "crystal-infused nectars" altered the theological orientations of new converts to the Brotherhood of the New Life or Summum might be difficult to assess. What is more certain is that wine loosens the hold of our normal patterns of waking thought and thereby encourages the very kind of intellectual experimentation that is a prerequisite to making a conscious decision to embrace variant religious beliefs.

Third, and finally, wine promotes the formation of religious groups by providing individuals with a sense of emotional expansiveness. Recent study suggests that Jesus' ministry promoted just such emotional expansiveness through the commensal sharing of food and wine. This, in turn, became part of Christian worship, just as Judaism and other Mediterranean religions had long recognized wine's symbolic association with spiritual ecstasy. Alcoholic bever-

ages help create the sensation that we have momentarily transcended our ordinary mental and emotional powers. Whether pronounced or mild, the ecstasy occasioned by wine thus reinforces the
conviction that one has suddenly been granted superior intellect
and enhanced spiritual well-being. This enthusiasm tends to lessen
the inhibitions that might otherwise counter any inclination to go
against prevailing community opinion and embrace a novel religious path. The Mormons, for example, passed around cake and
wine until it "was the season to speak in tongues." Members of the
Brotherhood of the New Life consumed wine for the purpose of
achieving "an organic openness to the pure Breath of God," and
Summum initiates drink wine, meditate, and expect the Summum
Bonum to permeate their very being. It would seem that the more
variant a religious group's theology or communal ethics are, the
more likely the group is to benefit from their members' communal
drinking of wine.

As already noted, the very properties of wine that have fostered its
incorporation into some American religious communities simultaneously account for why other religious groups have considered
wine drinking a taboo. Jews, recognizing the "social jollification" attendant upon wine drinking, have evolved strict kosher regulations
that minimize the chances of social fraternization leading to marriage between Jew and non-Jew. Joseph Smith received a revelation
stipulating that Latter-day Saints refrain from drinking wine "not
made new among you." Religious groups, particularly newly emerging or minority religious groups, must be especially attentive to the
maintenance of group boundaries. We saw this, too, in the prohibition of wine drinking among many conservative Protestant groups
such as the Baptists, Assemblies of God, and the Church of the
Nazarene. These groups call for a prophetic stand against the secularizing influences of modern society. They seek to instill a moral
piety based on the withdrawal from the intellectual trends (e.g.,
Darwinism and secular humanism), social trends (e.g., immigration
and the breakdown of traditional authority structures), and lifestyle
trends (e.g., the widespread repudiation of traditional moral
codes) of modern life. The taboo against wine drinking, then, functions to preserve a certain "over and againstness" through which
these groups differentiate themselves from the potential corruptions of an apostate world.

There is, of course, also a theological dimension to these groups'
opposition to the consumption of wine. Strict evangelical faith considers improperly directed emotions to be the root of much of hu-

manity's sinful behavior. The theological conceptions of salvation found in most American religious groups that oppose wine drinking are predominately evangelical. Evangelical faith entails the conviction that there is nothing that humans can do to merit salvation. Because salvation is thought to proceed only from God's saving grace, it follow that no ritual action or emotional "opening" on the part of humans can, in and of itself, bring humans closer to God. It is interesting to note in this context that both Mary Douglas and Mircea Eliade have observed that a community's conceptions of taboo and uncleanliness frequently entail efforts to prevent individuals from having direct access to the divine. Evangelical faith is predicated upon a wide gulf separating humanity from God, bridgeable only by the saving grace of Christ. From this perspective, the "spontaneous communitas" directly produced by wine is not only a misdirection of humanity's desire for communion with the sacred but an action that is intrinsically unclean or even diabolic. In short, wine drinking is an act associated with those "outside" the boundaries of conservative evangelical faith.

In all, then, the use of wine provides a fascinating handle on the origin, identity creation, and boundary-setting behaviors of American religious communities. The distinctive patterns of use—and nonuse—of wine by a wide variety of religious groups provide an additional perspective on the continuing creativity of American culture in giving rise to new forms of religious enthusiasm.

Drugs, Aesthetics, and Unchurched Spirituality

The previous chapter examined how a particular drug, wine, has contributed to the historical development of a wide variety of American religious groups. Equally important in American religious life, however, are the religious thought and experiences that exist outside of formal religious organizations. Unchurched American religion also has a rich history.[1] One fascinating chapter in this history is the connection between drugs and the emergence of many of the most innovative forms of American spirituality.

Estimates of the percentage of the American populace that has no affiliation with a church vary a great deal. One of the most thorough studies of religious affiliation throughout American history concludes that about 38 percent of the American population is currently unchurched.[2] The size of America's unchurched population is itself not very surprising. But what is surprising about unchurched Americans is that they are for the most part just as likely to be personally religious as those who have formal church affiliation.[3] That is, unchurched Americans are just as likely as their churched counterparts to claim belief in God and to espouse religiously based values. The main difference between the two groups appears to be that unchurched Americans lack confidence in traditional religious institutions' ability to meet their personal spiritual needs.

It is difficult to make too many generalizations about a full 38 percent of the United States population. But sociologist Wade Clark Roof has paid considerable attention to the unchurched population belonging to the Baby Boom generation. According to Roof, about a fourth of unchurched Americans—a number that also amounts to 9 percent of all Baby Boomers—can be classified under the category he labels "highly active seekers."[4] Roof found that members of this sizable segment of the Baby Boom generation are deeply committed to their own personal religious journeys but do so wholly outside established Jewish or Christian religious organizations. Most prefer to think of themselves as "spiritual" rather than "religious." They are put off by what they view as the legalistic, bureaucratic, and experientially empty nature of most churches. Roof further found that these highly active seekers tend to be well educated, economically successful, liberal-minded professionals.

The fact that these individuals are so highly spiritual is somewhat unexpected since their educational and economic backgrounds have located them in the very social and intellectual strata that scholars typically associate with secularization, the gradual decline of religion in favor of scientific rationality. Yet this sizable group of Baby Boomers has an almost insatiable curiosity about a variety of spiritual ideas and practices. Their exposure to so-called secularizing cultural forces appears to have shifted, rather than eradicated, their religious tendencies. Roof's highly active seekers look outside the churches in their pursuit of spiritual fulfillment, turning instead to such sources of religious edification as Eastern religions, Western mystical philosophies, and transpersonal psychologies. In other words, about one-fourth of the unchurched population is actively seeking spiritual nourishment, albeit through unconventional avenues.

It goes without saying that most of America's unchurched population, especially those whom Roof calls highly active seekers, have religious needs and curiosities that fall outside the domain of the nation's established churches. Furthermore, many of those who do belong to a church are also motivated to look outside of formal religious institutions for additional sources of spiritual fulfillment. That is, even many churched Americans have a keen interest in unchurched forms of spirituality. Studies indicate that Baby Boomers have less loyalty to their particular denomination than did church members in previous generations. Many contemporary Americans become involved with formal religious organizations in order to meet their practical needs (e.g., helping them raise children, giving some semblance of meaning, or providing an experience of community) but believe that no single group captures the whole of religious truth or meets all of their spiritual needs.[5] Although it would be difficult to estimate the exact number, many of these church-going Americans supplement the teachings of their churches by exploring other, often quite unconventional spiritual traditions. Thus unprecedented numbers of Americans—churched and unchurched alike—are currently seeking spiritual inspiration from a wide variety of cultural sources. Popular psychologies, self-help paperback books, meditation seminars, New Age organizations, theories about near-death or out-of-body experiences, and the study of world religions have all emerged to supplement Americans' understandings of how they might find harmony with the "highest" power of the universe. Indeed, perhaps the most fascinating chapter in recent American history is the progressive growth of unchurched forms of spirituality.[6]

Historian Robert Ellwood has noted that the very social and intellectual forces that have weakened Americans' loyalty to religious institutions have simultaneously enabled spirituality "to exist principally, possibly even to prosper unprecedentedly, within subjectivity and in small groups."[7] Unfortunately, however, few historians other than Ellwood have paid attention to the various ways in which drugs have enhanced the kinds of subjectivity and small-group camaraderie that foster the growth of unchurched spirituality.

Coffee, marijuana, and wine serve as ready examples of how certain patterns of drug use have enabled spirituality to exist, indeed flourish, within subjectivity and in small groups. The principal reason is undoubtedly the fact that these particular drugs are frequently used in ways that open up an aesthetic or nonrational way of perceiving the universe. Although cannabis and alcohol undoubtedly hamper persons' logical faculties, they (as with caffeine) stimulate the senses and seemingly awaken us to ranges of experience that are normally excluded from waking awareness. Even mild forms of drug-induced stimulation are thus able to reinforce belief that we possess the potential for greater degrees of happiness and inner fulfillment. And, too, even relatively mild drugs such as coffee, wine, and marijuana provide experiences that address modern individuals' hunger for a felt sense of participation in a wider spiritual reality. Meanwhile, the social settings in which these drugs are usually taken respond to the equally important religious need to belong to a community of fellow seekers. The use of coffee, marijuana, and wine has introduced Americans to social settings and mood-altering rituals that meet a range of otherwise neglected emotional and spiritual needs. All three are vehicles for sustaining certain modes of spirituality even among those individuals who have little or no affiliation with the nation's churches.

The emergence of several new, drug-related forms of "unchurched" religion can be traced to the 1950s, the very decade that is often thought to be the heyday of churched religion in the United States. Americans emerged from World War II with a sense of optimism, enjoying the prosperity generated by their rejuvenated industrial economy. Church attendance hit a historical high in these years as the mainstream denominations grew at an unprecedented rate. Membership in a mainstream denomination denoted conformity with the American way of life and all the material prosperity it promised. God and country, Bible and Constitution, cross and flag collectively symbolized "consensus" American culture.

Yet even in these years when church membership reached its zenith, alternative voices could be heard. A group commonly referred to as "the Beats" were among the first "dropouts" from middle-class culture and mainstream denominational religion. The Beats emphasized individuality over conformity. Their penchant for the exotic sowed the seeds of youthful rebellion against authority of all kinds. A decade later the Beats' nonconformity resurfaced in the so-called hippie movement. Calling upon youth to "do their own thing," the hippies spurned the capitalistic values of the American middle class and instead promoted love, peace, and unity with nature.

Throughout the 1950s and 1960s a growing group of Americans became spiritually restless. Historian Robert Ellwood demonstrates that many new forms of unchurched American religion emerged in this era due to the availability of new social settings and new rituals that provided opportunities for the spiritually restless to "bond" with alternative religious philosophies. Ellwood suggests that a great deal of what we now associate with unchurched spirituality emerged out of three kinds of social and intellectual bonding:

1. Male bonding in contrast to the dominant nuclear family. Rebels needed to complete their process of rebellion by finding their clan. The spiritual underground needed places and rituals for bonding outside the religious mainstream.
2. Bonding around the ideal of religion as the inner-directed following of an interiorized myth or mystical experience. Such bonding had to have an ecstatic element, leading to individuation and creative expression rather than upholding consensual values of society. This is why Carl Jung, Joseph Campbell, and "mystics" like Alan Watts or Aldous Huxley were important to the spiritual underground; they were purveyors of the alternative myths and pathways to spiritual experience.

3. Bonding around exotic rather than normative religious symbols. Attraction to Zen Buddhism, Vedanta Hinduism, and Native
American shamanism expressed self-conscious commitment to
countercultural social roles. Exotic symbols bespoke ecstasy—
stepping outside of the normal to embrace that which is transcendent and original.[8]

The ritual presence and mood-altering activity of drugs was frequently contributed to the effectiveness of these countercultural
"bondings." Coffeehouses, the passing of marijuana cigarettes, and
the sharing of wine in close-knit groups have all promoted various
forms of bonding outside the mainstream. The settings in which
Americans consume coffee, marijuana, and wine carve out separate
cultural spaces that have permitted spirituality to survive, and even
prosper, in subjectivity and in small groups. They permit intimacy
and communal affirmation in ways that—especially for males—are
rarely possible in everyday social interaction. They have also fostered ecstatic emotional episodes that encourage a feeling of connectedness with a "higher reality." These and similar drugs have enabled millions of Americans to appreciate ranges of aesthetic
thought and feeling that might otherwise remain closed to them. In
so doing, they have provided the experiential basis for a variety of
forms of unchurched American spirituality.

Coffee as Sacramental Beverage

Throughout world history certain beverages have come to be celebrated in myth, ritual, and sacred speculation. Milk, for example, is
almost universally associated with both the sustenance of life and
family nurturance. In many passages of Hebrew scripture, milk is
depicted as a paradisiacal fluid, and Israel is even referred to as "the
land of milk and honey." Among the Masai and other cattle-herding
peoples of East Africa, milk is revered as a life-bestowing elixir. Intoxicating beverages have achieved even greater mythic status. The
ancient Greeks considered wine to be the nectar of the gods and associated this pleasing beverage with Dionysus. South American cultures valued the vision-bestowing properties of the hallucinogenic
yajé.

Of further interest is the reverence with which the Japanese have
regarded tea. It is reputed that Zen monks brought heavily caffeinated tea with them from China for the purpose of staying awake
for extended periods of meditation.[9] After prolonged meditation

and copious amounts of tea, these monks would experience the flash of insight that Zen terms *satori*. Although satori brings "a sense of the beyond," it is not considered by Zen practitioners to be an experience of any supernatural realm. It is, instead, an experience of the totality of the present, natural world. Satori comes from radically opening up to the world of immediate experience. It imparts the conviction that the whole of reality is sacred, if we can but learn to see it that way.

Zen claims that we must begin our quest for spiritual insight by learning to dismantle the mind's dualistic structure. That is, the vast bulk of our lives are spent in the ego-centered perspective that divides life into "I"/"not-me"; subject/object; self/world; and actor/action. Satori can be experienced only by going beyond these dichotomies and restoring the original unity of experience in which all things are linked together in a seamless ontological whole. The key to Zen enlightenment is to learn to view life from the perspective of being connected with all things. The experience that results, satori, produces the conviction that the holy is present in the here and now of everyday life if we but let go of the ego and allow ourselves to see or experience it.

Zen enlightenment thus has nothing to do with escaping the natural world or making contact with some supernatural realm. Instead, Zen satori entails radically opening up to one's present world of experience. Because caffeine is a stimulant rather than hallucinogen, it is a vehicle to just such sensations of enthusiasm, clarified vision, and accelerated participation in life. It is said that satori was first discovered by monks who, in order to keep a night-long meditational vigil, consumed large quantities of highly caffeinated tea.

A perfect illustration of how Zen theology and the mood-enhancing properties of caffeine blend together is the traditional Japanese tea ceremony. The Japanese tea ceremony is an art form all its own, a kind of ritual activity that helps persons see old things or the world in general from an angle of perception entirely and most refreshingly new. The art of the tea ceremony is the aestheticism of stark simplicity. In the tea ceremony the very common activities of preparing, serving, and drinking tea are done with quiet simplicity, with special ritual implements, and in a serene setting. The whole activity is invested with a sacred significance in which common things are seen and done in a new light. As religious historian Bruce Lincoln observed, Japanese tea masters are able to create "nothing less than a perfect microcosm, a thoroughly harmonious environment in which one might take refuge from the tribulation of the external world and encounter the Buddha nature that lies beyond the conflicts and fluctuations of life in the material world."[10]

Caffeine, in the form of coffee beverages, has been no less important to Western culture's efforts to symbolize the union of divine and human activities. The legends that recount the early discovery of coffee are undoubtedly apocryphal, but they are striking in their mythic association of this exhilarating beverage with the ecstasy to be found in prayerful communion with God. Perhaps the best known of these legends tells of a young Abyssinian goatherd named Kaldi.[11] At sunset his goats usually slept, lying motionless with outstretched limbs. On one particular night, however, they cavorted uncontrollably, bleating and chasing one another. Kaldi watched as the goats darted to and fro, pausing only long enough to nibble the red berries from a nearby shrub. Kaldi inspected the shrub and was enticed by the jasmine scent of the plant's flowers. He decided to try a few of the berries for himself. Kaldi found himself wide awake. His hunger was gone. He felt alert and excited. Kaldi forgot all of his worldly troubles and realized that he was the happiest man in all of "happy Arabia." He brought a few of the berries to the imam, or prayer leader, of the local monastery. The imam then made a tea from these unusual berries. Immediately upon drinking this tea the imam felt that he had been strengthened by heavenly food, a gift from the angels of paradise. He would never have to sleep again. He proclaimed that this beverage would be used to keep the faithful awake during the evening prayer services. He called it *kahveh*, "the stimulating and invigorating." His fellow monks began to drink kahveh on a regular basis, staying up all night to pray and reaching exhilarating states of ecstasy.

The historical record suggests that coffee was originally consumed as a food among African tribes. Ripe cherries from coffee bushes were crushed in stone mortars and then mixed with animal fat. War parties consumed these balls of coffee and fat for their calories and stimulation. It appears that about 900 C.E., Ethiopians began to make a wine from the fermented pulp of coffee berries. The beverage was called *qahwah* (meaning "spirit drink") in Arabic, the forerunner of the term *kahveh* in Turkish, *café* in French, *kaffee* in German, and *caffè* in Italian. Because alcohol was soon to be forbidden among Muslims, it was most fortunate that these coffee berries were able to produce a hot, nonalcoholic beverage capable of inducing feelings of pleasure and stimulation.

The practice of boiling green berries in water to create a liquid resembling our modern coffee started about 1000 C.E., possibly as a means of softening the hard beans. The word *qahwah* or *kahveh* was transferred to this new beverage toward the end of the thirteenth century. Claudia Roden observes that one reason for the hot coffee beverage receiving the poetic name formally used for fermented wine "is that coffee, first inaugurated in Sufi mystic circles, had come to replace the forbidden wine as a drink during religious ceremonies. Delighted by the wakefulness the new drink produced and the help it gave them in their nightly prayers, the early Muslims honored it by giving it the poetic endearment with which they had sung the praise of wine."[12] Coffee was particularly appealing to the Sufis, who practiced one of the most mystically oriented forms of the Muslim faith. Sufi mystics, often called dervishes, adopted coffee as an adjunct to their long ceremonies, which used music and dancing to induce mystic exaltation. The dervishes passed huge jars of coffee around and chanted prayers as they danced and sang until sunlight.

Secular demand for coffee gradually developed, and thus coffee-houses, or *qahveh khaneh*, sprang up in Mecca about 1470 C.E. These coffeehouses were associated with music, gambling, and freewheeling discussions of the day's religious and political issues. Muslim clerics criticized the coffeehouses for fostering licentiousness and immorality. Coffee was blamed for turning people away from religious orthodoxy. For a time, the government of Mecca tried to forbid the sale and consumption of coffee but finally relented under mounting public pressure. The secular consumption of coffee spread, and the coffeehouses of Constantinople and Damascus, known as *cafenets*, became the prototypes of modern Western coffeehouses.[13] The *cafenets* displayed artistically designed prints and rugs on their walls and offered aesthetically appointed areas in which friends could meet to share the excitement of the city or play games of cards, chess, and backgammon. Similar coffeehouses spread to Italy and, from there, to the rest of Western Europe. Of note is the fact that Italian priests initially accused coffee of being the "bitter invention of Satan." The priests maintained that Satan had forbidden the infidel Muslims to use wine, because it was used in the Christian Eucharist, and instead given them this hellish black brew. A contingent of priests requested that the pope, Clement VIII, condemn this beverage of heretics. Pope Clement VIII decided to first try the beverage for himself and rebutted, "Why, this Satan's drink is so delicious that it would be a pity to let the infidels have exclusive use of it. We shall cheat Satan by baptizing it."[14] With full papal sanction, coffee was interjected into the spiritual centers of Western Europe.

The golden age of the coffeehouse coincided with the intellectual and artistic fervor of the Enlightenment era. The Enlightenment was a time of unprecedented scientific and philosophical creativity. Intellectuals across Europe shared a common sense of discovery and breakthrough. The secrets of nature seemed to be yielding to human ingenuity. Traditional religious beliefs about human weakness were taking a back seat to this wave of confidence in human powers and the inevitability of worldly progress. Coffeehouses provided a forum for the era's scholars and artists to gather to share their creative efforts. The coffeehouse was, as David Joel and Karl Schapira have noted, "pulpit, courtroom, stage, and classroom."[15] In Paris, the symbolic center of the era's intellectual ferment, Rousseau, Beaumarchais, Diderot, and Voltaire (who is reputed to have drunk up to fifty cups of coffee per day) were all patrons of the café. In London, Will's and Button's were the gathering places for the literary intelligentsia, including Dryden, Dr. Johnson, Boswell, Pepys, Addison, Steele, Congreve, and Swift. European coffeehouses exuded an atmosphere of heightened spiritual and mental awareness. In England, where admission cost a penny, coffeehouses were referred to as "penny universities," where it was said that a man could "pick up more useful knowledge than he could if applying himself to his book for a whole month."[16]

The coffeehouse was also a vehicle for disseminating progressive thought among the newly created middle class. Joel and Schapira chronicle how "men needed centers of social intercourse where they could learn the news and discuss it. The time was shaping a unique and powerful group of men—middle-class in terms of wealth and values, well-educated and with progressive ideas."[17] The coffeehouse was thus the cultural center of a major shift in Western religious and political thought. Freed from the restrictive influence of the church's theology and the king's politics, a new class of individuals met to share coffee and generate the worldview that would give rise to liberal democracies and progressive religious outlooks.

On December 16, 1773, at the very height of the European Enlightenment, an event took place in Boston harbor that was to create an entire nation of coffee drinkers. The colonial patriots who undertook the Boston Tea Party planted an aversion to tea deep within American culinary preferences. And in doing so, they opened up strong coffee markets, first for French and Dutch trade merchants, and eventually for Americans who established trade routes to the Caribbean.

Coffee had been introduced to the American colonies early in their history. Captain John Smith who had learned about coffee in his travels to Turkey was probably the first to introduce the beverage to North America. Records indicate that coffee was being drunk regularly in New York by the 1680s when many began to substitute it for beer at their breakfast meal. Yet, for reasons that are not completely clear, separate coffeehouses never flourished in the United States as they did in Europe. Coffee was served at taverns, inns, restaurants, and private clubs. The serving and enjoyment of coffee did not, however, impart a distinctive ethos to any of these forums for public gathering. The number of "pure" coffeehouses continued to decline throughout the nineteenth and twentieth centuries. To be sure, Americans still wished to congregate around a good cup of coffee. But the American cafe was essentially a small roadside restaurant. Indeed, doughnut shops were probably the closest thing in American culture to a special setting where sweets and coffee could be enjoyed while gathering with others to share gossip and opinions. Coffee continued to be connected with informal forms of sociality among Americans, but few frequented coffeehouses that in any way embodied a distinctive, countercultural ethos.

The renaissance of coffeehouses in the United States dovetailed almost perfectly with the counterculture movement among youth between the late 1950s and the early 1970s. Artists and writers living in New York City during the late 1950s adopted coffeehouses as the forum for their "beat" take on life. In New York's Greenwich Village, the Figaro and Caffè Reggio attracted artists, musicians, poets, and others living on a shoestring.[18] By the 1960s more and more coffeehouses appeared and attracted those who sought to bond with other critics of bourgeois American culture. Coffeehouses launched experimental theater productions, displayed the work of local artists, arranged for poetry readings, and introduced urban audiences to the emerging genre of politically charged folk music. Arlo Guthrie, James Taylor, and Pete Seeger were among those who gained early followings at a coffeehouse known as the Bitter End. Poets and eclectic philosophers like Allen Ginsberg frequently premiered their work at coffeehouses in New York and San Francisco, transforming coffeehouses into an icon of the hip outlook on life.

The coffeehouse was the symbolic meeting center of the countercultural movement, where initiates were exposed to existentialism, Eastern religion, and metaphysical interpretations of life's mysteries. Existentialism, in its most strident forms, denied the existence of absolute truths that somehow exist over and beyond the relativities of human life. Existentialism insisted that the only truths are those that we create by our own thought and actions. The early Beats were trying to think through moral and religious issues anew and thus found existentialism an attractive springboard to novel intellectual formulations. Although some devotees of existentialism affirmed its nihilistic and antireligious implications, most embraced only its call to test ideas by determining whether they make sense in terms of our own personal existence. The lure of existentialism, then, was not so much to deny ultimate meaning as to insist that it be found in lived human existence.

Eastern religions, with their emphasis upon introspection and enlightened states of awareness, had a natural appeal to those attracted by the early counterculture. The expanded awareness described in Eastern mystical literature appealed to those who found their inherited religious traditions sadly irrelevant to their own metaphysical yearnings. Gathering in coffeehouses, the early members of the American "religious underground" became exposed to entirely new spiritual possibilities. Emboldened by the exhilaration and sense of expanded well-being generated by hours of consuming coffee in such settings, many abandoned their former religious beliefs and instead embraced exotic new approaches to spiritual discovery.

San Francisco's emergence as epicenter of a major cultural shift was aided by such early coffeehouses as Caffè Trieste and Malvina Caffè. North Beach coffeehouses provided the physical space where the era's most progressive thinkers could congregate and forge some kind of palpable community among the era's philosophical rebels. In the mid-1960s, the Blue Unicorn opened up in San Francisco's Haight-Ashbury district and was soon stimulating the hippie movement with heavy doses of caffeine. The Blue Unicorn advertised the lowest prices of any coffeehouse in town, plus "food, books, music and art" and—boldly announcing its intention to eschew all traces of conventional youth culture—"no jukebox."[19] The purpose wasn't really to make money. The owner, Bob Stubbs, wanted to provide a space for social interaction and philosophical exchange. He put in an old sofa to hang out on, chessboards, and a free secondhand clothes box. He even held mail for regular customers who didn't have regular addresses. This wasn't a commercial venture so much as an attempt to foster community. Stubbs allowed the Legalize Marijuana (LEMAR) movement to hold its meetings there, including their weekly Wednesday-night poetry readings. The Sexual Freedom League also met there and even used the Blue Unicorn for its press conference following one of their nude wade-ins. Stubbs even issued pamphlets that explained the "Unicorn Philosophy," which he described as "essentially a striving for realization of one's relationship to life and other people."[20]

Other coffeehouses were quick to emerge alongside Haight-Ashbury's row of psychedelic shops, health food stores, and mod clothing boutiques. The Drugstore, soon to be renamed the Drogstore under police pressure, opened with paisley-decorated tabletops. An instructor at San Francisco State University opened a coffee shop called the I/Thou. Patrons frequently had to stand in line for long periods of time to gain entrance. These coffeehouses provided the physical space that enabled members of the early hippie movement to gather and share their particular take on the "Turn On, Tune In, and Drop Out" philosophy that was gaining momentum in their midst. They could share a cup of coffee and clarify their own unique relationship to life and to other people. Bookshelves along the walls exposed the clientele to the philosophies that would define the era's alternative spirituality: Hindu meditation systems, Zen Buddhism, the *Dao de Ching*, the writings of such purveyors of alternative wisdom as Carl Jung or Alan Watts, and sundry works related to the Western occult tradition. These books, combined with the avant garde art that covered coffeehouse walls, defined a distinct, separate space into which one could retreat to find a more intense "realization of one's relationship to life and other people." Coffeehouses, then, permitted a kind of social and intellectual "bonding" that contrasted sharply with the shallowness that many American youth associated with bourgeois American society.

Coffee generated community among the hippies in a way that hallucinogens never really could. A typical cup of coffee delivers about 100 milligrams of caffeine to the central nervous system (compared to about 40 milligrams in a cup of tea). Caffeine has a stimulating effect upon the central nervous system, almost immediately stimulating the heart, blood vessels, and kidneys. Caffeine has been shown to increase alertness, improve motor performance, enhance sensory activity, and decrease fatigue. All of these yield a sense of elation, mild euphoria, and interest in engaging life more energetically.

It is important to note that caffeine really isn't a stimulant per se. It binds to cells in the brain in such a way as to block the effect of adenosine, a chemical that ordinarily has a quieting effect upon the brain.[21] Like many other drugs, caffeine is thus an indirect stimulant; by itself, it can't stimulate anything. By blocking the quieting effect of adenosine, it impairs the brain's ability to keep its own excitatory neurotransmitters in check. In this way, caffeine clears the way for the brain's own stimulants—neurotransmitters such as glutamate, dopamine, and the endorphins—to do their job without interference. Coffee drinkers thus "get wired" only to the extent that their own natural excitatory neurotransmitters transmit exhilarating signals. Caffeine might consequently be viewed as a pharmaceutical agent of nature religion. That is, it puts us in a position to respond to nature's own hidden riches. Caffeine enables us to appreciate the exhilaration that emanates from nature itself; this, in turn, enhances our aesthetic rapport with our surroundings in such a way that we might see common things in a new and more vibrant way.

It is in this context that the selection of the name I/Thou was so befitting a countercultural enterprise in Haight-Ashbury. The Jewish philosopher Martin Buber published a book titled *I and Thou* that provided a mystical perspective on human relationships. Buber noted that most human relationships fall into the categories of either I/It or I/You encounters characterized by the active presence of the ego and efforts to "use" others for our own personal gain. In contrast, I/Thou relationships have a sacred quality to them. They emerge when we surrender ego and approach life in a fresh, more aesthetically enriched way. I/Thou relationships recognize and affirm others for their own intrinsic value. They are characterized by free-flowing, spontaneous, and mutually enriching dialogue.

More to the point, Buber maintained that such flowing human relationships are themselves experiences of an immanent divinity. Buber, the mystical prophet, argued that God is to be sought not on remote mountaintops but rather in the midst of immediate experience. According to Buber, God can therefore be found in the birth of a child, in a tree, or in a human relationship if we can but learn to open ourselves up to this deeper spiritual presence. Coffeehouses, like the I/Thou coffeehouse in Haight-Ashbury, are places set apart from everyday life where persons go yearning for such intimacy and spiritual well-being. The flowing, mutually enriching dialogue between individuals becomes a kind of stepping-stone to a divine-human encounter.

Coffeehouse encounters, much like those connected with Japanese tea ceremonies, are highly ritualized. Both set and setting create expectations of rising above ordinary human consciousness and tapping into some mysterious reservoir of creativity and enchantment. The pervasive presence of artistic, musical, and literary compositions elicits an aesthetic response. Even the preparation of the coffee has a ritual element. The careful activities associated with selecting and grinding an appropriate blend of coffee beans creates a distinctive ritual atmosphere. So, too, does the attention given to the use of special cups and saucers associated only with the use of coffee. This ritual element helps lift persons out of their workaday mind-sets and prepares them to embrace the "finer" things in life. The physiological effects of caffeine consumption, no less than the set or setting, also help produce a Zen-like "fresh way of seeing things." Enhanced mental alertness and increased sensory alertness combine to help us appreciate new dimensions or an added richness to what are otherwise ordinary experiences.[22] Few Americans consume coffee in social or ritual contexts that might transform their experience into one of quite the same spiritual magnitude as Zen Buddhism's satori. Yet by the hundreds of thousands they have found coffee drinking to be crucial to such spiritual activities as flowing conversation, intimate reading, and intellectual discovery. And in this sense these Americans have found that coffee, in a matter at least approximating Zen satori, is capable of awakening them to the fact that the sacred (i.e., what is precious, truly important, intrinsically worthwhile) is in the here and now of everyday life if we can but learn to see it.

The number of coffeehouses in the United States has grown dramatically in recent years. During the decade of the 1990s, the number of coffeehouses in the United States grew from 200 to over 8,000. The Starbucks chain alone has about 1,500 coffeehouses in North America, generating more than $700 million in sales annually. There can be little doubt but that the growing dominance of the "sanitized" coffeehouses such as Starbucks is in direct proportion to the decline of the role of coffeehouses as purveyors of "alternative spirituality." Indeed, many modern coffeehouses are built in locations chosen solely for their proximity to places of work. Forces of capitalism regulate Americans' coffee consumption as much, or possibly more, than any spiritual urges, no matter how loosely the concept of spirituality is defined. Most of those who patronize America's burgeoning array of coffeehouses are by no means interested in "bonding" to the countercultural values that flourished in the late fifties and sixties. In this sense, then, the popularity of upscale coffeehouses reflects the tendency of American middle-class culture to adopt the accoutrements of the counterculture, while having little intention of adopting its ideological substance.

Yet even given the commercial forces underlying partronage of contemporary American coffeehouses, they nonetheless continue to provide the social settings and mood-altering rituals in which unchurched spirituality continues to prosper. In his study of the way in which commercial enterprises have commodified elements of the hippie movement, Thomas Frank notes that the sixties counterculture projected a "myth of personal transformation through ecstatic nonconformity."[23] To be sure, most of the 8,000 coffeehouses in the United States do not understand themselves to be in the business of providing experiences of ecstatic nonconformity. But many do, especially those located near college campuses or in urban areas that attract persons who identify with the arts and intellectual discovery.

Even a chain of coffeehouses as driven by commercial forces as Starbucks nonetheless understands its mission to include providing a setting conducive to personal transformation and intimate relationships. Starbucks's chairman and CEO claims that is has been their mission to provide urban Americans with what sociologist Ray Oldenburg calls a *third* place, that is, a place distinct from home and work that permits a forum for informal public life.[24] Part of Starbucks's founding mission is to provide precisely such a comfortable, sociable gathering place in which individuals come for the atmosphere and the camaraderie as much as they do the coffee.[25] It is the function of a third place—a great good place—to provide a "neutral" ground where the mood is playful and conversation is the main activity. In such a setting we find a form of sociality that is unencumbered by the kinds of role stratification found at home or work and that stimulates us with the "spiritual tonic" that comes from flowing human discourse.

And while many coffeehouses exude a genuinely "bohemian" ethos, still others provide at least a studied commodification of countercultural themes. For example, Starbucks stores sell compact discs with a selection of reggae or rock songs. Peace symbols or other expressions of sixties youth culture often bedeck the walls and windows. The Starbucks logo (based on a sixteenth-century woodcut of a two-tailed, bare-breasted mermaid) has an exotic flare and is meant to be "unique and mystical, yet purely American."[26] And thus however attenuated the ethos created by Starbucks and other contemporary coffeehouses might be, it nonetheless strikes a certain resonance with many of the themes of alternative spirituality and the myth of "personal transformation through ecstatic non-conformity."

As the forces of secularization march on, educated and artistically oriented Americans yearn for ways to assuage their "wholeness hunger" through experiences that flourish in subjectivity and small groups. The popularity of coffeehouses (whether of the upscale or hippie variety) reveals a continuing connection between coffee and spirituality—and more particularly, a spirituality that flourishes outside our official religious institutions. Corner coffee shops, sixties-ish coffeehouses, and even the neighborhood kaffeklatsch provide a forum for spirited—and spiritual—human exchange. For that matter, even America's churches have recognized the value of a "coffee hour" promptly after the conclusion of weekly worship services. The "coffee hour" provides an opportunity for church members to linger after the formal worship service, engage in informal conversation, and quite literally feel the exhilaration of the faith they came to renew.

The act of drinking a cup of coffee structures a special setting removed from the world of everyday psychological maneuvering. We might consider, for example, how best friends or even lovers make arrangements to nourish their relationships by gathering at a favorite coffeehouse. The ritual of sharing coffee permits them to stimulate their senses and to see one another in a fresh, invigorated light. Alcoholics Anonymous, which is without doubt one of the most powerful sources of unchurched spirituality in America, has often been described as "a couple of drunks meeting over a cup of coffee." Alcoholics Anonymous, which espouses the necessity of being spiritual even if not conventionally religious, has long recognized the power of coffee to uplift spirits, forge a supportive community, and enhance a sense of connection with a Higher Power.[27] Even many Web pages offer a "café" link where those who log on can communicate at a more personal level and share aspects of their personal lives (the icons for these café chat rooms is often the image of a cup of coffee). For example, the popular American Buddhist journal *Tricycle* touts a Web site called "Café Nirvana," which includes a "bookshelf" listing recent publications related to Buddhist thought.

Indeed, coffeehouses of all types are testimony to Americans' desire to expand their aesthetic engagement with life. The aromas and tastes often border on the exotic, beckoning us to develop whole new repertoires of "sensing" ability. The arrangement of tables and chairs sets up a social space where we can simply chat with friends or share the most intimate of feelings. And yet it is finally the caffeine itself that is most responsible for catapulting persons to new and more intense enjoyment of life's simple pleasures of conversation, reading, or listening to music. The sharing of coffee is a sacrament that enables humans to discover and celebrate the divine already implanted in the natural order. In this sense, coffee provides Americans with a vehicle for enjoying the attitudes and sensibility we term nature religion. Yet coffee drinking often becomes an ecstatic form of nature religion; it imparts a heightened sense of power and well-being. Caffeine elevates people's spirits and evokes aesthetic experiences that blur the distinction between self (the subject) and what we are experiencing (the object). In this way, coffee consumption affords many the sense that they are at least temporarily attuned to the divine "ground of being." Although existing well outside the doors of our institutional churches, the enjoyment of coffee is for many Americans a form of spirituality that flourishes in subjectivity and in small groups.

Marijuana and the Celebration of Interiority

The 1950s spiritual underground focused new attention on subjectivity. In contrast to mainstream religion's concern with public creeds and outer ritual, the counterculture championed an inner-directed spirituality. Those who promoted an alternative spirituality in the United States drew heavily upon the mystical writings of Zen Buddhism and Vedanta Hinduism. They consequently believed that authentic religion is something inward, having to do with mystic receptivity. Sensing that mainline religion lacked a mystical dimension, these idealists proclaimed that spirituality must be based on firsthand experience of a higher reality. Youthful seekers yearned to open up to the hidden reaches of the universe. First, however, they had to learn to expand personal awareness.

Marijuana became the counterculture's drug of choice. Although marijuana lacked the hallucinatory or vision-giving powers of the major hallucinogens such as LSD or psilocybin, it could be used more casually and more frequently. Smoking marijuana created unique social settings that allowed young cultural rebels to "bond" with a countercultural community centered around the spiritual goal of personal growth or individuation (even if at the expense of traditional cultural values). In fact, a great deal of what persons experience in a "marijuana high" is learned in a social context. And as Howard Becker has demonstrated in his classic studies of marijuana use, these social groups typically focus new users' attention on emotions and attitudes that have a distinctively countercultural flair to them.[28] Experienced users report an almost childlike openness to inner sensations) Using marijuana gives persons the impression that they are finally getting in touch with themselves and with the deeper currents of nature./By flooding the senses, marijuana use deepens a person's appreciation of interiority.'(In this way, marijuana facilitated what Ellwood describes as "bonding" around the ideal of religion as the inner-directed pursuit of mystical experience./

Marijuana has had a long historical association with religious "interiority." Known by such other terms as *bhang, ganja, hashish,* and *chara,* the resin and resin-bearing parts of this hearty hemp plant have been sacramentally employed all over the world. Hindu holy men have for centuries regarded bhang to be the giver of long life and a vehicle for establishing communion with the divine spirit. Smoked or made into a liquid concoction, bhang is thought to establish harmony between the divine and human realms. A governmental report on marijuana use in India prepared in the 1890s began by recognizing its age-old religious importance:

> To the Hindu the hemp plant is holy. A guardian lives in bhang. . . . Bhang is the joy giver, the sky flier, the heavenly guide, the poor man's heaven, the soother of grief. . . . No god or man is as good as the religious drinker of bhang. The students of the scriptures of Benares are given bhang before they sit to study. At Benares, Ujjain and other holy places, yogis take deep draughts of bhang that they may center their thoughts on the Eternal.[29]

Marijuana, particularly in its potent form of hashish, also has a long history of use in Muslim society, which prohibits use of alcohol.\One legend, undoubtedly apocryphal, recounts that in the year 1155 C.E. a Sufi ascetic discovered the marijuana plant while dancing in the heat of a summer day. He learned to make a wine from the leaves of plant and found that this drink made him laugh uncontrollably. His merriment proved contagious and soon other Sufis were drinking from his "emerald" cup. Although the use of hashish began to spread among Muslim holy men, medieval Muslim authorities disapproved of the plant. As Ronald Siegel commented, "floating to heaven in a hashish stupor was bad enough, but laughing riotously about it was unacceptable."[30] Hashish intoxication, like alcohol, was officially forbidden. It was claimed that hashish sapped the user's willingness to work and was thus a danger to the social fabric. It was also claimed that hashish opened up sexual desire. Sufi ascetics nonetheless continued to use the plant to induce ecstatic glimpses of the holy, and it appears that authorities' efforts to curb its use were intermittent and half-hearted.[31]

In the nineteenth century, European physicians used marijuana as a painkiller and mild tranquilizer. In all, hundreds of thousands of patients were treated with no record of adverse effects on their work ethic, social relationships, or moral demeanor.[32] Medical records indicated that marijuana was not addictive and did not lead to involvement with other, more potent narcotics. The medical use of marijuana gradually diminished for a number of reasons, including the variability in its potency, its lack of solubility and consequent inability to be administered through injection, and the increasing use of "competing" drugs such as aspirin and morphine.

The marijuana plant was apparently brought to North America by the Spanish in the sixteenth century as a commercial crop. The hemp fiber from the plant was used to make rope for boats and, later, for the wagons that moved settlers to the western frontiers. Of historical interest is the fact that a portion of George Washington's Mount Vernon estate was devoted to the cultivation of marijuana plants for the purpose of selling hemp fiber. It is generally thought that the recreational smoking of marijuana in the United States began in the southwestern states when Mexican workers crossed the Texas border in the early part of the twentieth century.[33] By 1910, New Orleans became the center of marijuana activity as boats from Havana, Tampico, and Vera Cruz brought large quantities of the intoxicating plant to American shores. In the early years of the century, marijuana was almost exclusively confined to minority groups, particularly African Americans and Mexican Americans. When the use of marijuana continued to increase in the southern states during the 1920s, the U.S. Federal Bureau of Narcotics conducted a campaign to eradicate it that resulted in the Marijuana Tax Act of 1937. The Tax Act stipulated that anyone using marijuana for industrial or medical purposes needed to register and pay a tax of $1.00 per ounce. Anyone wishing to use marijuana for any other purpose needed to pay a tax of $100 per ounce, effectively forcing recreational users to rely on an illegal, underground market. As the century progressed, marijuana was frequently used by jazz musicians and its use gradually spread to others in the fields of music, entertainment, and the creative arts. It was not, however, until the 1960s that its use spread to middle class, white Americans. By 1970, more than eight million Americans had smoked this intoxicating "weed." And by 1980, that figure had probably reached twenty million.

The popularity of marijuana as a recreational drug is not difficult to understand. The plant, known scientifically as *cannabis sativa*, produces an isomer known as 1-delta-9-tetrahydrocannabinol (commonly referred to as THC), which is thought to be the principal agent responsible for the physiological and psychological effects of marijuana use. The THC content of marijuana plants varies considerably, from about 0.5 percent to over 6 percent; the THC content of hashish oil (made from the resin of the plant's flower tops) is often as high as 50 percent. The actual physiological effects of smoking a marijuana cigarette are poorly understood. In fact, the only two established facts concerning marijuana smoking are that it causes a mild reddening of the eyes and a temporary increase in heartbeat. The psychological effects vary from person to person, but a commission appointed to study marijuana use by the Canadian government found that typical reports by users included the following:

"happiness, increased conviviality, a feeling of enhanced interpersonal rapport and communication, heightened sensitivity to humour, free play of the imagination, unusual cognitive and ideational associations, a sense of extraordinary reality, a tendency to notice aspects of the environment of which one is normally unaware, enhanced visual imagery, an altered sense of time in which minutes may seem like hours, enrichment of sensory experiences, increased personal understanding and religious insight, mild excitement and energy . . . [34] "

These psychological effects combine to give individuals a sense of having stepped beyond their ordinary limits. Unleashing what the report calls "unusual cognitive and ideational associations," marijuana use imparts the subjective feel of creativity and aesthetic insight. THC has no chemical resemblance to other drugs associated with the sixties counterculture, such as LSD, mescaline, or psilocybin. As Johns Hopkins School of Medicine professor Solomon Snyder concluded, "the impression emerges from current research that marijuana is a mild intoxicant. Moderate users, when high, have rich fantasies and enhanced perception, but are generally in control of their thoughts and actions and can behave quite normally if the need arises."[35]

The effects of marijuana on a person's mental and social functioning hold important clues about its role in "bonding" individuals to alternative religious beliefs and to small groups of fellow seekers. Charles Tart's intensive study of the experience of "being stoned" confirmed Snyder's observation concerning marijuana's ability to incite rich fantasies and enhanced perception. Tart's subjects saw patterns and designs more sharply and noticed subtle differences in shades of color better than when they were "straight."[36] Subjects reported an enhanced sense of touch, noticing more tactual imagery and finding tactual sensations to be more exciting. Marijuana subjects' sense of taste and smell were likewise more vivid and intense. Perhaps more importantly, Tart found that persons under the influence appear to have an intensified awareness of their own thought processes. Being stoned tends to give persons the sense that their thoughts are more original, intuitive, and profound (although many researchers note that these same individuals often later think that marijuana only gave them the *feeling* of being more original). Tart concluded that, on the whole, "marijuana intoxication characteristically produces a childlike openness to experience and a sense of wonder and awe, in contrast to the usual businesslike manner in which we classify events and people strictly in terms of their importance to us."[37] This childlike openness to experience opens the doors of aesthetic appreciation of life's intrinsic meaning and beauty. It expands persons' sense of interiority, helping them to feel that they have momentarily established what Emerson called "an original relationship to the universe."

William Novak's study of the role that marijuana has played in the lives of Americans makes another telling point about the connection between drugs and alternative spirituality. Novak wrote that "for some, marijuana has served as a teacher whose principal lesson has been that life holds multiple forms of reality."[38] Marijuana, it seems, was instrumental in helping many Baby Boomers adopt the belief that logic and science are not the only valid paths to understanding reality. Much like the use of cocaine structured states of consciousness that made Freud's "discovery" of psychoanalysis all but inevitable, marijuana produces psychological states that favor pluralism and a tendency to embrace some form of nature religion.[39] Marijuana affords its users a "pluralism of perspectives." In our normal waking state, we process sensory data by connecting "incoming information" with the most appropriate set of ideas or concepts. Marijuana users, however, report that they find themselves connecting the same sensory data to two or more different sets of concepts. This gives them the sensation that there is not just one reality but several realities, depending upon one's current frame of mind. One subject reported to Novak, "When I'm very stoned, I find myself switching constantly between two or more frames of mind."[40] Another subject commented that "When I'm high, the ideas keep on coming. Sometimes I wonder whether marijuana actually creates these ideas—or whether, perhaps, it functions more like a magnet, drawing together the various iron filings of thought from different parts of my mind and bringing them together."[41] These multiple associations give experience a highly symbolic character. Marijuana users frequently conclude that life is multidimensional. While the waking state of consciousness attends to the "material" meaning of experience, there are nonetheless other levels of experience more capable of yielding insights about life's intrinsic beauty and spiritual purpose.

The "multiple perspectives" that emerge when smoking marijuana helped newcomers to the religious counterculture bond with alternative myths and worldviews. The pluralistic way of viewing experience they learned from using marijuana turned many away from religious belief systems that proclaim one, absolute truth. Instead, many marijuana users tended to see beliefs as symbolic rather than literal. Smoking marijuana was in this sense a ritual that helped connect young seekers to the mystical philosophies of Alan Watts, Aldous Huxley, Carl Jung, Carlos Castenada, Zen Buddhism, or Vedanta Hinduism. These exotic forms of spirituality all suggested that the core of authentic spirituality is the inner experience of a sacred reality. They also implied that the mainline churches had somehow lost touch with the experiential basis of genuine spirituality. Many of those who were introduced to smoking marijuana were simultaneously introduced to some element of these mystical philosophies. Learning to get high was thus simultaneously learning to identify one's inner sensations and one's relationship to the universe in a new spiritual vocabulary. As one user put it,

> It's difficult to talk about marijuana and religion because I have a hard time separating them out. Authentic religion, when you sweep away all the extraneous stuff of politics and institutions, is about transcendence, heightened awareness, ecstasy, and goodness. Religion and marijuana both involve going beyond the rational, material, and normative concerns of existence. Religion is the original altered state of consciousness.[42]

Some researchers, such as Charles Tart, went out of their way to suggest that marijuana provides an "access" to such brazenly occult or parapsychological phenomena as out-of-body experiences, ESP, precognition, and direct awareness of the mystical centers or chakras that interconnect our physical and astral bodies.[43] Despite the fact that a very small percentage of his subjects reported such paranormal experiences, Tart maintained that marijuana use could lead to contact with transpersonal dimensions of reality. These were, however, never typical of the kinds of religious experience associated with marijuana use in the sixties and seventies. Instead, marijuana seemed to appeal to persons' aesthetic rapport with their natural surroundings. Smoking marijuana turned people's attention away from the extrinsic and instrumental meanings of experience and toward reflection on life's intrinsic beauty and significance. Just as Ralph Waldo Emerson's walks through the woods helped him to let go of his egocentric way of viewing the world and instead to behold the divinity that flows through all things, marijuana enabled many to attain a similar kind of aesthetic spirituality. Consider, for example, the report of a woman who went into a field to meditate after using marijuana.

> I sat down and looked slowly around in appreciation. Everything hushed, except the many huge tall trees, which were stirred by breezes. As I looked more and more at them, I seemed to see each leaf, and saw each one sway, and I felt it was the presence of the Holy Spirit breathing on them, making them move so apart, so together, so perfectly.[44]

Marijuana users formed a distinct American subculture. They were more likely to be liberal in politics and less likely than other Americans to be affiliated with a religious organization.[45] The longer and more often people smoked marijuana, the more likely they were to bond or connect with the eclectic cluster of metaphysical ideas underlying the era's "alternative spirituality" movement.[46] In the sixties and seventies, the actual act of smoking marijuana was something like a rite of initiation into the religious underground. Persons who took their first "joint" were aware that they were thereby signifying their desire to join an elitist, clandestine, and self-consciously countercultural segment of American society. They knew that they were joining a community that valued nonconformity, peacefulness, and quiet introspection. By the late seventies and eighties, marijuana smoking had largely lost this countercultural element. As marijuana became more pervasive in American society, it lost any special significance and became just one more intoxicant alongside others. It no longer served to bond individuals into a distinct counterculture, and thus marijuana intoxication became less and less distinguishable from the rowdiness associated with adolescent beer drinking.

For a short time the drug MDMA, often known as Ecstasy, performed cultural functions similar to those of marijuana. MDMA, which is related to both amphetamines and mescaline, is not a hallucinogen and rarely distorts sensory perception. Instead, it generates a sense of overall well-being, of being animated and energetic. But many found that MDMA seemed to enhance their sense of closeness and communication with others. Indeed, Ecstasy frequently gave persons a sense of connection with all of nature and humankind and was thus not surprisingly associated with persons who were exploring New Age spirituality. MDMA, much like marijuana and even coffee, fit naturally with experimental philosophies that teach persons to love themselves, understand and communicate with others, and to find deeper harmony with the universe. As one user of MDMA explained, "It's an experience of the core self or sometimes called the God-space or the peaceful center, or somebody once described it as experiencing themselves being held in the hands of God."[47] Much like marijuana, however, MDMA did not retain a close connection with New Age subculture and instead gradually became known as a "dancing drug" due to its use at bars and nightclubs.

Marijuana was for the most part associated with a wholly informal, unchurched form of spirituality. Joints were passed around in small groups that gathered together in dormitory rooms or apartment living rooms. As it began to "enhance visual imagery," "enrich sensory experience," and create "a free play of the imagination," these small groups made it possible for individuals to witness to their changing religious and philosophical beliefs. Informal gatherings of marijuana smokers provided a forum for the transmission of the various mystical philosophies that made up the era's alternative spirituality (and that were in large part to become the nucleus of the New Age spirituality of the eighties and nineties). The "increased conviviality" and "feeling of enhanced interpersonal rapport and communication" associated with marijuana use grounded these newly acquired beliefs in a sense of community and thus gave them greater credibility or support.

There were a few attempts to "institutionalize" the religious use of marijuana. Chapter 3 made reference to the emergence of several "dope churches" in California during the 1960s. Most were fairly short-lived, and it is almost impossible to assess the sincerity of their members' spiritual motives. The Psychedelic Venus Church, for example, formed in 1969 as an outgrowth of what had formerly been known as the Shiva Fellowship (worshiping the Hindu god, Shiva, who was historically associated with the smoking of bhang or hashish). In its incarnation as the Psychedelic Venus Church, this groups described itself as a "pantheistic nature religion, humanist hedonism, a religious pursuit of bodily pleasure through sex and marijuana."[48] Typical worship ceremonies would being with the sacrament—smoking marijuana—followed by a sensitivity session and partying in the nude. Although it claimed 1,000 members by 1971, the groups had completely disappeared by the end of the decade.

A more serious form of spirituality incorporating marijuana is to be found in the Rastafarians, a Jamaican religious group that has about 3,000 adherents in the United States. The Rastafarians are a Jamaican black nationalist movement that emerged in the 1920s and 1930s. The movement has direct ties to Marcus Garvey, who focused protest against Jamaica's historical master-slave arrangements and turned the attention of blacks both in Jamaica and in the United States to their spiritual homeland, Africa. (Another Jamaican religious group associated with Garvey, the Ethiopian Zion Coptic Church, has also used marijuana in its ceremonies and may still have as many as two hundred adherents in the United States.)[49] In 1927, Garvey predicted that the crowning of a black king in Africa was near and that this would be a sign heralding the redemption of black people from white oppression. In 1935, Ras Tafari (meaning "prince" of the "new empire of Ethiopia") was coronated emperor of Ethiopia, seemingly fulfilling Garvey's prediction. Ras Tafari took the name Haile Selassie, which meant "Power or Might of the Trinity," placing himself in the legendary line of King Solomon. In Jamaica, a group of black nationalists formed the Rastafarian movement clustered around six principal beliefs: (1) Haile Selassie is the living god; (2) the Black person is the reincarnation of ancient Israel, who, at the hand of the White person, has been in exile in Jamaica; (3) the White person is inferior to the Black person; (4) the Jamaican situation is a hopeless hell and heaven is to be looked for in Ethiopia, which is now under the leadership of King Solomon's Black descendent; (5) the Invincible Emperor of Ethiopia is now arranging for expatriated persons of African origin to return to Ethiopia; and (6) in the near future Blacks shall rule the world.[50]

Over time the Rastafarians evolved rituals that helped them establish their distinctive doctrinal and social "boundaries." Their principal rituals are known as "groundings," from the verb "to grounds," meaning to get along well. A major form of grounding, referred to as a reasoning, is an informal gathering at which a small group of brethren share in the smoking of the holy weed, ganja, and engage in lofty discussions.[51] As the brethren sit around in a circle, the host cuts up the marijuana and mixes it with a small amount of tobacco before placing it into the chillum of a water pipe (called a *huka* by the East Indians, from whom the whole ganja complex was borrowed). The Rastafarians call their water pipe a cup or chalice, likening their ritual to the Christian communion service. The host lights the pipe, or chalice, and recites a short prayer and then passes it counterclockwise around the circle, until all have "supped."

One of the Rastafarian movement's historians, Leonard Barrett, described how ganja "produces visions, heightens unity and communal feelings, dispels gloom and fear, and brings tranquillity to the mind of the dispossessed."[52] In the words of one Rastafarian, ganja "give I a good meditation; it is a door inside, when it is open, you see everything that is good."[53] The use of ganja to promote mystic reverie was combined with other boundary-setting behaviors, such as the weaving of hair into "dreadlocks" and the playing of reggae music (with its slow, undulating, hesitant beat reinforcing ganja's ability to excite the senses). Marijuana smoking thus served to promote internal community and preserve the Rastafarians' witness to the ecstasy they hoped would soon be theirs.

Although groups such as the Psychedelic Venus Church and the Rastafarians have had little effect on American religious life, the use of marijuana certainly contributed to the counterculture's celebration of interiority. It opened Americans to a vision of the world in which there are multiple perspectives, multiple truths. By sharpening users' aesthetic rapport with their surroundings, marijuana provided an experiential mooring for many of the new teachings associated with unchurched sources of modern religious thought. Indeed, marijuana use flourished among precisely those whose educational background and political orientations made them unlikely to affiliate with established churches. For good or for bad, using marijuana enabled these individuals to find new grounds for being actively interested in spirituality, even if they remained singularly uninterested in church affiliation. A major reason was undoubtedly that using marijuana gave millions of Americans access to a range of aesthetic experiences in which spirituality could exist, even prosper, within subjectivity and in small groups.

Wine and Aesthetic Sensibility

The late 1960s witnessed the phenomenal growth in popularity of yet another mood-altering substance, wine. Annual wine consumption in the United States grew from a low of about 0.3 gallons per capita at the end of World War II to about 2.2 gallons in the early 1980s. Throughout the 1950s and early 1960s Americans ordered cocktails while having dinner at a restaurant; yet, by the 1970s and 1980s they became used to ordering wine while dining out. At home, too, a glass of wine in the evening frequently replaced beer or highballs. Accompanying this rapid increase in per capita consumption of wine has been a decided shift to more sophisticated wines. As Americans became better educated about wine, there was a new and sustained consumer demand for wines made from premier varietal grapes. Indeed, it was not until 1968 that what might be called "dinner wines" outsold the sweet or even syrupy wines that emerged with Prohibition.

The growing appreciation of wine in the United States has given rise to what might be called a distinctive "wine culture." That is, although Europeans have for centuries associated wine with such things as gourmet cuisine, art, and romance, it has only recently become an integral part of Americans' perception of the good life. Gourmet dinner clubs and small wine tasting groups have sprouted up in nearly every city in the country, bringing people together to share their personal reactions to the sensory experiences afforded by drinking fine wine. Proper etiquette at such social functions entails learning to attend to the subtle nuances of the wine's aromatic bouquet or its peculiar taste sensations. Not only is wine frequently served at receptions for the fine and performing arts, but even the labels adorning bottles of wine have become associated with artistic expression. And Americans, too, have come to think of wine as the most romantic of beverages. The traditional saying, "a jug of wine, a loaf of bread, and thou," inspires hillside picnics as well as candlelight dinners intended to create an ethos of intimacy and affection.

We often think of religion—whether institutional or popular—as having creeds, a moral code, and a distinctive form of worship or cultus. Contemporary enthusiasm over wine exhibits all three. Of course, most Americans who consume wine are not full participants in the entire range of wine culture. But a sufficient core of enthusiasts have helped communicate the creeds, code, and cultus of wine appreciation to a surprisingly large number of those who have learned to delight in a glass of well-crafted wine. The creeds of wine culture are numerous. They pertain first and foremost to beliefs about what makes any given wine truly excellent. Learning these creeds requires years of catechism-like study and instruction. Sectarian opinions exist, of course, but there is nonetheless a kind of inherited orthodoxy about the respective roles of climate, soil, fermentation techniques, and so forth. There are also creeds pertaining to the qualities and abilities that persons must acquire before they become "worthy" of appreciating the subtle nuances that distinguish a good wine from a truly great wine. Acquired mastery of such cultural lore is even thought to be a prerequisite to entrance into the higher orders of wine-tasting delight. H. Warner Allen suggested that "our joy of the world is increased by an understanding of the artistic pleasure that a great wine can give, and a great wine cannot be fully appreciated without some knowledge of its composition."[54]

Associated with these creeds is the code that governs etiquette or propriety among wine drinkers. The code specifies behavioral norms that are to be disregarded only at grave cost to one's "enological purity." Among other things, this code stipulates proper techniques for storing wine, removing the cork, decanting and pouring wine, the selection of appropriate glasses, and the pairing of wines with appropriate foods. It also stipulates behaviors that are to be avoided (e.g., smoking or excessive alcohol consumption) because they will impair the palate and corrupt the wine-tasting experience as such.

What most clearly distinguishes the religious dimensions of contemporary wine consumption is the ritual, or cultus, of tasting. Wine tasting provides an almost paradigmatic example of what anthropologist Victor Turner has described as the transformative power of rituals.[55] Turner noted that rituals enable persons to move back and forth between the two basic modes of human relationship. The first of these he called "structure." The "structural" dimension of human existence refers to the laws, rules, and formal institutions that regulate social existence. Because humans will always compete for limited economic resources, there is a need for social structures capable of regulating our relationships in ways that minimize conflict. The structures of society impose certain roles, responsibilities, ethical duties, and behavioral codes upon us for the purpose of communal stability. The very structures, however, accentuate the differences between us and have an inherent tendency to drain us of spontaneous friendship or love. Further, because social structures channel our relationships with others into role-bound patterns of interaction, they foster a certain impersonality in communal life. In this sense, "structure" tends to deplete us of our most human qualities and over time leads to resentments, friction, and dispiritedness.

Turner refers to the second major mode of human existence as "communitas." Communitas consists of those spontaneous bonds of friendship and love without which there could be no society. It is the spirit of our fundamental unity with others that fosters care and concern for our fellow human beings. According to Turner, communitas is felt as a distinct mode of consciousness, set apart from our workaday life amidst social structures. Communitas breaks into human lives in those moments when we have temporarily suspended our structured habits of thought and action. There is a distinctively religious quality to the experience of communitas, and in fact, Turner noted that almost everywhere humans attribute communitas to the influx of a divine spirit into the human realm. Communitas reinvigorates lives that have been drained of vitality by the rigidities of social structure. It transforms the "I-It" character of role-structured relationships into "I-Thou" encounters characterized by selfless love. And finally, communitas infects individual life with a sense of boundless, mystical power capable of stimulating us to new levels of growth and creativity.

What rituals do, according to Turner, is to release individuals temporarily from life in structure and provide them with a felt sense of communitas. Rituals thus function within a culture by providing a framework for reinvigorating individual life and renewing our sensibility for the precious quality of interpersonal relationships. The sharing of wine—no less than coffee or marijuana—is particularly suited to ritual transformation. The act of sharing wine brings individuals together outside their accustomed social and economic roles to savor something of exquisite beauty. The action has no real utilitarian purpose. It aims instead at appreciating life's intrinsic pleasures. It was in this connection that the journalist and man of letters George Saintsbury recollected that when the wines he had consumed "were good they pleased my senses, cheered my spirits, improved my moral and intellectual powers, besides enabling me to confer the same benefits on other people."[56]

Wine tasting's ritualistic features also foster its aesthetic dimension. Wine engages the senses and invites individuals to perceive and appreciate natural pleasures. As with other art forms such as music, dance, or painting, the appreciation of wine provides fresh, new ways of perceiving reality. Yet wine, because it is quite literally consumed and produces novel physiological effects, elicits a more pronounced sense of aesthetic delight than most any other art form. Wine's moderate level of alcohol is sufficient to alter the subject-object structure of everyday consciousness and bestow a new radiance upon the surrounding field of experience.

Wine tasting, as with other artistic experiences, invites persons to experience beauty or excellence. One of the age-old questions pertaining to the appreciation of beauty is whether the quality of beauty lies in the object or in the beholder. This question draws attention to the particular way in which the aesthetic dimension of tasting wine borders on religious mysticism. Wine tasting, more than any other artistic experience, blurs any final distinction between the aesthetic object (the wine) and the experiencing subject (the self). Such a fusion of subject and object is the prototypical characteristic of all mystical experiences. This mystical, or at the very least quasi-mystical, experience is undoubtedly caused in part by the alcohol content of wine. It is also nurtured by the ritualized activity surrounding the tasting experience. The ceremonial opening of the bottle, the long period of expectancy while the wine is allowed to "breathe," and each successive step of judging the wine's color, bouquet, and impressions on the palate all create a unique setting in which the individual ritually merges with the object of his or her devotion. And, too, this ritual serves to "fund" the immediate sensory experience with memories and acquired knowledge. Each sensation engages memories of previous tastings, which, in turn, contribute to the fund of sensory impressions. For a brief moment, the wine taster struggles to abstract specific elements from the immediate sensory experience and to consider how they might correlate with an acquired repertoire of knowledge concerning the possible ways in which climate, soil, production technology, specific varietal characteristics, bottle aging, or temperature influence a wine's sensory qualities. These memories and abstract considerations in turn focus attention in ways that restructure, heighten, and invest our sensory experience with meaning. In and through this aesthetic experience, the individual is alternating rapidly between a mode of receptivity to incoming stimuli and an active attempt to sort out and interpret this stimuli. The experience is, for this reason, often thought to be exhilarating. It unites a person's intellectual and experiential faculties in such a way as to impart a sense of synergy and vibrancy.

The lure of this wine-tasting ritual is not hard to understand. The aesthetic dimension of human experience—the sense of opening up to and being affected by a higher order of beauty or excellence—is perhaps the least developed element in the American psyche. Our competitive capitalism and our highly ascetic (i.e., moralistic) religious ethos do little to help individuals learn to let down the rigid boundaries of ego and to merge experientially with some nonphysical, or "higher," reality. A major reason for the popularity of wine drinking is that it nourishes Americans' aesthetic sensibilities. At the very least, wine tasting allows individuals to appreciate natural pleasures. It permits momentary freedom from routine mental functioning. In the contemplation of an elegant wine, persons become free to play with their imaginations and to exercise their capacities to delight in beauty for its own sake. In his analysis of the formal philosophical properties of aesthetics, Charles Senn Taylor wrote, "A wine which truly animates the representative powers does so through the complex smells, tastes, and colors which it provides for contemplation. The more complex those factors are, the more we are likely to linger over them, to meditate upon them—and the more the wine will be able to keep up with, to sustain, to even strengthen our meditation."[57]

This connection between aesthetics and spirituality is important to understanding the zeal with which many contemporary Americans pursue their immersion into "wine culture." The enjoyment of wine is a ritual that makes it possible for individuals to suspend their secular identities and to create an awareness of levels of natural beauty that exist at a level too subtle to be appreciated by the calculating ego of our normal waking consciousness. In his masterpiece on humanity's propensity for religion, *The Varieties of Religious Experience*, William James noted that alcohol produces a distinct altered stated of consciousness that should be considered "one bit of the mystic consciousness, and our total opinion of it must find its place in our opinion of that larger whole."[58] James believed that

the sway of alcohol over mankind is unquestionably due to its power to stimulate the mystical faculties of human nature, usually crushed to earth by the cold facts and dry criticism of the sober hour. Sobriety diminishes, discriminates, and says no; drunkenness expands, unites, and says yes. It is in fact the great exciter of the *Yes* function in man. It brings its votary from the chill periphery of things to the radiant core. It makes him for the moment one with the truth.[59]

As James suggested, alcohol helps dismantle what might be called our "general reality orientation." It mutes our built-in cognitive mechanisms for separating reality into discrete bits or into objects of experience that can be manipulated for the purpose of better adapting to our material environment. Wine does this in a much less pronounced way than hard liquor. The self, therefore, is not so much dissolved as reconfigured in ways that make possible a more aesthetic sense of relatedness. Instrumental reason is temporarily in abeyance, and awareness is instead flooded with a sense of relatedness to life's intrinsic meanings and pleasures. In James's words, mild alcohol intoxication produces a form of consciousness in which "the centre and periphery of things seem to come together. The ego and its objects, the *meum* and the *teum*, are one."[60] This aesthetic sense of union and communion is the experiential basis of the religious longing for initiation into the furthest reaches of nature. The enthusiasm over wine tasting, as with other forms of American popular religion, simply carries this yearning for a deeper harmony with nature into a less overtly "religious" setting than do the sacraments of our established churches. Yet, this form of American popular religion, no less than this country's "churched" religion, embodies and combines our desire for immediate contact with nature and for the creation of community.

In sum, the increasing interest in wine—just as with coffee and marijuana—is connected with Americans' interest in social settings and rituals that foster an unchurched form of modern spirituality. The kinds of aesthetic delight and closer connection to natural pleasures induced by wine tasting obviously do not compete with, or in any way replace, "theological" religion and its important articulation of doctrinal and moral guides to life. But the emergence of a "wine culture" in the United States has helped many reinvigorate the long-neglected aesthetic side of American cultural life. In the aesthetic experience of enjoying wine, many Americans have found a ritual for opening themselves to a flood of novel sensations and for sharing these inner experiences in a communal context.

The Quest for Ecstasy

Humans are a curious species. In addition to being capable of serious rational deliberation, we actively pursue drug-induced intoxication. The UCLA psychopharmacologist Ronald Siegel put this quite clearly when he observed that "throughout our entire history as a species, intoxication has functioned like the basic drives of hunger, thirst, or sex, sometimes overshadowing all other activities in life. Intoxication is the fourth drive."[1] Siegel probably overstates the case a bit when he declares the pursuit of intoxication to be a fourth major drive. After all, many persons deliberately avoid intoxication. But he is surely correct in drawing attention to its persistence as a prime motivator of human behavior. One reason for the persistence of this drive is its survival value.[2] Intoxication produces sensory and physiological disturbances that can alert individuals to the toxic nature of a plant, even causing ingested items to be regurgitated. Intoxication, then, provides a warning system for detecting the presence of toxic substances and helps protect individuals from more serious harm.

Alerting us to toxic plants is only one of the reasons that this "fourth drive" has had such an extraordinary influence upon human behavior. It would seem that intoxication is a pleasure that many humans seek for its own sake. For example, dizziness is frequently regarded as a pleasurable sensation. Children will spend hours on a merry-go-round or twirl themselves into frenzies of dizziness. Adults will pay large amounts of money for amusement-park rides for the sheer exhilaration of being whirled into a state of disorientation. Not surprisingly, then, humans tend to find that drugs such as marijuana, peyote, alcohol, nitrous oxide, and LSD produce episodes of dizziness that are curiously pleasurable. A good many other pleasurable physical and psychological effects are also associated with drug use. Most intoxicating drugs stimulate the brain's natural production of pleasure-giving agents such as dopamine and endorphins. They also tend to enhance sensory experience; not only do colors seem brighter, but smells are more intense, music seems richer, and foods taste more complex and delectable. Such experiences provide a temporary retreat from adult worries and responsibilities. The result is a feeling of returning to childlike spontaneity and happiness. Laughter and general giddiness are common. All in all, the "fourth drive" is sustained by physical and psychological pleasures. Humanity's pursuit of drug-induced paradise is closely connected with our penchant for simple hedonism.

The principal objective of this book has been to document that there is a spiritual dimension to this "fourth drive." The previous chapters have demonstrated that Americans' interest in drugs can also be understood as an expression of our spiritual hopes and feelings. The use of drugs for spiritual purposes goes as far back in American history as religion itself. Native Americans, for example, have historically valued ecstatic states that facilitate access to both natural and supernatural powers. Native American cultures developed ritual structures that have connected the use of such intoxicating substances as tobacco, sacred mushrooms, datura, and peyote with this quest for spiritual power. Jews, meanwhile, incorporate wine into the rituals that hallow significant moments in life such as a Sabbath meal or wedding celebration. Many Christians use wine to connect themselves mysteriously with Christ's atoning sacrifice, whereas others—such as the Mormons and the Amana colonists—have recognized its value for "gladdening the heart" and fostering communal solidarity. The counterculture of the sixties and seventies found that both LSD and marijuana made it possible to turn on, tune in, and drop out at critical moments in their personal religious journeys. And finally, much of the allure of coffee and coffeehouses in contemporary American culture is due to caffeine's ability to impart a fresh perspective on the activities of everyday life.

It is thus clear that the ecstatic experiences induced by drugs are a persistent feature of American religious history. What is not clear is how this quest for ecstasy should be interpreted and evaluated. The questions raised by the connection between drugs and religion are almost endless: Is the quest for ecstasy compatible with the highest goals of religion? Are the insights gained from drug-induced ecstasies "true"? Given the threat that drugs pose to society, can we afford to let individuals procure, distribute, and use them under the banner of religious freedom? Are drug-induced experiences compatible with mature spiritual development?

There are no easy answers to these questions. History is not always a place we might go to determine what is best or what is right. The *fact* that Americans have persistently found drugs to be of religious value does not establish the principle that they *should* continue to do so. Yet history is a place we might go to gain perspective. The story of Americans' pursuit of ecstasy can at least help us identify the most important issues.

Ecstasy and Spiritual Living

The previous chapters in this book have provided numerous examples of the role that "elixirs of ecstasy" have performed in eliciting personal religious experience and in promoting religious community. It is true, of course, that a great deal of drug use is wholly devoid of any kind of spirituality. Indeed, most drug use would appear to be almost exclusively motivated by the pursuit of hedonistic pleasure. It is also true that both the indiscriminate use of psychedelics and alcohol abuse have led many Americans to states of personal brokenness, eventually leading them to abandon all drug use and to embrace forms of conservative religious piety that strictly monitor our tendency to seek ecstasy. And still other patterns of drug use produce behaviors that perpetuate a capitalist economy. These, too, are important stories and offer their own fascinating lenses through which to view American culture. Yet the historical record clearly illustrates the enduring connection between drug-induced ecstasy and the broader patterns of American religious life. It is important, then, to offer at least a partial summary of the special role that drugs have played in accentuating the ecstatic element in American spirituality.

In her book *Ecstasy, Ritual, and Alternate Reality,* anthropologist Felicitas Goodman observed that nearly every culture possesses religious rituals that are specifically designed to induce altered states of consciousness. The purpose of these rituals is to induce a trance that permits a particular kind of brain "tuning" in which individuals might make contact with an alternate reality.[3] These ritually induced altered states of consciousness make it possible for an entirely different order of existence to "break into" our everyday world of experience. Such ecstatic encounters forever change our understanding of the nature and meaning of existence. They initiate persons into an awareness that their lives are in some mysterious way enveloped by an alternate reality. Forces and powers whose existence had never before been suspected are now understood to be crucial variables affecting our quest for wholeness and fulfillment.

The value of drugs for inducing such religious states of consciousness can hardly be questioned. It is difficult, however, to make neat generalizations about how drug-induced ecstasies contribute to spiritual living. Even the same drug in roughly the same dosage can facilitate contact with quite different "alternate realities," depending upon set and setting. In some settings Native American tribes might use datura or psychoactive mushrooms to make contact with a tutelary spirit that appears in the form of a bird or animal. In other settings these and similar drugs might establish contact with ancestral spirits. Mescaline-rich peyote can be used for either of the above purposes, for healing, or for communing with the God of Christianity. Yet when Aldous Huxley took mescaline in his Los Angeles home, he made contact with an alternate reality more in keeping with the metaphysical categories he had picked up in his reading of Vedanta Hinduism, Zen, and Western occultism. Huxley met no tutelary spirits. Instead, he encountered the "Istigkeit" or "isness" that permeates the whole of material existence. To Huxley, cleansing the doors of perception enables us to see a world where everything shines with Inner Light and is infinite in significance. Meanwhile, another psychedelic researcher, Stanislav Grof, found that LSD leads us on a journey through the successively deeper levels of our own psyche. Grof's subjects were led to the startling discovery—indeed, epiphany—that the human unconscious extends far beyond the boundaries of their finite personalities. Accessing this transpersonal dimension of their psyches triggered such paranormal phenomena as clairvoyance, out-of-body experiences, and conversing with suprahuman spiritual entities.

The sheer variety of drug-induced experiences is testimony to the plasticity of human experience. After reviewing dozens of vivid and fantasy-like descriptions of the "unseen reality" disclosed in mystical states of awareness, the psychologist William James concluded: "Such is the human ontological imagination, and such is the convincingness of what it brings to birth. Unpicturable beings are realized, and realized with an intensity almost like that of an hallucination."[4]

Indeed, such is the human ontological imagination. And such is the convincingness of what it brings forth. The fantasy-like imagery that humans "see" in drug-induced states of consciousness varies from culture to culture, even person to person. Both the set (i.e., the individual's theological background, the mythic vocabulary to which the individual has been exposed, expectations of the experience, the individual's personality traits, etc.) and the setting (i.e., the immediate environment and the subtle influences that it exerts on both the individual's experience and on his or her verbal account of the experience) exert powerful influences upon our ontological sensibilities. And yet these experiences, however plastic their form, have many underlying similarities. First, drug-induced ecstasy is generally characterized by the feeling of subjective richness. The sense of interiority is enhanced. The "inner life" of immediate experience seems intensified and more vibrant.

Second, the religious states of consciousness prompted by drugs typically have an aesthetic quality. Drugs heighten our sensitivity to sensory impressions, thereby enabling us to find new fascination and delight in even the most ordinary of objects. They also seem to lessen, or even dissolve, the subject-object structure that characterizes most of our rational, waking-state experiences. That is, the duality between self and world begins to fade. The experiencing subject and the experienced object become more intimately connected. Because experience is no longer structured according to the dichotomy between I/Not-I, Self/World, or Actor/Action, persons tend toward the perception that the universe is instead a seamless ontological whole. This aesthetic quality renders drug-induced states of consciousness as intrinsically enjoyable as the appreciation of art or music. Because these states of ecstasy are enjoyed for their own sake rather than for any utilitarian purposes, they have a natural affinity with humanity's spiritual propensities.

A third characteristic of drug-induced states of consciousness is that they have a life-altering convincingness about them. As James observed, such mystical states "are as convincing to those who have them as any direct sensible experiences can be, and they are, as a rule, much more convincing than results established by mere logic ever are." Although most of us will go through life without ever having had such an experience, nonetheless those who do have them "cannot help regarding them as genuine perceptions of truth, as revelations of a kind of reality which no adverse argument . . . can expel from belief."[5]

It is easy to see, then, how drugs lift us out of our ordinary mode of apprehending reality in such a way as to enhance the ecstatic element of personal religious experience. Yet it is also the case that drugs have historically served to accentuate the ecstatic character of religious community. Most persons who adopt a sacred orientation to the world do so because of the socializing influence of the religious community they live in. Rituals, community activities, and doctrinal education combine to pattern a religious way of life. Ecstasy-bestowing drugs, too, play a part in the process of religious socialization. Examples from American religious history are plentiful: the communal sharing of tobacco at virtually all solemn Native American ceremonies; the presence of wine at the Jewish Sabbath and Seder meals; the sharing of wine by members of the Amana colonies at communion, during the work day, and at informal wine tastings; the passing of a marijuana joint as a bonding ritual among fellow "seekers"; or the gathering of two friends at a coffeehouse to share intimate details of one's life or to engage in spirited discussion. Intoxication—whether mild or strong—is exhilarating. It arouses largely pleasurable emotions, which become associated with the set and setting in which they are taken. In this way, individuals come to identify in an almost physical way with a larger community that is based upon the affirmation of distinctive beliefs and moral codes.

Because of their ability to accentuate the ecstatic element of religious experience, drugs have a natural affinity with the efforts of religious communities to incorporate persons into a distinctively spiritual way of life. In Chapter 5, the relationship between drug-induced ecstasy and religious communities was explained by drawing upon the work of anthropologist Victor Turner.[6] Turner, we might recall, referred to the experience of ecstasy as *spontaneous communitas*. Spontaneous communitas is an existential condition. Turner described it as the experience of "more than human powers." It is the fleeting glimpse of reality that transcends all human social structures. Spontaneous communitas can rarely be sustained for long periods of time. The need to organize members of society to perform social tasks eventually dissipates the ecstatic elements of a person's or community's orientation to life. Thus, over time, spontaneous communitas gives way to a set of doctrines and moral codes that Turner calls *ideological communitas:* "Ideological communitas is at once an attempt to describe the external and visible effects—the outward form, it might be said—of an inward experience of existential communitas, and to spell out the optimal social conditions under which such experiences might be expected to flourish and multiply."[7] The purpose of doctrines and moral codes (ideological communitas) is to preserve and communicate what is otherwise an isolated experience of this "more than human" reality. There is, however, an unfortunate tendency for ideological systems to stagnate over time. Moral and religious doctrines inherently run the risk of losing any felt connection with the initial enthusiasm that gave rise to them, thereby robbing them of any ecstatic or distinctively spiritual quality.

One of the principal reasons that intoxicating substances are so commonly found in religious rituals is undoubtedly their capacity to infuse doctrines and moral codes with at least an aura of spontaneous communitas. Drugs are able to communicate a partial understanding of the ecstasy at the core of a religious community's sacred world. Tobacco, datura, mushrooms, peyote, mescaline, LSD, marijuana, and alcohol are all powerful stimulants. Their connection with religious rituals—and thereby a group's moral and doctrinal codes—preserves a religious community's connection with the initial enthusiasm of its founding members. Early Christianity, for example, was saturated with existential communitas. Converts such as Paul felt that they had literally been born again, that they were now inhabited by a cosmic spirit that somehow centered their personalities on an altogether higher plane of existence. And, too, Jesus' ministry had centered on a radical egalitarianism as symbolized by communal meals. The incorporation of bread and wine into the church's developing rituals preserved both the social and the spiritual dimensions of the communitas present in early Christianity. Wine—long associated with Middle Eastern cults of ecstasy—was put into the service of enabling the average parishioner to participate in the church's special relationship to sacred power or mystery. As exemplified in the Christian sacrament known as the Eucharist or Lord's Supper, mood-altering drugs are frequently part of the ritual processes through which religious communities socialize persons into a sacred way of life.

The presence of mood-altering drugs in religious rituals is also an effective means of procuring individuals' commitment to the group's moral structure. That is, drugs can be of particular value in helping persons *want* to believe or do what culture deems they *must* believe or do. Mood-altering drugs can be used to associate exhilarating or pleasurable emotions with adherence to specific moral codes. Intoxication, while normally illicit or antinomian, can thus be put into the service of eliciting commitment to society's core values. As Turner has written, many religious rituals use techniques designed "to arouse a gross quantity of affect—even of illicit affect—only to attach this quantum of affect . . . to licit and legitimate goals and values, with consequent restoration of moral quality, but this time positive instead of negative."[8] The incorporation of drugs into religious rituals ensures that such affective learning will take place. The ritual set and setting link aroused emotions with culturally valued beliefs and morals.

This is precisely what happened in the peyote ceremonies that spread among Native Americans in the late nineteenth and early twentieth centuries. Although vision-seeking and healing are surely among the motives behind peyotism, more striking is the overt emphasis upon preaching and moral instruction. Peyote produces physiological effects that reinforce participants' expectation of coming into contact with supernatural power. Vomiting, sweating, seeing kaleidoscopic patterns of light, and occasional hallucinations provide the visceral basis for believing that peyote transports persons to extraordinary regions of the universe. Yet, once such ecstasy has been achieved, the officiating roadman begins to admonish participants to forego vices and confess their sins. As Weston La Barre observed,

At intervals older men pray aloud, with affecting sincerity, often with tears running down their cheeks, their voices choked with emotion, and their bodies swaying with earnestness as they gesture and stretch out their arms to invoke the aid of Peyote. The tone is of a poor and pitiful person humbly asking the aid and pity of a great power, and absolutely no shame whatever is felt by anyone when a grown man breaks down into loud sobbing during his prayer.[9]

The roadman structures these episodes in such a way as to encourage participants to give up their "sinning" habits and to strengthen their moral resolve.

The use of LSD or marijuana by members of the American counterculture can also be seen as an example of how drugs procure commitment to a community's moral outlook. Drug use was explicitly connected with what Timothy Miller called an "ethics of dope." The sharing of ecstasy-producing substances facilitated bonding to a community organized around distinct notions of spiritual authenticity and moral integrity.[10] The "coffee hour" at the end of so many mainstream Christian worship services is yet another example of how religious communities utilize drugs to produce a sufficient hint of ecstasy to sustain its sacred commitments. The uplifted emotions and general exhilaration of the coffee hour undoubtedly make commitment to the church's normative vision more inviting. And, finally, the presence of wine at major Jewish holidays serves a similar purpose of linking pleasant physiological sensations with a religious group's moral outlook. Whether used to reinforce a culture's dominant moral system (e.g., Christian communion service, coffee hour, Jewish Sabbath dinner) or to lure individuals into the ethic of a peripheral cultural movement (e.g., marijuana use among the counterculture), drug-induced ecstasy has served the functional purpose of inducing loyalty to a community's particular moral vision.[11]

We might finally remind ourselves that the ritual use of mood-altering substances is also instrumental in creating some of the distinctive social attributes of religious communities. To rely once again on Victor Turner's terminology, the communitas that distinguishes religious communities is more than a purely psychological or existential condition. It is also a social condition, pertaining to the most spontaneous and free-flowing modes in which humans relate to one another. According to Turner, our social existence vacillates between two poles that he terms "structure" and "communitas." Life in structure refers to our location in a hierarchical social system that tends to make us rivals or competitors for limited economic goods. Insofar as we live in structure, we feel ourselves to be separate, defined by the roles and status of our location in the social hierarchy. In contrast, communitas is the feeling of shared identity. Communitas refers to the "human bond, without which there could be no society."[12]

The vitality of social life—particularly in religious groups—depends upon the periodic renewal of this fundamental sense of equality and connectedness. For this reason, religious rituals utilize a variety of techniques that encourage persons to step outside their normal social roles and to come together in a classless community. The sharing of intoxicating substances, because these substances tend to dissolve normal ego boundaries, is one such technique. The Apache tribes of Arizona and New Mexico, for example, used intoxicating beverages in rituals designed to forge communal solidarity. The Amana colonies, the Latter-day Saints, and historic Judaism have all found that the "social jollification" provided by wine drinking is an effective means of forging group cohesiveness. Coffeehouses, wine tastings, and small gatherings of people passing marijuana cigarettes are yet other ritual settings in which drugs help separate persons temporarily from their life "in structure" and permit more spontaneous forms of interpersonal relationships. Drug-induced states of consciousness have a leveling effect. They dismantle the cognitive structures around which our socially constructed ego is formed, thereby dissolving the psychological boundaries that separate persons from one another. Given the proper set and setting, drugs foster novel modes of interpersonal relationships. The ritual use of mood-altering drugs is thus among the most effective means of inducting persons into the ecstatic element of fellowship in a religious community.

Ecstasy and Truth

It is one thing to chronicle the historical record of the presence of drugs in American religious life. It is quite another thing, however, to ask whether there is any enduring significance to drug-induced ecstasies. There can be no question that many Americans believe that drugs have been of great value to them in their personal spiritual quests. Advocates typically claim that drugs have enabled them to extend the range of their senses so as to make possible the perception of truths that elude the waking ego. Carlos Castenada, for example, introduced his readers to the teachings of Don Juan, a Native American sorcerer who utilized psychedelic substances to "stop the world" of social conditioning. Castenada, once freed from the restrictive vision of the culturally defined ego, could journey to an alternate reality that was saturated with mystery and spiritual power. Christians, meanwhile, utilize wine in a sacrament understood to have the mystical capability of uniting believers with the invisible presence of Christ. And Aldous Huxley believed that mescaline has the power to cleanse the doors of perception. According to Huxley, the human brain ordinarily functions as a reducing valve, blocking out the wider range of sensations belonging to the Mind at Large. Huxley contended that psychedelic drugs temporarily suspend the brain's filtering activities, thereby revealing the infinite glory of the universe.

Yet how are we to discriminate between the ecstasy of spiritual awakening and mundane intoxication? What, if anything, distinguishes stairways to heaven from paths to skid row stupor? Are the insights that come from drug-induced ecstasies in any sense "true"? Do these insights have any intellectual significance for persons who have never been intoxicated in quite this way? After all, what does it mean if tiny doses of mescaline or LSD can instantly produce profound religious visions? Does this imply that every kind of religious mysticism is really nothing more than a mental aberration caused by the misfiring of our brain chemistry? Is "heaven" nothing more than the release of excessive quantities of neurochemical agents such as dopamine and endorphins? Or was Huxley right, that the world is indeed sacred and we but need to cleanse our doors of perception to find ourselves inhabiting a universe saturated with Divine Light?

Few of these questions can be answered with any certainty. The mind/body connection remains both a philosophical and scientific mystery. Despite all the advances in neurological science, we really don't understand what consciousness is. The vast amount of information we have about neurophysiology finally tells us little about why our brain cells produce self-awareness. Even though we know a great deal about the specific neurotransmitters responsible for "delivering" sensory data to the brain, we really don't understand how or why such data give rise to complex thinking processes. It follows that we know very little about why drugs produce the precise symptoms they do or why there can be such wide variance between different human subjects. Even if we can identify how a particular drug alters the brain's delicate chemistry, we are still a long way from understanding how these changes produce vivid experiences involving conversations with tutelary spirits, communion with the body and blood of Christ, or visions of a radiant "Inner Light."

We can begin to clarify some of these questions concerning the religious merits of drug-induced ecstasies by focusing on the way in which drugs alter our ability to organize and understand sensory data. Our normal waking state of consciousness is characterized by a fairly stable balance between the reception and interpretation of sensory information. That is, the normal waking state is characterized by a fairly steady flow of information delivered by the physical senses. The brain's primary function is to order, categorize, and label this flow of sensory information in such a way as to help us understand our environments and respond with appropriate behavior. The brain's effort to interpret sensory information may be likened to the way in which a computer's software programs organize information according to predetermined categories. Beginning at birth, individuals gradually acquire an entire set of interpretive categories. Socialization into a given culture's way of viewing the world provides persons with ready-made categories for making sense of their natural and social environments. Psychologist Ronald Shor has called this the development of a "generalized reality-orientation." Shor maintained that the normal waking state of consciousness "is characterized by the mobilization of a structured frame of reference in the background of attention which supports, interprets, and gives meaning to all experiences."[13] This generalized reality-orientation gives stability to the normal waking states of consciousness. It processes incoming sensory data in ways that not only predispose us to efficient behavior but also help us understand our environment in a shared, culturally reinforced manner.

Altered states of consciousness—whether induced by drugs, hypnosis, the onset of sleep, ritual activities, or fasting—are characterized by the destabilization of this generalized reality-orientation. Drugs alter brain physiology in ways that disrupt the normal ratio of "sensory intake" to "sensory processing."[14] For example, the physiological effect of a particular drug might be to accelerate or impede the flow of sensory impressions. In other instances, the chemical agents in a drug might alter the brain's own information-processing mechanisms. If sensory-processing activities are speeded up, a single sensory impression is rapidly given multiple meanings or interpretations (giving the individual the sense of the greatly symbolic or meaning-laden significance of her or his experience). Conversely, if sensory-processing activities are slowed down or interrupted, then sensory data won't be shaped into forms consistent with our generalized reality-orientation (frequently giving the individual the sense of the intrinsic significance of a simple object, which is now perceived independent of our more typical, utilitarian modes of understanding).

To repeat, then, one of the principal ways in which drugs alter consciousness is by changing the normal ratio of sensory intake to sensory processing. As a consequence, there is less stability in the way in which we configure our thoughts and emotions. Although confusion often reigns, there is also a heightened sense of the freshness or vitality of everything being experienced. Ronald Shor noted that in altered states of consciousness "(a) experiences cannot have their usual meanings; (b) experiences may have special meanings which result from their isolation from the totality of general experiences; and (c) special orientations or special tasks can function temporarily as the only possible reality for the subject in his phenomenal awareness as a result of their isolation from the totality of general experience."[15]

Shor's characterization of altered states of consciousness is important for our attempt to understand drug-induced ecstasy. As the generalized reality-orientation fades from awareness, experience simply cannot have its usual meaning. Instead, experiences have special meanings insofar as they are configured differently than we are accustomed. The experience is often one of utter disorientation. But if a person has previously been exposed to rituals, myths, or other "alternative" conceptual categories, he or she might well be able to make sense of the experience by imposing what Shor called a "special orientation" upon the flood of novel sensations. In this way, religious communities are often able to imbue drug-induced ecstasies with specific spiritual meanings. The implication would seem to be that validity or significance of a "drug experience" is finally determined by its social or ritual setting.

It is important to note, however, that this by no means rules out the possibility that drugs may introduce persons and groups to novel ways of constructing reality. Some research indicates that repeated experiences with a specific altered state may eventually lead to the adoption of a new, state-specific reality-orientation.[16] There is evidence to suggest that persons who use such drugs as peyote, marijuana, and LSD eventually become accustomed to the different levels of arousal in their nervous systems while under the influence of these drugs. Although their gradual acquisition of a drug-specific reality-orientation might well be explained in terms of socialization to a distinct subculture, it may also be the case that our generalized reality-orientation is but one of many possible reality-orientations, each with its own range of applicability. Arthur Deikman has noted that our generalized reality-orientation becomes a habitual part of our waking consciousness owing to its "maximum efficiency in achieving the basic goals of the individual: biological survival as an organism and psychological survival as an individual."[17] Yet, owing to the chemical activity of drugs, it is possible for us to enter "alternate modes of consciousness whose stimulus processing may be less efficient from a biological point of view but whose very inefficiency may permit the experience of aspects of the real world formerly excluded or ignored."[18] The following arguments about the validity or significance of drug-induced ecstasy finally boil down to our personal judgments about the significance of these "formerly excluded or ignored" aspects of the real world.

This brief overview of how drugs alter our way of apprehending reality sets the stage for the four principal arguments or debates concerning the validity of drug-induced ecstasies. The first of these debates is really quite simple. It can be argued that drug-induced ecstasies prompt individuals to confuse altered physiology with profound insight into truth. As drugs enter the nervous system they cause the release of several of the body's own neurotransmitters, including dopamine. Although such diverse drugs as alcohol, tobacco (nicotine), marijuana, and cocaine have different chemical effects on the nervous system, evidence suggests that the resultant effect is the same—a sharp increase in levels of dopamine. Dopamine is largely responsible for the exhilarating rush, pleasure, and elation that overtakes the nervous system after ingesting these drugs. It might be argued, then, that chemically induced euphoria is being confused with spiritual insight. This was precisely the point that the famed historian of religion Mircea Eliade wished to make in his classic study of shamanism. Eliade deemed the use of drug-induced ecstasies by some shamans to be a "vulgarization of a mystical technique." As he put it, "narcotic intoxication is called on to provide an *imitation* of a state that the shaman is no longer capable of attaining otherwise."[19] R. C. Zaehner, a scholar of Eastern religions, similarly asserted that drug-induced mysticism falls far short of the experiences of true saints and holy men. Zaehner argued that the emotions released by drugs are profane, not sacred. He maintained that drug-induced ecstasies should not be confused with the theistic states of genuine religious and mystical experience.[20]

Zaehner's condemnation of drug-induced mysticism as profane intoxication is clear and straightforward. It does not, however, lead us to any objective or solid philosophical ground. In fact, his condemnation is little more than a restatement of his own theological biases. Zaehner identified "genuine" religion with forms of theism that postulate the existence of a god or gods who in some way transcend the world of nature. Zaehner consequently could not envision a genuinely spiritual act transpiring solely in the material universe. Like Eliade, he maintained that drug-induced ecstasies are counterfeit imitations of true, nature-transcending mysticism. However, this misses the very point made by those who advocate one or another form of nature religion. Adherents of nature religion claim that the material world is itself a living, spiritual reality. They affirm that matter is, at heart, an expression of the ultimate spiritual force responsible for the whole of creation. Thus there can be no hard and fast distinction between matter and spirit, sacred and profane. In this view, the elation stemming from excitation of the nervous system need not be deemed in any way inferior. The human nervous system, as with every atom throughout the universe, is itself considered to be saturated with divinity. In other words, the physiological argument that drug-induced ecstasy is simply an artificial emotion contains a certain philosophical bias against ascribing ultimacy to the world of matter. Adherents of Western, biblically based religions and atheists alike are comfortable with this philosophical bias. But the advocates of nature religion take a different approach to the concepts of matter and spirit, and in this view, drug-induced ecstasies deserve to be understood as possible forms of a genuine spirituality.

A second argument that might be made about the validity of drug-induced ecstasy is that their so-called insights fail to measure up to basic philosophical and scientific standards for establishing truth. Indeed, the insights that arise from any kind of mystical experience might be seen as falling short of the intellectual rigor that modern culture has come to expect of attempts to arrive at truth. The philosopher Bertrand Russell's essay "Critique of Mysticism" is perhaps the most articulate expression of this argument against the validity of ecstasy as an avenue to truth. It was Russell's contention that ecstatic experiences cannot yield statements about reality that can be verified by other persons. He argues that modern philosophy, like modern science, demands that truth claims be capable of verification. For a statement to have any validity, it must stipulate the precise conditions under which it was derived so that other persons might test and verify it for themselves. A statement can be considered to be true only to the degree that it is capable of objective verification. A mystic, however, makes statements that emanate from his or her subjectivity. They consequently lack the kind of verifiability that modern thought uses to assess a statement's validity. Thus,

> Scientists, when they wish others to see what they have seen, arrange their microscope or telescope; that is to say, they make changes in the external world, but demand of the observer only normal eyesight. The mystic, on the other hand, demands changes in the observer, by fasting, by breathing exercises . . . [21]

Russell's point is that modern science and philosophy rely upon precise and uniform methods of observation. Mysticism, on the other hand, relies upon changing the observers themselves. Statements based upon altering the observer's capacity for perception cannot be publicly verified. Mystics' claims about truth therefore cannot be regarded as valid. Whether induced by fasting, meditation exercises, or drugs, ecstatic experiences are wholly unreliable paths to information about the nature of the universe. In Russell's words, each of these ways of altering the observer's perception "is an abnormal physical condition, and therefore has abnormal perceptions . . . [and] in abnormal perceptions there is no reason to expect . . . correspondence [with fact]."[22]

Russell's argument can be viewed as an understandable caution concerning the intellectual validity of drug-induced ecstatic experience. Yet it, too, presupposes certain rationalist and materialistic biases. Most importantly, Russell unquestioningly assumes that the normal waking state of consciousness is the final arbiter of all truth claims. And, as a corollary, Russell assumes that alterations of consciousness render truth claims unreliable. There is, however, no empirical warrant for these assumptions. Most individuals who use drugs for spiritual purposes would grant Russell that the normal waking state is best suited for adapting persons to the exigencies of our physical and social environments. The point is whether reality is limited to what can be known by the normal waking state of consciousness.

Those who find spiritual enrichment with the assistance of wine, coffee, marijuana, or peyote insist that by widening our capacity to engage reality we simultaneously put ourselves in a position to realize that a wider reality is there to be engaged. When Russell referred to arranging a microscope or telescope, he was admitting that many truths require us to extend the range of our nervous system and its sensory apparati. Microscopes and telescopes are, however, extensions only of the normal waking state of consciousness (which Russell unjustifiably prejudices as the only reliable modality of valid engagement with life). Yet who is to say that the "highest truths" can be apprehended through the range of activities associated solely with our normal waking state of consciousness?

We might consider here an important point made by William James when he considered the religious experiences of persons suffering from some kind of physical or psychological illness. James cautioned that we cannot dismiss an insight as invalid solely on the basis of the conditions under which it originated.

> Let us play fair in this whole matter, and be quite candid with ourselves and with the facts. When we think certain states of mind superior to others, is it ever because of what we know concerning their organic antecedents? No! It is always for two entirely different reasons. It is either because we take an immediate delight in them; or else it is because we believe them to bring us good consequential fruits for life. When we speak disparagingly of "feverish fancies," surely the fever-process as such is not the ground of our disesteem—for aught we know to the contrary, 103 degrees or 104 degrees Fahrenheit might be a much more favorable temperature for truths to germinate and sprout in, than the more ordinary blood-heat of 97 or 98 degrees.[23]

And James is right. For aught we know, the particular state of consciousness induced by a specific dose of a specific chemical agent is more favorable for truths to germinate and sprout in than the normal waking state. The real issue is whether we can take immediate delight in these altered states and whether they bring us good consequential fruits for life. No a priori bias toward the normal waking state can fairly consider these points. We will return to these two points in the final section of this chapter when we examine the relationship between ecstasy and spiritual maturity. For now, it is sufficient to recognize that the insights that come to persons in a drug-induced state of consciousness should not be dismissed by a premature bias in favor of the normal waking state.

A third way of evaluating the "true" nature of ecstatic experiences is to interpret them in terms of social and psychological forces that shape our waking lives. That is, it can be argued that an ecstatic experience is not an encounter with a metaphysical reality like it claims to be. Instead, altered states might be understood as projections of the social or psychological realities underlying an individual's conscious experience of the world. The sociological version of this argument is probably best expressed in I. M. Lewis's classic, *Ecstatic Religion*. Although Lewis studied spirit possession and shamanism rather than drug-induced states per se, he maintained that ecstatic states can be wholly explained in terms of their social setting. He noted, for example, that most ecstatic states function to induce compliance with a culture's "main morality." Lewis explained that those entrusted with preserving a culture's official moral code use ecstatic states to legitimate their own claim to be in special connection with supernatural powers and wisdom. By entering into ecstatic states, these individuals reinforce their culture's belief that their moral codes have a more-than-human authority. It is important, however, that the ecstatic element be carefully restricted if these ecstatic states are to function in a culturally conservative manner. As Lewis observed, "New faiths may announce their advent with a flourish of ecstatic revelation, but once they become securely established they have little time or toleration for enthusiasm."[24] Ecstasy-born enthusiasm is always a threat to the established religious order. As we saw in Chapter 4, this may well account for why wine-induced enthusiasm was pronounced in early Mormonism (or such groups as the Brotherhood of the New Life) but became subdued in later Mormonism and in all mainstream Christian groups.

Lewis noted that ecstatic trances can also emerge on those at the "periphery" of the dominant social group. In such cases, the content of ecstatic experiences can be seen to be an oblique form of social protest, expressing the interests of the weak and downtrodden. Lewis, in fact, viewed LSD users as just such a peripheral protest group, whose interests pitted them directly against the religious and cultural establishment.[25] The so-called revelations that come to drug users who are outside the cultural establishment, then, are attempts to give the illusion of supernatural significance for a countercultural philosophy. Lewis's point is that whether ecstatic experiences function to reinforce a culture's "main morality" or a "peripheral morality," it is always possible to see how they function in the service of motivations that are ultimately political or social—rather than metaphysical—in nature.

It is also possible to understand the "true" nature of drug-induced ecstasies by tracing them back to unacknowledged motives that are psychological in nature. A ready example is G. Reichel-Dolmatoff's study of ecstatic shamanism among the Indians of Colombia. Reichel-Dolmatoff was fascinated with the imagery with which Colombian shamans described their experiences under the influence of the hallucinatory beverage *yajé*. What particularly caught his attention was the frequency with which shamans claimed to see jaguars roaming mysteriously and frighteningly through their visions. Reichel-Dolmatoff approached this jaguar imagery from the psychoanalytic perspective, which traces the specific content of mental fantasies back to our underlying psychological tensions and drives. Reichel-Dolmatoff was able to show how the jaguar represents "that other part of humanity's personality that resists and rejects cultural conventions. The jaguar of the hallucinatory sphere, the jaguar-monster of Tuikano tales, is a person's alter ego, now roaming free and untrammeled, and acting out our deepest desires and fears."[26] The implication for understanding the "real" meaning of drug-induced ecstasy is clear:

> We have said that narcotic drugs are used to establish contact with the "supernatural" sphere. This Otherworld is, of course, nothing but a projection of the individual mind, activated by the drug. Unconscious mental processes—fears and desires—are brought into focus and are projected upon the shapes and colors of the visions, and the interpretations given to this imagery by the viewer . . . refer in all essence to problems of food, sex, disease, and aggression, that is, to problems of physical survival.[27]

Such social and psychological perspectives are valuable for understanding the historical connections between drugs and religion. The real question is just how far to push these perspectives. How much should be attributed to the social and psychological background of the ecstasy-seeking subject and how much should be attributed to the physiological effects of the drug? Is this to be understood as a "soft claim," merely stating that subjects color their experience with themes drawn from the social and psychological forces at work in their lives? Or is this intended as a "hard claim," contending that social and psychological factors can exhaustively account for the entire experience? If it is the latter, then we must surely be willing to acknowledge that drug-induced ecstasies have tremendously broadened our understanding of human nature. It would be one thing if drug use revealed only humanity's propensity toward sensual indulgence or social aggression. But when drugs are taken in specific ritual patterns that imbue these experiences with religious meanings, they have also revealed humanity's propensity toward aesthetic delight and social cooperation. Indeed, the American experience with coffee, wine, tobacco, peyote, marijuana, and LSD all indicate a profound human propensity to relate to one another in what Victor Turner described as the modality of communitas. And if drug-induced ecstasies are to be exclusively understood in terms of underlying psychological drives, then how are we to interpret Stanislav Grof's contention that repeated uses of LSD led his subjects to move "beyond" the psychological level dominated by sex or aggression and revealed a level that is transpersonal or spiritual in nature? It is not clear that drug-induced ecstasies can be reduced to psychological and sociological factors without requiring a considerable revision of all existing theory in those fields. If drugs often facilitate the release or projection of such sublime social and psychological themes, then they may well be shedding new light on the highest possibilities of human nature.

The final perspective from which we can assess the validity of ecstasy as a mode of human knowing is the most thought-provoking. Steven Katz, Robert Gimello, and Hans Penner are among a cadre of scholars who maintain that mystical ecstasies are just as determined by their cultural settings as any other experience.[28] This is in sharp contrast to the traditional view that mystical experience is unconnected with everyday social life. Mysticism has traditionally been understood as a direct encounter with a reality that is in itself "wholly other" than our social reality. Because mystical experiences are usually thought to be a direct encounter with an altogether "other" dimension of being, they are assumed to originate in a mode of knowing that goes beyond all words or verbal precision. It is thus customarily claimed that all verbal descriptions and interpretations come after the direct experience; they are incidental to the "real" mystical experience, which is itself beyond ordinary conceptual categories.

Katz, Penner, and Gimello have disputed this claim. Coming out of a philosophical tradition influenced by Heidegger, Wittgenstein, Foucault, and Derrida, they maintain that all experience—including mystical experience—is produced in a specific social context. Their position, generally referred to as constructivism, argues that all of our thoughts and experiences are constructed by our background of beliefs and concepts. In Gimello's words, "Mysticism is inextricably bound up with, dependent upon, and usually subservient to the deeper beliefs and values of the tradition, cultures, and historical milieux which harbour it."[29] The point that Gimello and others are making is that the language, doctrines, and beliefs with which mystics describe their experience do not come *after* the mystical experience, they *produce* it. According to Gimello, "'interpretation' is actually ingredient in and constitutive of mystical experience. All mystical experiences, like all experiences generally, have specific structure."[30] The concepts, beliefs, values, and expectations already held by the mystic actually engender the experience. As Steven Katz put it, every experience—whether mystical or not—is the product or outcome of one's prior history and activity. Mystical experience, like all others, must "involve memory, apprehension, expectation, language, accumulation of prior experience, concepts, and expectations, with each experience being built on the back of all these elements and being shaped anew by each fresh experience."[31] Mystical experiences "are, at least in respect of some determinative aspects, culturally and ideologically grounded."[32]

The constructivists are making a fairly radical claim about the truth and significance of ecstatic experiences.[33] They are not simply claiming that the "set" and "setting" influence an ecstatic experience. They are, instead, making the bolder claim that the "set" and "setting" actually *generate* the experience. In other words, meaning and truth are not apprehended by members of a society; they are produced by that society.

Interpreting ecstasy in terms of its social context has obvious merits. This approach explains why the same drug produces such different experiences in different social contexts. We have already noted, for example, that Aldous Huxley took mescaline and reported an experience perfectly congruous with his background in Hindu Vedantism, whereas Native Americans take the same chemical and report experiences consistent with their respective religious heritages. The constructivist perspective can account for the varying content of drug-induced ecstasies at least as well as traditional theorists who assume that ecstatic experience is centered in the apprehension of a "higher" truth. Moreover, the social-generation theory of ecstasy is simpler, requiring no metaphysical belief or speculation on our part. It contends that ecstatic experience can be best explained in terms of sociohistorical contexts that can be examined in rational, scholarly terms. No concessions need to be made to claims that ecstatic experience somehow gives rise to "higher" modes of knowing that exude a special authority all their own.

It is not clear, however, whether the views advocated by Katz, Penner, and Gimello fully apply to drug-induced ecstasy. Their theory presupposes the existence of a generalized reality-orientation that mediates and structures all experience. Yet the most distinguishing feature of drug-induced ecstasy is the destabilization of the generalized reality-orientation. Drug-induced ecstasies, by definition, are not as "culturally and ideologically" grounded as the normal waking state of consciousness. To the degree that the subject's generalized reality-orientation has faded from awareness, the individual having an ecstatic experience is relatively free of the very set of culturally engendered conceptions that Katz and others insist structure all experience.

Robert Furman and other scholars have maintained that the constructivist perspective breaks down when applied to the kinds of mystical states produced by drugs. Furman concluded "that some experiences—notably the silent mystical experiences of pure consciousness—do not seem to be shaped or formed by the language system. Through a process akin to forgetting, one may be able to let go of one's concepts and conceptual baggage and come to an experience that is both nonconceptual and not shaped by concepts and beliefs."[34] There is also strong evidence to suggest that persons gradually develop new, state-specific vocabularies to correspond to these novel experiences. Ecstatic experiences not only enable individuals to organize information about the world in novel ways but, as Arthur Deikman alerted us, also permit them to experience aspects of the world ordinarily excluded or ignored. That is, ecstasy by its very nature centers on information about the universe that—while possibly irrelevant from a biological or sociological point of view and thus absent from our generalized reality-orientation—may nonetheless have other kinds of intellectual validity.

There is nothing in the historical record of Americans' use of drugs that can decisively settle these and other debates about the truth status of mystical ecstasy. In every case, the arguments turn on philosophical assumptions that resist easy refutation by an appeal to the verbal accounts of mystics themselves. We might, however, remind ourselves of William James's counsel concerning the relationship between ecstasy and truth. James's advice on this matter, which he specifically intended to include the kinds of drug-induced ecstasy covered in this book, was divided into three parts.[35] First, James noted that mystical states usually are, and have the right to be, absolutely authoritative over those who have them. Despite any grumbling by rationalists or materialists, it is a psychological fact that well-pronounced ecstatic experiences prove formative in shaping an individual's conception of the universe. As James put it, such experiences impart "a *sense of reality, a feeling of objective presence, a perception* of what we may call '*something there*,' more deep and more general than any of the special and particular 'sense' by which the current psychology supposes existent realities to be originally revealed."[36] These sensations are as vivid and real as any sensations ever are. Persons having such an experience thus understandably assign them validity and significance. For this reason, ecstatic experiences are psychologically authoritative for those who have them. What is more, James argued, from an empirical standpoint these experiences *should* be philosophically authoritative to those who have them.

A second conclusion that James came to about the validity of ecstatic experiences is that nonmystics are under no obligation to acknowledge them as possessing any superior authority. Ecstatic experiences have no special status that compels those who stand outside of them to accept them (or claims based upon them) uncritically. Just as we should not dismiss an insight as invalid solely because of our biases toward the conditions under which it originated, we should not uncritically accept truth claims solely because of the conditions under which it originated. Instead, the claims emanating from ecstatic experiences must be evaluated in the same manner we would evaluate any other statements in the area of religion and metaphysics. And, as we shall see in the concluding section, this is largely by appealing to their consequences. We must ascertain for ourselves whether an ecstatic experience brings immediate delight or good consequential fruits for life. Put differently, the validity of an ecstatic experience is measured by the degree to which it yields a fuller, more satisfactory life.

Third, and perhaps most importantly, the very existence of mystical states such as those described in earlier chapters overthrows the pretension of the normal waking state of consciousness to be the sole and ultimate dictator of what we may believe. The normal waking state is but one kind of consciousness. It remains an open question whether various kinds of ecstatic states are superior points of view, windows through which the mind looks out upon a more extensive and inclusive world. It is true that such ecstatic states do not necessarily deliver authoritative claims about our world. But they do offer new hypotheses about our world. James pointed out that if we choose to ignore these hypotheses because of our commitment to prefixed notions of rationality, we do so at our own risk. It is at least possible, after all, that they hold the truest of insights into the meaning of life.

Drugs and the Free Exercise of Religion

Evaluating the claim that drug-induced ecstasies constitute a path toward "higher" truths forces us to think through a number of thorny philosophical issues. Just as thorny, however, are the legal issues that Americans confront when trying to determine when, and under what conditions, it might be necessary for the government to restrict the use of drugs. This is particularly the case when such restriction might cause some people to believe that their right to freedom of religion has been infringed. Indeed, the freedom of religion is considered a defining element of the American way of life. Americans so treasure the freedom of religion that it was, along with the freedom of speech, singled out and protected in the First Amendment appended to the Constitution. The First Amendment provides that "Congress shall make no law respecting an establishment of religion, or prohibiting the free exercise thereof." The Constitution's Bill of Rights thus grants every citizen the right to believe and profess whatever religious doctrine he or she chooses. The free exercise provision ensures that the government may not compel affirmation of religious belief, punish the expression of religious doctrines it believes to be false, impose special disabilities on the basis of religious views, or lend its power to one side or the other in a religious controversy.

The free exercise of religion is not only about beliefs. It also includes the freedom to perform—or abstain from—religious acts. Religious actions include congregating for the purpose of worship, wearing distinctive clothing, proselytizing, and abstaining from certain foods, among others. The purpose of the First Amendment (and the Fourteenth Amendment, which empowers Congress to see that every state enforces the protection of individual rights) is to see that no branch of government bans such actions because of one's religious beliefs. Yet this has never meant that persons are free to do anything they want just by claiming it is part of their religion. Those who framed our legal tradition realized that there would be certain circumstances in which the government would have to regulate at least some forms of religiously motivated behavior.

George Mason and James Madison were perhaps the most articulate on this subject. In 1776, they were both participating in the Virginia Constitution Convention and urged their colleagues to adopt a protection of religious liberty. Mason proposed a particularly eloquent summary of Americans' right to the free exercise of religion:

> That religion, or the duty which we owe to our CREATOR, and the manner of discharging it, can be (directed) only by reason and conviction, not by force or violence; and therefore, that *all men should enjoy the fullest toleration in the exercise of religion . . . unless, under colour of religion, any man disturb the peace, the happiness, or safety of society.* And that it is the mutual duty of all to practice Christian forbearance, love, and charity towards each other.[37]

Mason's concern for religious freedom was typical of many of those who framed the United States Constitution. He trusted that a spirit of toleration would prevail in American society. He also took it for granted that nearly all Americans would belong to a small number of Christian religious organizations. And finally, it was clear to Mason that the free exercise of religion was not an absolute right. The right to the free exercise of religion does not exist in a vacuum. It is a right that must be understood in the larger context of the government's preservation of "the peace, the happiness, or safety of society."

Mason's colleague, James Madison, thought that religious freedom needed to be protected in stronger language. Madison wanted to shift the language of toleration to a language of rights. And he also wished to narrow the conditions under which government might interfere with the right of the free exercise of religion. Madison, who became one of the principal architects of the Constitution's Bill of Rights, suggested that the Virginia Constitutional Convention adopt instead the following revision:

> That religion, or the duty we owe our Creator, and the manner of discharging it, being under the direction of reason and conviction only, not of violence or compulsion, all men are *equally entitled* to the full and free exercise of it, ac-

cording to the dictates of conscience; .. . . *unless under color of religion the preservation of equal liberty, and the existence of the State be manifestly endangered.*[38]

Not only was Madison insisting that our government recognize the freedom of religion as a legal entitlement, but he was also restricting the conditions that might justify governmental infringement on this right. To Madison's way of thinking, the state could interfere in a believer's free exercise only if the state would otherwise "be manifestly endangered." The changes in wording were only slight, but they nonetheless focused attention on the legal problem of when and where the government is justified in regulating religiously motivated behavior.

The members of the Virginia Legislature weren't any more confident about where this line should be drawn than we are today. The legislators ultimately decided to be silent on the more controversial issues and instead settled for a simple clause mentioning that all persons are equally entitled to the free exercise of religion. Mason's and Madison's writings nevertheless reveal how clearly the framers of our legal tradition recognized potential conflicts of interest between the free exercise of religion and the right of the government to protect the overall interests of society. The free exercise of religion would always have to be balanced against the interests of society. No precise formula could be derived to help us decide conclusively just where the line should be drawn in any given case.

Challenges to the free exercise clause have come in every conceivable form. For example, courts have had to decide whether the government can mandate that an autopsy be performed on a person belonging to a religious group that considers such actions to be sacrilegious. Other cases involved the issues of whether members of a religious group can refuse immunizations against disease even if this endangered the health of other citizens and whether members of a religious group can prohibit their children from receiving blood transfusions and thereby endanger the life of a minor. Courts have had to decide whether the "peace, happiness, and safety" of society is endangered by a religious group that practices animal sacrifice or by religious groups whose members insist upon retaining their long hair in the armed services. The kinds of dilemmas generated by the First Amendment free exercise clause remind us of the inherent difficulty in balancing individual rights and the welfare of society.

Some of the most difficult cases involving interpretations of the free exercise clause have dealt with the religious use of drugs. Few

Americans would dispute the government's need to identify and control substances that are harmful to public health. True, there are some who take the extreme libertarian position that government intervention in the lives of citizens is rarely justifiable. But most Americans support the government's efforts to regulate what are termed "controlled substances." Ranging from prescription medicines to "street" intoxicants, there are any number of drugs whose potential for bodily harm warrants their placement on the list of substances to be regulated by government agencies.

Whereas caffeine, tobacco, and alcohol have generally been exempted from government control, marijuana, LSD, cocaine, heroin, and mescaline are all identified as drugs that have great potential for endangering the public welfare. Current estimates indicate that over 200,000 Americans use heroin, 1.5 million Americans use cocaine, 800,000 use illegal amphetamines, and 10 million smoke marijuana. Of the "legal" drugs, caffeine is the most popular. Caffeine is contained in tea, coffee, chocolate products, most soft drinks, and over 2,000 nonprescription drugs. Roughly 80 percent of Americans consume caffeine in one form or another on a daily basis. Meanwhile, 61 million Americans use nicotine in the form of tobacco. And, finally, approximately 60 percent of adult Americans consume alcohol at least occasionally. With the possible exception of caffeine, all of these substances are either addictive or at least habit-forming in ways that become injurious to a person's health or ability to function well in society. Most Americans understand the physical, economic, and social repercussions of drug abuse and for this reason support the basic principle of the government's "war on drugs."

Generally speaking, the government has the authority to control the use of drugs that it determines to be dangerous, even if those drugs are used for religious purposes.[39] Courts have consistently ruled that the government's need to protect society by enforcing drug laws is more compelling than, for example, an individual's right to smoke marijuana as part of a religious practice. As might be expected, there has been no shortage of cases in which persons charged with possession of a controlled substance have offered a religious defense. For example, a follower of the Black Muslim faith was arrested for smuggling both heroin and marijuana and argued (unsuccessfully) that these substances were necessary for meditation. A priest of the Holy American Church likewise claimed religious purposes for the marijuana he had attempted to sell to an undercover narcotics agent. A person charged with the use and distribution of marijuana claimed to be practicing Tantric Buddhism at the time of his arrest in the restroom of a nightclub. In yet another case, a person charged with possession of marijuana unsuccessfully claimed that he was a minister of something called the Universal Industrial Church of the New World Comforter, which viewed the use of marijuana as a sacrament. In all of these cases, the courts determined that the state had a compelling interest in restricting a controlled substance and that this concern for the welfare of society was sufficient to override the defendant's free exercise argument. In some of these cases, the courts have ruled that the use of a prohibited substance is not absolutely essential to the defendant's ability to practice his or her religious faith. Courts have, in fact, ruled that the desire to heighten awareness or to enable oneself to "have new dimensions opened" does not constitute a legitimate religious purpose sufficient to invoke the free exercise clause.

Neither the government nor the courts have been very consistent in defining the principles that might distinguish between instances when the use of a controlled substance for religious purposes is and is not permissible. For example, the federal government has decided to exempt the religious use of peyote from restrictive legislation. In the case of peyote (as we shall examine more closely), the government completely reversed itself and upheld the right to use a drug intended to heighten awareness and open new dimensions, finding it indispensable to religious practice. Peyote, then, has been given quite different legal treatment than LSD or marijuana. Alcohol and coffee, which are both regularly found in America's churches precisely because of their historical role as mood-altering substances, are also exempted from federal control. It seems apparent that political and cultural forces dictate the distinction between drugs that are indispensable to religious practice and drugs that are not. A drug thought indispensable to a religion practiced by a socially dominant group (or a group whose interests are considered "politically correct" by a socially dominant group—see discussion of peyote use below) is much less likely to be deemed a threat to the welfare of society than a drug deemed important to the religious practices of a social minority.

A fascinating example of the social dimensions of Americans' (failed) efforts to define a drug as inimical to religious practice is the history of Prohibition. Throughout the nineteenth century, a cluster of evangelical Protestant denominations became ever more visible as America's self-proclaimed "moral majority."[40] The white,

Anglo-Saxon, Protestant members of the American populace were confident that they were creating a society pleasing to God. Bible-toting citizens formed together into small societies to promote a variety of causes aimed at promoting moral perfection and Christian progress. Abolition societies, groups working for educational improvements, and ministries to the sick and poor were all examples of Protestant piety seeking ways to spread its vision of a well-ordered society. So, too, were societies trying to curb what was deemed the intemperate use of alcohol. Evangelical religion was suspicious of uncontrolled emotions. Alcohol compounds humanity's natural dispositions toward sinning rebellion against God's will. Drunkenness impairs human reason, weakens our conscience, dissipates our fear of God, and prompts us to commit vices of most every kind. The formation of temperance societies was thus an important part of American Protestantism's official mission of saving souls and incorporating these persons into a well-regulated community.

The gradual escalation of temperance efforts into a demand for the complete prohibition of alcohol spanned several decades. These years witnessed a number of social and economic changes that made it increasingly more plausible for America's WASP middle class to view alcohol as a social threat. First, immigrants continued to flow into the United States at a rate almost unprecedented in Western history. Moreover, a good many of these immigrants were Germans, Poles, Italians, Jews, and Irish who didn't share the Protestant vision of their Yankee hosts. The Protestant majority viewed these "foreigners" with disdain. They were, after all, often poor, ill educated, and living in the squalor of urban ghettos. With the exception of Jewish immigrants, among whom drinking outside of family and religious observances was quite rare, the new immigrants were notable for their public drinking. This drinking became a symbol of what Protestants viewed as their coarse or uncivilized way of life. The push to a total prohibition of alcohol, then, had a very pronounced social dimension as it pitted the established middle class against the seemingly unredeemable masses of persons who stood in the way of the formation of a perfect Protestant society.[41]

Religious and social prejudices were only part of the story behind Prohibition. Rapid industrialization prompted even nonreligious members of the middle and upper classes to favor moral codes that would foster efficiency, self-discipline, and orderly conduct among workers. The second decade of the twentieth century also witnessed the birth of the Progressive Movement among scholars, legislators, and social reformers who shared a vision of improving the political and economic conditions of the poor. They, too, saw alcohol as a social menace because it despoiled human reason, undermined representative government, and eroded the moral foundations of our religious and cultural heritage.[42] Alcohol abuse was associated with the disintegration of families, domestic violence, and the perpetuation of poverty. All in all, alcohol was a symbol of the impediments that stood in the way of a more efficient, orderly America.

The combined clout of Protestant reformers and political progressivists was sufficient to create the political consensus needed to pass the Volstead Act enforcing Prohibition in the United States from 1920 until its repeal in 1933. Prohibition was by almost any reckoning a colossal failure. It spawned waves of crime and violence. Backroom batches of alcohol posed a public health problem of considerable magnitude. Prohibition also generated a great deal of dissension about the relationships between alcohol and the practice of both Christianity and Judaism. Even before the Volstead Act, many temperance advocates had called for total abstention from alcohol. This meant that wine, which had for almost two thousand years been regarded as symbolic of the very substance of Christ, was now being labeled a poison that was particularly abominable in the eyes of God. The "wine question" divided congregations throughout the country. Ritual-oriented denominations such as the Episcopalians, Lutherans, and Roman Catholics were the least persuaded. But most evangelical Protestants jettisoned wine from their worship services. Bible teachers at conservative seminaries actually advanced the argument that when the Bible mentions wine it is only referring to unfermented grape juice. A Methodist minister turned dentist, Thomas Welch, was so convinced that alcohol was unacceptable in the Christian sacrament of the Lord's Supper that he perfected a process to produce "Dr. Welch's Unfermented Wine." His son, Charles, later observed that Welch Company and its well-known brand of grape juice "was born in 1869 out of a passion to serve God by helping His Church to give its communion 'the fruit of the vine,' instead of the 'cup of devils.'"[43] To this day, American Christians cannot agree on the moral or theological correctness of using an alcohol-containing substance in its central act of worship.

Passage of the Volstead Act was possible only by amending it to recognize the "legitimate" use of wine for the purpose of religious worship. Its provisions allowed for bonded wineries to sell wine "for sacramental purposes or like religious rites" to individuals such as "a rabbi, minister of the gospel, priest, or an officer duly authorized for the purpose by any church or congregation."[44] The principal point here is that the members of ritual-oriented Christian groups possessed sufficient political clout to ensure their continued use of wine. At the time the Volstead Act was passed, the vast majority of Americans had at least some family connection to the Christian faith (and about 2 percent were Jewish). Wine, used for such religious purposes as heightening awareness and opening up the dimension of God's gracious spirit, would be considered a legitimate exemption to the otherwise applicable prohibition of any alcoholic beverage. Might made right.

As mentioned briefly above, there has been another fascinating test of the free exercise clause in connection with otherwise controlled substances. This time it was peyote, not wine, that focused attention on the precarious balance between public welfare and the free exercise of religion. The government and courts have become increasingly sensitive to the historical mistreatment of Native Americans. New statutes were enacted that were specifically designed to preserve traditional religions of Native Americans. Some statutes, for example, ensured access to and ceremonial use of sites considered sacred by Indian religious practitioners. Twenty-eight states also enacted laws that exempted ritual use of peyote from its drug enforcement codes. Most of them did so recognizing, as the federal government did in the 1990s, that "the traditional ceremonial use of the peyote cactus as a religious sacrament has for centuries been integral to a way of life, and significant in perpetuating Indian tribes and cultures."[45] It didn't seem to matter that ritual use of peyote north of the Rio Grande was fairly rare prior to the enforced relocation of Native Americans to reservations in the late 1800s. What probably was important, however, was that peyote rituals are quite compatible with white, middle-class culture. Legislatures and courts alike stressed that peyote rituals promoted the adoption of biblical morality, taught peaceful coexistence with neighbors, and discouraged the use of alcohol, which is frequently a problem among the male populations on reservations. In short, the protection of peyote rituals not only was consistent with the moral aims of preserving Native American culture but also had the value of protecting a free exercise right that really didn't clash with middle-class values anyway.

A Supreme Court decision in 1990 revisited the free exercise clause, particularly in relationship to the right to use peyote in Native American religious ceremonies. The case, titled *Employment Division v. Smith*, pertained to two individuals who had been employed as drug rehabilitation counselors at a private drug rehabilitation organization in Oregon.[46] Each had signed an agreement as a condition of employment not to use illegal drugs but were later found to have ingested peyote for sacramental purposes at a ceremony of the Native American Church. In Oregon, the possession of peyote is a felony. When the drug counselors applied for unemployment compensation, the Oregon agency held them to be ineligible under a state rule that disqualifies employees discharged for work-related misconduct. The drug counselors appealed the agency's ruling, basing their defense on a few important cases that had found that a state cannot withhold unemployment benefits if an individual had been fired for actions directly related to his or her religion. The most important of these cases had been a Supreme Court ruling in 1963, *Sherbert v. Verner.*

While not dealing with drug-related issues, *Sherbert* was one of the strongest statements ever made by the Supreme Court in enunciating the principle that the government must justify any curtailment of an American citizen's right to the free exercise of religion. More specifically, *Sherbert* maintained that there must be a compelling government interest to justify placing any burden upon religious practice. Furthermore, *Sherbert* required that such laws must hold up under the "strict scrutiny" test. The concept of "strict scrutiny" not only required that the law be necessary for ensuring a compelling government interest but that it also be the least restrictive means of doing so.

It at first appeared that the courts would find no government interest sufficiently compelling to prohibit the ritual use of peyote by the Native American Church. Oregon's state appellate court reversed the decision on the basis of *Sherbert* and upheld the payment of unemployment benefits. The case was then taken to the Oregon Supreme Court, which also ruled in favor of the drug counselors on the grounds of the federal guarantee of the free exercise of religion. Eventually the case made its way to the United States Supreme Court, which, in a narrow 5–4 decision, ruled in favor of the unemployment agency, finding that the state prohibition of the religious use of peyote is permissible under the free exercise clause. Justice Scalia wrote for the slim majority, explaining that the law prohibiting the use of peyote was not enacted with the intention of either promoting or restricting religious beliefs. The prohibition of peyote use was applicable to all citizens of Oregon and thus only incidentally affected those who sought to use peyote for religious purposes. Scalia argued that generally applicable laws are "one large step" removed from laws aimed at specific religious practices. Justice Scalia, as well as the other judges voting in the majority, believed that an orderly society cannot be attained when anyone can do as they please under the color of religious belief. Their point was that a person of religious conviction cannot become a law unto him- or herself. Scalia cited two previous Supreme Court cases to express this principle:

> Conscientious scruples have not, in the course of the long struggle for religious toleration, relieved the individual from obedience to a general law not aimed at the promotion or restriction of religious beliefs. The mere possession of religious convictions which contradict the relevant concerns of a political society does not relieve the citizen from the discharge of political responsibilities. . . . To permit this would be to make the professed doctrines of religious belief superior to the law of the land, and in effect to permit every citizen to become a law unto himself.[47]

The Court thus stipulated that the right of free exercise does not relieve an individual of the obligation to comply with a "valid and neutral law of general applicability." This decision alone was not controversial, except that in the *Smith* decision the Court refused to apply the "strict scrutiny" test that *Sherbert* had articulated. The Court was thereby shifting the emphasis back to the state's need to ensure the general public welfare rather than the individual's unrestricted free exercise rights. This ruling affirmed that if the state has an across-the-board criminal prohibition, it is not required to determine in every case whether it is the least restrictive method of ensuring the public welfare. Scalia reasoned that "the government's ability to enforce generally applicable prohibitions of socially harmful conduct, like its ability to carry out other aspects of public policy, cannot depend on measuring the effects of a governmental action on a religious objector's spiritual development."[48] And here is why:

> Any society adopting such a system would be courting anarchy, but that danger increases in direct proportion to the society's diversity of religious beliefs, and its determination to coerce or suppress none of them. Precisely because we are a cosmopolitan nation made up of people of almost every conceivable religious preference, and precisely because we value and protect that religious divergence, we cannot afford the luxury of deeming presumptively invalid, as applied to the religious objector, every regulation of conduct that does not protect an interest of the highest order.[49]

Justice Scalia contended that anarchy would reign if individuals could disobey otherwise applicable laws owing to their private religious beliefs. There is too much religious diversity in the United States to permit individuals to avoid compliance with civic obligations for religious reasons. The government would no longer be able to go about its business of seeing that its citizens pay taxes, obey traffic laws, get driver's licenses, abide by animal cruelty statutes, receive compulsory vaccinations, abide by child labor or child neglect laws, and so forth. The government must therefore be able to prohibit, without justification, conduct mandated by an individual's religious beliefs, so long as that prohibition is generally applicable.

Justice Blackmun wrote for the four dissenting members of the Court. He believed that the Court had erred in not reaffirming the *Sherbert* requirement of a compelling government interest, and one that is safeguarded in a way that least restricts persons' religious rights. First, Blackmun noted that there is no evidence that the religious use of peyote has ever harmed anyone. He noted that although peyote is on Oregon's schedule of controlled substances, even the federal government exempts peyote for religious use. The Native American Church's use of peyote is so ritually structured that there is no real concern for health and safety. Furthermore, there is no evidence that the religious use of peyote leads to further drug use. On the contrary, members of the Native American Church receive such spiritual and social support that it has been an effective instrument in combating the tragic effects of alcoholism on the Native American population. In sum, Blackmun maintained that "peyote simply is not a popular drug; its distribution for use in religious rituals has nothing to do with the vast and violent traffic in illegal narcotics that plagues this country."[50]

Over and beyond his contention that the religious use of peyote does not constitute a compelling threat to the government, Blackmun's dissent staked out a second point of objection. Blackmun believed that setting aside the *Sherbert* principle of strict scrutiny was a major mistake. The majority of the Court had decided that strict scrutiny of a state law burdening the free exercise of religion is a luxury that a well-ordered society cannot afford. In Blackmun's view the Court's ruling reflected the opinion that the repression of minority religions is an unavoidable consequence of democratic government. Blackmun dissented. He wrote, "I do not believe the Founders thought their dearly bought freedom from religious persecution a 'luxury,' but an essential element of liberty—and they could not have thought religious intolerance 'unavoidable.'"[51]

A substantial number of Americans agreed with Blackmun's dissenting opinion. Some were staunch advocates of the free exercise clause. Others were motivated more by an ideological opposition to government interference in the lives of private citizens. An unusual alliance between political liberals who sought the protection of minority rights and political conservatives who traditionally view the courts as an enemy of religion led to a battle between Congress and the Supreme Court.

Three years later Congress passed the Religious Freedom Restoration Act (RFRA). Congress was distressed over the *Smith* decision, which virtually eliminated the requirement that the government justify burdens on the free exercise of religion. By passing the RFRA, Congress sought to underscore the free exercise of religion as an unalienable right. The law specifically prohibits the government from substantially burdening a person's exercise of religion, even if the burden results from a rule of general applicability, unless the government can demonstrate that the burden (1) is in furtherance of a compelling governmental interest, and (2) is the least restrictive means of furthering that compelling governmental interest.[52]

Congress was, in essence, trying to restore the strict scrutiny test elucidated in the 1963 *Sherbert* case. Interestingly, the House of Representative voted unanimously to approve the RFRA, and the Senate passed it with a 97–3 margin. Given that the *Smith* case factored so prominently in the declaration of purpose that serves as a preamble to this legislation, it seems there is a general consensus among the nation's elected representatives to protect the religious use of peyote as a fundamental part of Americans' free exercise rights. Yet no support was heard for those who wished to use marijuana or LSD for essentially similar purposes. Just where the line of compelling interest lies is thus still a matter of social and political ambiguity.

Another test of the free exercise clause made it to the Supreme Court in 1997. Although this case, *City of Boerne v. Flores*, did not involve the right to use otherwise controlled substances for religious purposes, it was a case intended to clarify the discrepancy between the RFRA's provisions and the *Smith* decision of 1990.[53] In a 6–3 decision, the Court ruled that the RFRA was "out of proportion" to the kinds of problems it sought to remedy. The Court reiterated that it could find no examples of generally applicable laws passed because of religious bigotry and, hence, RFRA was unnecessarily and unjustifiably tipping the balance away from the government's ability to ensure the orderliness and welfare of society.

A major portion of the *Boerne* decision focused on the Court's opinion that Congress had overstepped the bounds of the Fourteenth Amendment by going beyond enforcing rights to actually defining them. But the *Boerne* decision revisited the larger ideological battle and suggested that if "compelling interest" really means what it says, then many laws (e.g., those dealing with traffic violations, animal welfare, licensing statutes, etc.) would not meet the test. Hence, the kind of thinking that the RFRA reflected "would open the prospect of constitutionally required religious exemptions from civic obligations of almost every conceivable kind."[54] The fear, again, was that religious beliefs would become superior to the laws of society and that every citizen would become a law unto her- or himself.

It is clear that Americans will continue to debate the limits of our commitment to the free exercise of religion for years to come. The Supreme Court almost seems to have invited backers of the RFRA to bring it a more legitimate test case than the *Boerne* case presented. In her dissenting opinion, Justice Sandra Day O'Connor reminded us that "the Religion Clauses of the Constitution represent a profound commitment to religious liberty."[55] In her view, we have not yet gone far enough in preserving this important liberty. Along with the protection of free speech, no other right so fully expresses the noblest aspirations of American culture. There are few persons among us who can confidently claim to know what in every conceivable situation would determine a "compelling interest" and just how far government must go to make its prohibitions the least restrictive possible. As the public debate engendered in both the RFRA and the *Smith* (and *Boerne*) decision attests, most Americans realize that the free exercise of religion is a precious right, but one that doesn't exist in a vacuum. Difficult judgments must be made, and made in the hope of balancing the need for protecting the free exercise of religion with the need for a well-ordered society that avoids anarchy under the color of religion.

The final section of this chapter reflects on a portion of the issues that are at stake in making sound judgments about the use of drugs in the exercise of religion. Justice Scalia had hoped to find a general principle that would help the government avoid "measuring the effects of a governmental action on a religious objector's spiritual development." But that is one of the most important issues at stake in determining just when certain drugs are, or are not, compatible with the overall welfare of society. The spiritual development of citizens should surely be considered relevant to the general welfare of society. Judgments about whether certain patterns of drug use are helpful or harmful to spiritual development—no matter how difficult to make—are unavoidable if we are to take every conceivable step to preserve the right to the free exercise of religion while maintaining a well-ordered society.

Drugs and Spiritual Maturity

The quest for ecstasy is a quest to go beyond one's ordinary mental and emotional boundaries. It is a quest for greater subjective richness, a more intense mode of experiencing life. The pursuit of ecstasy thus has a natural affinity with human spirituality. Spirituality, too, is rooted in the desire to expand one's range of experience and action. The very word spirituality is derived from the Latin verb *spirare,* to breathe. Spirituality is therefore about "breathing" life into an otherwise inanimate universe. As such, spirituality has both a receptive and active side. First, being spiritual is about becoming receptive to the principle or power that infuses vitality into our world. A vital spirituality requires that we expand our ordinary sensibilities so as to be receptive to the sacred power underlying the whole of creation. Second, spirituality also means becoming an agent of this principle of vitality. Spirituality is connected with the desire to express life, and to express it more abundantly. It is about energetically performing actions that "breathe" life into our world. To be spiritual, then, is to be an effective agent of wholeness-making and world-building activity. This entails considerable responsibility. Misguided or ineffective action cannot translate even the most sublime of subjective intentions into tangible expressions of wholeness-making behavior. Being an agent of world-building activity requires intelligence, discipline, and moral reflection. Anything less falls short of effective spiritual agency.

Many drugs would appear to enhance the first aspect of spirituality. Wine, peyote, tobacco, marijuana, LSD, and coffee have all functioned in American life as means of enhancing spiritual receptivity. Drugs facilitate states in which we feel momentarily united with a more sacred dimension of reality. This is a fact that should not be overlooked in assessing humanity's "fourth drive." Indeed, William James opined that the power that intoxicating substances have over humans "is unquestionably due to their power to stimulate the mystical faculties of human nature." The ecstasy afforded by drugs makes us "for the moment one with truth. Not through mere perversity do men run after it. . . . The [drug-induced] consciousness is one bit of the mystic consciousness, and our total opinion of it must find its place in our opinion of that larger whole."[56]

The philosopher and religious studies scholar Huston Smith was himself drawn to psychedelics precisely for this very reason. They provided him a long-desired vehicle for achieving mystical states of consciousness. Smith wrote that "drugs unquestionably can occasion Otto's mysterium tremendum, majestas, mysterium fascinans; in a phrase the phenomenon of religious awe."[57] This ability to disclose dimensions of the universe normally screened from our conscious experience gives drugs tremendous religious import. Smith laments that the scientific and materialistic bent of modern Western culture has made spiritual receptivity a rare commodity. He joins theologian Paul Tillich in arguing that the greatest threat to genuine spirituality in our age is the general absence of such a mystical sensibility. As Tillich put it, "the question our century puts before us [is]: Is it possible to regain the lost dimension, the encounter with the Holy, the dimension which cuts through the world of subjectivity and objectivity and goes down to that which is not world but is the mystery of the Ground of Being?"[58]

Spirituality cannot survive in the absence of such mystical experiences. The ritual use of certain drugs seems to create conditions favorable to "regaining" the lost dimension that Tillich referred to. And for this reason it seems likely that at least some drugs will continue to be connected with the spiritual quest for the foreseeable future. Wine and coffee, for example, have proven themselves particularly capable of nourishing the "aesthetic sensibility" that underlies all genuine spirituality. This is true both in connection with their use by formal religious institutions and as part of the unchurched varieties of popular or nature religion that flourish in American life. The ritual use of peyote by the Native American Church is yet another instance in which drugs help elicit the kind of mystical experiences without which spirituality cannot survive in the modern era. However, the climate that formerly connected the use of marijuana and LSD with the pursuit of "metaphysical illumination" has somewhat dissipated in recent years. It appears that these and other street drugs (e.g., MDMA, cocaine, mushrooms, or mescaline) are predominantly used for the experience of intoxication rather than in connection with specifically spiritual motives. Nonetheless, these drugs, too, can in the right circumstances surely enhance the kinds of receptivity that provide the foundations for a vibrant spirituality. And thus to this extent, the use of drugs may well be conducive to at least one vital aspect of spiritual development.

The final test of mature spirituality, however, is the degree to which persons are transformed into effective agents of wholeness-making and world-building activity. And it is here that the most serious reservations arise about the value of drugs for nurturing a mature spirituality. As Huston Smith put it, "short cuts may become short circuits."[59] Spirituality does not consist solely of spiritual experience. It also consists of participating in ongoing process whereby life is "breathed" into our universe. The quest for spiritual insight, as with any other human desire or motivation, must finally be judged by its long-term consequences. Metaphysical illuminations must ultimately be judged by their ability to direct us toward sustained wholeness-making behavior. And thus, as William James observed of his own experiments with nitrous oxide, "what blunts the mind and weakens the will is no full channel for truth, even if it assists us to a view of a certain aspect of it."[60] Reaching private heavens through drug-induced ecstasies is itself not fully spiritual. Spiritual receptivity needs to be connected with an ethical outlook sanctioned by an intact community that has successfully met the developmental needs of an ongoing sequence of generations. Without this, spiritual receptivity is unlikely to give rise to effective spiritual agency. And hence, all too often drug use is unlikely to measure up to the second test of a vital spirituality.

Most cultures have recognized the importance of connecting spiritual receptivity with a commitment to a normative world vision. Felicitas Goodman, in her cross-cultural study of ecstatic states, noted how "religious communities that use drugs to [induce ecstasy] teach their members how to switch from intoxication to religious trance."[61] Most societies not only value certain drugs for contributing to the spiritual development of their members but provide a cultural context that structures such development. And this is precisely what most Jewish and Christian congregations do with their ritual use of wine. The Native American Church similarly connects the use of peyote with elements of both Indian and Christian morality in such a way as to foster its members commitment to wholeness-making activity. To some extent the youth counterculture of the sixties and early seventies accomplished this too. Coffeehouses, Be-Ins, and small groups gathering to "turn on" and discuss Eastern philosophy all established supportive social and intellectual climates for linking the quest for ecstasy with the ongoing process of spiritual development. In the right cultural and ritual context, then, the religious use of drugs has historically proven capable of fostering spiritual development.

It is interesting that the courts, despite Justice Scalia's desire to avoid such judgments, have in fact attempted to assess the likelihood that drug use will contribute to an individual's spiritual development. Indeed, our government saw fit to exempt religious communities from Prohibition precisely because of an implicit judgment that these communities could, in Goodman's words, "teach their members how to switch from intoxication to religious trance." The government expressly invoked these kinds of considerations in exempting the Native American Church from its otherwise applicable statutes prohibiting the use of peyote. On the other hand, the government has implicitly decided that many other religious groups are less likely to structure drug use in ways that are likely to foster spiritual development. Unfortunately, neither legislatures nor courts have been very explicit about how they arrived at their overall estimate of the "legitimacy" of drug-related religious rituals. In many cases, the law has probably mirrored middle-class prejudices against minority religious groups. Such organizations as the Aquarian Brotherhood Church, the Universal Industrial Church of the New World Comforter, or the Psychedelic Venus Church are unlikely to benefit from the same presumptive judgments that mainline Christian churches enjoy in American culture.

This is not, however, to suggest mean-spiritedness, heavy-handedness, or even closed-mindedness on the part of those who have deemed it necessary to prohibit some groups from using otherwise controlled substances in their religious activities. A good many of those who sought the right to use drugs "under the colour" of religion did—and continue to do so—disingenuously. And other groups, while utterly sincere in their efforts to enhance spiritual receptivity, were nonetheless naively underestimating the danger that these drugs might actually curtail their members' overall spiritual development. The historical record shows that the government has indeed attempted to estimate "the effects of a governmental action on a religious objector's spiritual development." This is not only unavoidable but necessary for a government that wishes to preserve and even promote its citizens' spiritual well-being.

History also seems to indicate that the conceptions of "spiritual development" held by socially empowered groups are more likely to be given legal sanction than those of social minorities. But we can make efforts to remedy that unfortunate tendency of democratic government. It is possible to engage in open, democratic debate over the effects of specific patterns of drug use in promoting both spiritual receptivity and spiritual agency. The debate will rarely focus on the ability of drugs to render persons more receptive to the private heavens of religious belief and experience. Instead, the more contested issues will have to do with whether specific patterns of drug use promote sustained spiritual agency. And here the government must weigh the evidence carefully to ascertain whether the patterns of drug use in question are likely to foster long-term spiritual development. Indeed, drug-related disputes concerning the free exercise clause can be greatly clarified by appealing to empirical studies dealing with the development of addiction and habit-forming behaviors. Quantitative data alone, of course, will not dictate either spiritual or legal judgments. Yet social scientific research can tell us much about whether certain patterns of drug use are statistically likely to be conducive to wholeness-making behavior on a consistent basis. This information, open to public debate and scrutiny, can tell us much about whether certain patterns of drug use will prompt persons to become effective agents of world-building activity or victims of habit-forming chemical processes.

If we, like Justice O'Connor, believe that the commitment religious liberty is one of the noblest aspirations of the American legal system, then we must be willing to enter into the difficult process of judging the effects of governmental actions on a religious objector's spiritual development. We must be prepared to recognize that certain patterns of drug use have indeed proven supportive of spiritual maturity. The historical record does not support those neo-Prohibitionists who find any and all expressions of the plant kingdom to be inimical to humanity's introduction to the Kingdom of God. We must, however, also be prepared to recognize compelling interests of society that might well prompt us to curtail the right to certain behaviors under the colour of religion. The spiritual well-being of society requires the existence of safeguards to ensure the triumph of wholeness-making and world-building processes over sickness-engendering and world-dissolving addictions.

Americans have, for centuries, viewed drugs as stairways to heaven. These stairways have, on occasion, opened up a pathway to a paradise of mystical delight. For some, these stairways never led any further. What initially appeared to be a paradise of intoxication all too often becomes a self-imposed exile from the wider life of spiritual activity. Yet, in other contexts, these stairways have led not only to enhanced spiritual receptivity but also to a revitalized capacity to serve as an agent of life-affirming activity. Although history alone cannot tell us what actions are truthful or right, let us hope that it can provide us at least a little more wisdom in understanding this enduring impulse in American religious life.

NOTES

Chapter 1

1. The most helpful introduction to the religious and cultural history of hallucinogenic drugs is Richard Evans Schultes and Albert Hofmann, *Plants of the Gods: Origins of Hallucinogenic Use* (New York: McGraw-Hill, 1979). My introductory section relies heavily upon their work.

2. Readers may also wish to consult Ronald Siegel's valuable study on the cultural history of drug use, *Intoxication: Life in Pursuit of Artificial Paradise* (New York: E. P. Dutton, 1989).

3. A discussion of the origin and scholarly use of the term entheogen can be found in the introduction to Robert Forte, ed., *Entheogens and the Future of Religion* (San Francisco: Council on Spiritual Practices, 1997). As Forte indicates, the term entheogen is used "to distinguish the religious nature of these substances and the experiences they evoke from their effects in other contexts, for which there are other terms, psychedelic or hallucinogen" (p. 1).

4. The most important studies of the religious use of hallucinogenic mushrooms have been written by R. Gordon Wasson. See his *Soma: Divine Mushroom of Immortality* (New York: Harcourt Brace Jovanovich, 1968), *The Wondrous Mushroom: Mycolatry in Mesoamerica* (New York: McGraw-Hill, 1980), and *The Road to Eleusis: Unveiling the Secret of the Mysteries* (New York: Harcourt Brace Jovanovich, 1979).

5. See Barbara Meyerhoff, *Peyote Hunt: The Sacred Journey of the Huichol Indians* (Ithaca: Cornell University Press, 1974), and Kathleen Berrin, ed., *Art of the Huichol Indians* (New York: Abrams, 1979).

6. Mircea Eliade, *The Sacred and the Profane* (New York: Harper, 1961), p. 14. Further discussions of the distinction between the sacred and the profane can be found in Arnold van Gennep's *The Rites of Passage* (Chicago: University of Chicago Press, 1960), and Emile Durkheim's *The Elementary Forms of the Religious Life* (New York: Free Press, 1965).

7. Rudolf Otto, *The Idea of the Holy* (New York: Oxford University Press, 1958).

8. Eliade, *The Sacred and the Profane*, p. 12.

9. Larry D. Shinn, *Two Sacred Worlds: Experience and Structure in the World's Religions* (Nashville, TN: Abingdon Press, 1977). This section on drugs and "two sacred worlds" relies heavily upon Shinn's discussion of experience and structure in the world's religions.

10. Ibid., p. 15.

11. Felicitas Goodman, *Ecstasy, Ritual, and Alternate Reality* (Bloomington: Indiana University Press, 1988).

12. Marlene Dobkin de Rios, *Hallucinogens: Cross-Cultural Perspectives* (Albuquerque: University of New Mexico Press, 1984), p. 203.

13. See Catherine Albanese, *Nature Religion in America* (Chicago: University of Chicago Press, 1990).

14. Mary Douglas, *Purity and Danger* (New York: Penguin, 1970), p. 18.

15. William Clebsch, *American Religious Thought* (Chicago: University of Chicago Press, 1973), p. 2.

16. Ralph Waldo Emerson, *The Complete Works of Ralph Waldo Emerson*, 12 vols. (New York: AMS Press, 1968), 1: 10.

17. Ralph Waldo Emerson, *The Early Lectures of Ralph Waldo Emerson*, 3 vols. (Cambridge: Harvard University Press, 1959), 2: 89.

18. Emerson, *Complete Works*, 1: 63. A more thorough discussion of how this fascination with the religious or metaphysical dimensions of the "recesses of the mind" has influenced the subsequent history of both American psychological thought and American religious thought can be found in Robert C. Fuller, *Americans and the Unconscious* (New York: Oxford University Press, 1986).

Chapter 2

1. Carlos Castenada, *The Teachings of Don Juan: A Yaqui Way of Knowledge* (Berkeley: University of California Press, 1968); *A Separate Reality: Further Teachings with Don Juan* (New York: Simon and Schuster, 1971); *Journey to Ixtlan: The Lessons of Don Juan* (New York: Simon and Schuster, 1972). A good starting point to review the scholarly controversy surrounding Castenada's books is Weston La Barre's appendix in the fourth edition of *The Peyote Cult* (New York: Archon Books, 1975), pp. 271–275. See also Paul Riesman's review of Castenada's works in *The New York Times Book Review* (October 22, 1972), and R. Gordon Wasson's review in *Economic Botany* 26 (January-March 1972), pp. 98–99.

2. From Walter Goldschmidt's foreword to the 1990 edition of *The Teachings of Don Juan* (New York: Pocket Books, 1990), p. 10.

3. From the inside cover of *A Separate Reality* (New York: Pocket Books, 1972).

4. Ake Hultkrantz, *The Religions of the American Indians* (Berkeley: University of California Press, 1967), p. 15.

5. Lewis M. Hopfe, *Religions of the World* (Beverly Hills, CA: Glencoe Press, 1976), p. 35.

6. Hultkrantz, *The Religions of the American Indians*, p. 75.

7. An extended discussion of the distinction between the terms medicine man and shaman can be found in Ake Hultkrantz, "The Shaman and the Medicine-Man," *Social Sciences and Medicine* 20 (1985): 511–515.

8. We might consider, for example, how a shaman affects cure when a person has become ill due to soul loss. The diagnosis presupposes that the sick person's soul has left the body. This may have occurred by the soul's free choice—the soul simply

wandered off into the natural surroundings. At other times, the soul may have been snatched away by malevolent spirits, possibly at the prompting of a rival shaman or sorcerer. In these cases, the shaman must send his own soul or perhaps one of his guardian spirits to retrieve the runaway or captured soul. Occasionally the soul has been carried away by the dead. When this occurs the sick person, whose soul has now crossed over into the land of the dead, dies. A skillful shaman is capable of entering the land of the dead and bringing the soul back. Such a feat is accomplished in spite of great personal danger. Legends tell of shamans being attacked by the dead and forced to battle for their very lives. In any event, such heroic rescues of lost souls require that a shaman be able to enter an exceptional trance state. Only by entering into an ecstatic trance can the shaman release his own soul from his body, cross the threshold into the invisible spirit world, and thus recapture the patient's soul. See Hultkrantz, *The Religions of the American Indians*, pp. 89–91.

9. Mircea Eliade, *Shamanism: Archaic Techniques of Ecstasy* (Princeton: Princeton University Press, 1972), p. 401.

10. Discussions of the history of hallucinogenic botanical substances can be found in Richard E. Schultes and Albert Hofmann, *Plants of the Gods: Origins of Hallucinogenic Use* (New York: McGraw-Hill, 1979); Weston La Barre, "Hallucinogens and the Shamanic Origins of Religion," in Peter Furst, ed., *The Flesh of the Gods: The Ritual Use of Hallucinogens* (New York: Praeger, 1972); and R. Gordon Wasson, *SOMA: Divine Mushroom of Immortality* (New York: Harcourt Brace Jovanovich, 1968).

11. See Richard E. Schultes, "Hallucinogenic Plants of the New World," *Harvard Review* 1 (1963): 18–32, and "Botanical Sources of the New World Narcotics," *Psychedelic Review* 1 (1963): 145–166.

12. See Weston La Barre's appendix "The New World Narcotic Complex," in *The Peyote Cult*, 4th ed., pp. 263–265; La Barre's article "The Narcotic Complex of the New World," *Diogenes* 48 (1964): 125–138, and his article "Hallucinogens and the Shamanic Origins of Religion," in Furst, ed., *Flesh of the Gods*, pp. 261–278.

13. La Barre, "Hallucinogens and the Shamanic Origins of Religion," p. 272.

14. See Johan Huizinga, *The Waning of the Middle Ages* (New York: Doubleday, 1954).

15. An investigation into witchcraft in 1324 reported that "in rifleing the closet of the ladie, they found a Pipe of oyntment, wherewith she greased a staffe, upon which she ambled and galloped through thick and thin, when and in what manner she listed." Later, in the fifteenth century, a similar account stated: "But the vulgar believe and the witches confess, than on certain days and nights they annoint a staff and ride on it to the appointed place or annoint themselves under the arms and in other hairy places and sometimes carry charms under the hair." See Schultes and Hofmann, *Plants of the Gods*, pp. 88–90.

16. Weston La Barre, "Old and New World Narcotics: A Statistical Question and an Ethnological Reply," *Economic Botany* 24 (1970): 79.

17. A discussion of the physical effects of ingesting *Banisteriopsis* can be found in Richard Schultes, "Hallucinogens in the Western Hemisphere," in Furst, ed., *Flesh of the Gods*, pp. 33–40.

18. Ibid., p. 35.

19. G. Reichel-Dolmatoff, *The Shaman and the Jaguar: A Study of Narcotic Drugs Among the Indians of Colombia* (Philadelphia: Temple University Press, 1975), p. 133.

20. Ibid., p. 201.

21. Ibid., p. 202.

22. Weston La Barre, "Native American Beers," *American Anthropologist* 40 (1938): 224–234.

23. Ibid., p. 232.

24. Schultes and Hofmann, *Plants of the Gods,* p. 85.

25. Ibid., p. 148.

26. Schultes, "Hallucinogens in the Western Hemisphere," p. 11.

27. Schultes and Hofmann, *Plants of the Gods,* p. 111.

28. See La Barre, *The Peyote Cult,* pp. 134–136.

29. Schultes and Hofmann, *Plants of the Gods,* p. 111.

30. La Barre, *The Peyote Cult,* p. 136. La Barre's account draws upon the work of A. H. Gayton, *The Narcotic Plant Datura in Aboriginal American Culture* (Thesis, University of California Library, 1926).

31. See Schultes and Hofmann, *Plants of the Gods,* p. 111.

32. James Howard, "The Mescal Bean Cult of the Central and Southern Plains," *American Anthropologist* 59 (1957): 75–87.

33. We might also draw attention to the roles that the coca plant and marijuana played in Native American religious life. In South America, the coca plant is deified and its stimulating properties thought to be a gift of the gods. Although it has not factored into North American native cultures, it is quite possible that the chewing of tobacco by American Indian groups was historically connected to the South American practice of chewing coca leaves. See W. Golden Mortimer, *Peru: History of Coca, "The Divine Plant" of the Incas* (New York: J. H. Vail, 1901); and Ronald Siegel, *Intoxication: Life in Pursuit of Artificial Paradise* (New York: E. P. Dutton, 1989). It seems that marijuana was associated with Native American visionary and prophetic states. It was also carried to counteract sorcery. In some instances, marijuana has been substituted for peyote in peyote ceremonies. See Weston La Barre's discussion of Native American use of marijuana in *The Peyote Cult,* pp. 20–22, 133–135.

34. La Barre, "Hallucinogens and the Origins of Religion," p. 276.

35. See Ralph Linton, *Use of Tobacco Among North American Indians* (Chicago: Field Museum of Natural History, 1924).

36. See Joseph Epes Brown, ed., *The Sacred Pipe: Black Elk's Account of the Seven Rites of the Oglala Sioux* (Baltimore: Penguin Books, 1971).

37. For analyses of the physiological effects of nicotine, see D. J. K. Balfour, ed., *Nicotine and the Smoking Habit* (New York: Pergamon Press, 1984).

38. La Barre, "The Narcotic Complex of the New World," p. 129.

39. See Francis Robicsek, *The Smoking Gods* (Norman: University of Oklahoma Press, 1978). Another work on shamans' use of tobacco is Johannes Wilbert's *Tobacco and Shamanism in South America* (New Haven: Yale University Press, 1987).

40. Paul Radin, *The Winnebago Tribe* (Lincoln: University of Nebraska Press, 1970), p. 97.

41. Willard Park, *Shamanism in Western North America* (Evanston, IL: Northwestern University Press, 1938).

42. William K. Powers, *Yuwipi* (Lincoln: University of Nebraska Press, 1982), p. 29.

43. Linton, *Use of Tobacco Among North American Indians,* pp. 25–26.

44. Brown, ed., *The Sacred Pipe,* p. 21.

45. The three best accounts of North American peyote rituals (especially owing to their excellent bibliographies) are J. S. Slotkin, *The Peyote Religion: A Study in Indian-White Relations* (Glencoe, IL: Free Press, 1956); La Barre, *The Peyote Cult;* and Omer Stewart, *Peyote Religion: A History* (Norman: University of Oklahoma Press, 1987).

46. Overviews of the pharmacological properties of peyote can be found in La Barre, *The Peyote Cult,* pp. 138–150; and Schultes and Hofmann, *Plants of the Gods,* pp. 132–143.

47. An interesting anecdote concerning peyote's tendency to produce extreme nausea concerns the famous American philosopher-psychologist William James. In 1896 James received some buttons of peyote from S. Weir Mitchell, who was among those in the medical community to whom the United States government had distributed a supply of peyote buttons for general research purposes. Mitchell had ingested peyote and had visions of jewel-like color. James took just one button and, as he later wrote his brother Henry, became "violently sick for 24 hours." He had "no other symptom whatever" except a hangover the next day. Vowing never to subject himself to such nausea again, he wrote Henry that "I will take the visions on trust." See Hal Bridges, *American Mysticism* (New York: Harper & Row, 1970), p. 16.

48. The most detailed account of Huichol peyote use is Barbara Myerhoff's *Peyote Hunt: The Sacred Journey of the Huichol Indians* (Ithaca: Cornell University Press, 1974). Also valuable resources are Stacy B. Schaefer and Peter T. Furst, eds., *People of the Peyote: Huichol Indian History, Religion, and Survival* (Albuquerque: University of New Mexico Press, 1996); and Kathleen Berrin, ed., *Art of the Huichol Indians* (New York: Harry N. Abrams, 1978).

49. Barbara Myerhoff, "Peyote and the Mystic Vision," in Berrin, ed., *Art of the Huichol Indians,* p. 56.

50. Excellent analyses of the diffusion of peyote rituals among North American Indians can be found in Ruth Shonle, "Peyote, The Giver of Visions," *American Anthropologist* 27 (1925): 53–75; David Aberle and Omer Stewart, *Navaho and Ute Peyotism: A Chronological and Distributional Study* (Boulder: University of Colorado Press, 1957); and Omer Stewart and David Aberle, *Peyotism in the West* (Salt Lake City: University of Utah Press, 1984).

51. Shonle, "Peyote, The Giver of Visions," p. 57.

52. Ibid., p. 59.

53. La Barre, *The Peyote Cult,* p. 51; and Slotkin, *The Peyote Religion,* p. 29.

54. More detailed descriptions of peyote rites are to be found in La Barre, *The Peyote Cult,* pp. 43ff; Slotkin, *The Peyote Religion,* pp. 22ff; and Stewart and Aberle, *Peyotism in the West.*

55. From La Barre, *The Peyote Cult,* p. 48.

56. Ibid., p. 50.

57. Ibid., p. 166.

58. See the discussion of white efforts to ban peyote use in Slotkin, *The Peyote Religion,* pp. 50–57.

59. Ibid., p. 55.

60. See the discussion of "The Native American Church and the Law," in La Barre, *The Peyote Cult,* pp. 265–266.

61. The Peyote Way Church of God is a 160 acre religious sanctuary dedicated to the sacramental use of peyote. Although its formal membership in the 1990s was estimated to be approximately eighty or ninety members, it maintains an active web site presence dedicated to the promotion of books and pamphlets advocating the spiritual use of peyote and other entheogens.

62. Omer Stewart and David Aberle offer an interesting analysis of the "ideology of peyote" in *Peyote in the West,* p. 64.

63. The best analysis of the social functions performed by peyotism is to be found in Slotkin, *The Peyote Religion,* pp. 18–21, 35–45.

64. Myerhoff, "Peyote and the Mystic Vision," p. 56.

Chapter 3

1. Thomas De Quincey, *Confessions of an English Opium-Eater* (New York: Oxford University Press, 1955), p. 211.

2. Martin Booth, *Opium: A History* (London: Simon & Schuster, 1996), p. 35.

3. See David T. Courtwright, *Dark Paradise: Opiate Addiction in America Before 1940* (Cambridge: Harvard University Press, 1982), p. 9. See also Caroline Jean Acker, "From All-Purpose Anodyne to Marker of Deviance: Physicians' Attitudes Towards Opiates in the U.S. from 1890 to 1940," and John Parascandola, "The Drug Habit: The Association of the Word 'Drug' with Abuse in American History," in Roy Porter and Mikulas Teich, eds., *Drugs and Narcotics in History* (Cambridge: Cambridge University Press, 1995). An excellent comparison of British and American patterns of drug use is the afterword of Terry Parssinen's *Secret Passions, Secret Remedies: Narcotic Drugs in British Society, 1820–1930* (Philadelphia: Institute for the Study of Human Issues, 1983).

4. Jill Jonnes, "The Rise of the Modern Addict," *American Journal of Public Health* 85 (August 1995), p. 1160.

5. See Martin Booth's summary of the twentieth-century spread of drugs in American society in *Opium,* pp. 190–202.

6. A discussion of Blood's nitrous oxide–induced mystical philosophy can be found in Hal Bridges, *American Mysticism* (New York: Harper & Row, 1970), pp. 15–19.

7. James's initial publication on nitrous oxide appeared in *Mind* 7 (1882): 186–208. It also appears in an abridged form as "Subjective Effects of Nitrous Oxide," in Charles Tart, ed., *Altered States of Consciousness* (Garden City, NY: John Wiley & Sons, 1969), pp. 367–370.

8. See Dmitri Tymoczko's "The Nitrous Oxide Philosopher," *Atlantic Monthly* (May 1996): 93–101. Although Tymoczko's article gives the mistaken impression that James frequently used nitrous oxide when there is no evidence to indicate that he ever used the gas more than his one initial experiment, the article does help to situate the experience within James's professional career and the larger cultural issues raised by the connection of drugs and mysticism.

9. William James, *The Varieties of Religious Experience* (Cambridge: Harvard University Press, 1985), p. 307.

10. Ibid., p. 308.

11. Ibid., p. 408.

12. Ibid., p. 308. Readers might wish to consult Eugene Taylor's *William James on Consciousness Beyond the Margin* (Princeton: Princeton University Press, 1996) for a discussion of how James's interest in extramarginal states of consciousness influenced his understandings of scientific psychology.

13. William James, *A Pluralistic Universe* (New York: E. P. Dutton, 1971), p. 264.

14. William Clebsch, *American Religious Thought* (Chicago: University of Chicago Press, 1973), p. 171.

15. Wade Clark Roof, *A Generation of Seekers: The Spiritual Journeys of the Baby Boom Generation* (San Francisco: HarperSanFrancisco, 1993).

16. Ibid., p. 22.

17. Perhaps the best overall account of the cultural drama enacted by the introduction of mescaline and LSD into American society is Jay Stevens's *Storming Heaven: LSD and the American Dream* (New York: Harper & Row, 1988). Stevens provides a well-written account of the meeting between Osmond and Huxley on pp. 44ff.

18. Aldous Huxley, *The Doors of Perception* (San Francisco: Harper & Row, 1954), p. 16.

19. Ibid., p. 17.

20. Ibid., p. 19.

21. Ibid., p. 22.

22. Quoted in Stevens, *Storming Heaven*, p. 49.

23. Albert Hofmann, *LSD: My Problem Child* (New York: McGraw-Hill, 1980), p. 15.

24. Stevens, *Storming Heaven*, p. 5.

25. Hofmann, *LSD*, p. 195.

26. Ibid., p. 198.

27. Ibid., p. 209.

28. This list is excerpted from the summation of psychological effects appearing in R. Masters and Jean Houston, *The Varieties of Psychedelic Experience* (New York: Holt, Rinehart and Winston, 1966), p. 5.

29. Martin M. Katz and Irene Waskow, "Characterizing the Psychological State Produced by LSD," *Journal of Abnormal Psychology* 73 (1963): 460–469.

30. Jane Dunlap, *Exploring Inner Space: Personal Experiences Under LSD–25* (New York: Harcourt, Brace & World, 1961), p. 196.

31. Timothy Leary, cited in Rick Fields, "A High History of Buddhism," *Tricycle: The Buddhist Review* (Fall 1996): p. 47. Readers interested in Leary's storied career

should read his two autobiographical accounts, *High Priest* (New York: World Publishing, 1968), and *Flashbacks* (Los Angeles: Tarcher, 1983). See also Jay Stevens's *Storming Heaven;* Robert Ellwood, *The Sixties Spiritual Awakening* (New Brunswick, NJ: Rutgers University Press, 1994), pp. 82–85, 151–153; and Robert S. DeRopp's entry on "Psychedelic Drugs," in Mircea Eliade, ed., *Encyclopedia of Religion*, vol. 12 (New York: Collier Macmillan, 1987), pp. 53–55.

32. See Walter Pahnke, "Drugs and Mysticism: An Analysis of the Relationship Between Psychedelic Drugs and the Mystical Consciousness (Unpublished doctoral dissertation, Harvard University, 1966). See also Walter N. Pahnke and William A. Richards, "Implications of LSD and Experimental Mysticism," *Journal of Religion and Health* 5 (1966): 175–208; and Walter Pahnke, "The Mystical and/or Religious Element in the Psychedelic Experience," in D. H. Salman and R. H. Prince, eds., *Do Psychedelics Have Religious Implications?* (Montreal: R. M. Bucke Memorial Society, 1967), pp. 41–56. Leary's account of the Marsh Chapel experiment can be found in his *High Priest*, pp. 291–318. An excellent overview of the psychological study of the religious dimensions of psychedelic drug use can be found in David Wulff, *Psychology of Religion* (New York: John Wiley & Sons, 1991).

33. Walter Clark, *Chemical Ecstasy: Psychedelic Drugs and Religion* (New York: Sheed & Ward, 1969), p. 77.

34. Ram Dass, *Remember. Be Here Now* (San Cristobal, NM: Lama Foundation, 1971). This unusual book contains an autobiographical account of Alpert's introduction to Leary and their subsequent collaboration prior to his spiritual metamorphosis.

35. See Ellwood, *The Sixties Spiritual Awakening*, p. 193. Ellwood suggests that the word hippie was popularized by the March 1967 article in *Ramparts* by Warren Hinckle, "The Social History of the Hippies."

36. Stevens, *Storming Heaven*, p. 208.

37. Timothy Leary, cited in Timothy Miller, *The Hippies and American Values* (Knoxville: University of Tennessee Press, 1991), p. 19. See the discussion of this same point in Ellwood, *The Sixties Spiritual Awakening*, p. 314.

38. Leary, *High Priest*, p. 154.

39. Alan Watts, *Cloud-Hidden, Whereabouts Unknown* (New York: Random House, 1973), p. 35.

40. Leary, *High Priest*, p. 285.

41. Sidney Cohen, *The Beyond Within: The LSD Story* (New York: Atheneum, 1965), p. 60.

42. Robert E. Mogar, "Current Status and Future Trends in Psychedelic (LSD) Research," *Journal of Humanistic Psychology* 2 (1965): 147–166.

43. Masters and Houston, *The Varieties of Psychedelic Experience*, p. 3.

44. Ibid., p. 316.

45. Leary, *High Priest*, p. 296.

46. Ram Dass, *Remember. Be Here Now*.

47. Masters and Houston, *The Varieties of Psychedelic Experience*, p. 148.

48. Ibid., p. 266.

49. The most succinct of Stanislav Grof's books is his *Realms of the Human Unconscious: Observations from LSD Research* (New York: Viking Press, 1975). Other important books include his *Beyond the Brain: Birth, Death, and Transcendence in Psychotherapy* (Albany: State University of New York Press, 1985), and his book with Joan Halifax, *The Human Encounter with Death* (New York: E. P. Dutton, 1978).

50. Grof, *Realms of the Human Unconscious*, p. 95.

51. Huston Smith, "Empirical Metaphysics," in Ralph Metzner, ed., *The Ecstatic Adventure* (New York: Macmillan, 1968), p. 72.

52. Huston Smith, *Forgotten Truth: The Common Vision of the World's Religions* (New York: HarperCollins, 1976).

53. Theodore Roszak, *The Making of a Counter Culture* (Garden City, NY: Doubleday, 1969).

54. See Ellwood, *The Sixties Spiritual Awakening*, pp. 10–15.

55. Spokespersons for the psychedelic or "altered states of consciousness" field of research frequently engaged in philosophical critique of Western scientific paradigms. Perhaps the most representative of these comes in Charles Tart's *States of Consciousness* (New York: Dutton, 1975).

56. Richard Alpert and Timothy Leary, in the foreword to Alan Watts, *The Joyous Cosmology* (New York: Vintage Books, 1965), p. x.

57. Aldous Huxley, article originally appearing in *Playboy*, reprinted as "Culture and the Individual," in David Solomon, ed., *LSD: The Consciousness Expanding Drug* (New York: G. P. Putnam's Sons, 1964), p. 32.

58. Marlene Dobkin de Rios, *Hallucinogens: Cross-Cultural Perspectives* (Albuquerque: University of New Mexico Press, 1984), p. 203.

59. Lewis Yablonsky, *The Hippie Trip* (New York: Pegasus, 1968), p. 35.

60. Warren Hinckle, "The Social History of the Hippies," cited in Ellwood, *The Sixties Spiritual Awakening*, p. 196.

61. See Charles Perry, *The Haight-Ashbury: A History* (New York: Random House, 1984).

62. Ibid., p. 122.

63. See Timothy Miller's discussion of "dope churches" in his *The Hippies and American Values*, pp. 31–34.

64. J. Gordon Melton, *The Encyclopedia of American Religions*, 5th ed. (Detroit: Gale Research, 1996), pp. 145ff.

65. Timothy Leary, quoted in Miller, *The Hippies and American Values*, p. 32.

66. Ibid., p. 19.

67. Timothy Leary, "The Religious Experience: Its Production and Interpretation," *Journal of Psychedelic Drugs* 1 (1967): 7.

68. In his *A Generation of Seekers*, Wade Clark Roof provides a segmented analysis of the spirituality of Baby Boomers by their degree of "exposure to the '60s." The greater the degree of exposure to the '60s counterculture, the greater the likelihood that individuals will describe themselves as "spiritual" rather than "religious." Exposure to the '60s is negatively correlated with putting value on "sticking to a faith," whereas it is positively correlated with valuing an ongoing "exploration of teachings." Furthermore, the greater the degree of exposure to the '60s, the less

likely individuals are to embrace conventional views of God and the more likely they are to embrace pantheistic or Eastern religious views.

69. William McLoughlin, *Revivals, Awakenings, and Reform* (Chicago: University of Chicago Press, 1978), p. xiii.

70. See the concluding chapter ("Final Reflections on the Sixties") of Robert Ellwood's *The Sixties Spiritual Awakening*, pp. 326–336.

71. Alan Watts, "Psychedelics and Religious Experience," in Bernard Aaronson and Humphry Osmond, eds., *Psychedelics* (Garden City, NY: Doubleday, 1970), p. 132. An article appearing in Timothy Leary's *Psychedelic Review* also reported the use of psychedelics to explore the nature of mystical experience. John Blofeld ingested one-half gram of mescaline to test Huxley's claim that mescaline can induce yogic experiences of a higher order. Blofeld reported that psychedelics can indeed enable us to discard our illusory egos and elicit bliss. His mescaline experience gave him (1) an awareness of undifferentiated unity, (2) a sense of unutterable bliss, and (3) a vivid awareness that all things are devoid of own-being as implied in the Buddhist doctrine of "dharma." See his "A High Yogic Experience Achieved with Mescaline," *Psychedelic Review* 3 (1966): 27–32.

72. Jack Kornfield, interview in *Tricycle: The Buddhist Review* (Fall 1996): 35.

73. Magazine and Web poll, reported in *Tricycle: The Buddhist Review* (Fall 1996): 44.

74. Ram Dass, interview in ibid., p. 102.

75. Joan Halifax, interview in ibid.

76. Dobkin de Rios, *Hallucinogens: Cross-Cultural Perspectives*, p. 203.

77. Watts, "Psychedelics and Religious Experience," p. 131.

78. Smith, *Forgotten Truth*, p. 168.

79. John Robertson, "Uncontainable Joy," in Metzner, ed., *The Ecstatic Adventure*, p. 86.

Chapter 4

1. See E. O. Wilson's discussion of how biologically rooted concepts such as tribalism, territorialism, and boundary setting explain human group behavior in *Sociobiology: The New Synthesis* (Cambridge, MA: Belknap Press, 1975), pp. 564–565.

2. This chapter is an integration of materials found in two of my earlier publications. Readers might wish to consult *Religion and Wine: A Cultural History of Wine Drinking in the United States* (Knoxville: University of Tennessee Press, 1996), and "Wine, Symbolic Boundary Setting, and American Religious Communities," *Journal of the American Academy of Religion* 63 (Fall 1995): 497–517. This article appears in a special thematic issue of the *Journal of the American Academy of Religion* that contains six other essays focusing on various issues pertaining to the relationship between religion and food.

3. Benjamin Franklin, cited in J. C. Furnas, *The Life and Times of the Late Demon Rum* (New York: Capricorn Books, 1973), p. 17. Below is the text of Franklin's "drinking song," penned about 1745. Honest old Noah first planted the Vine, And mended his Morals by drinking its Wine; And justly the drinking of water de-

cry'd; For he knew that all Mankind, by drinking it dy'd . . . From this Piece of history plainly we find That Water's good neither for Body nor Mind; That Virtue & Safety in Wine-bibbing's found While all that drink Water deserve to be drown'd. . . .

4. Benjamin Franklin, cited in Alexis Bespaloff, ed., *The Fireside Book of Wine: An Anthology for Wine Drinkers* (New York: Simon and Schuster, 1977), p. 219. Perhaps the most memorable of Franklin's theological discourses on wine was his 1779 letter to the Abbé Morellet. Morellet had earlier drafted a drinking song that suggested that the real reason for the American Revolution was Benjamin's desire to drink good French wine rather than drab English beer. In his letter, Franklin responded by arguing that only Divine Providence could account for the glorious location of the elbow. He proposed that the elbow is positive proof that God desires us to drink wine. After all, had God placed the elbow either lower or higher on the arm, we would not be able to lift our wine glass directly to our mouths. Yet, "from the actual situation of the elbow, we are enabled to drink at our ease, the glass going directly to the mouth. Let us, then, with glass in hand, adore this benevolent wisdom;—let us adore and drink!"

5. See John D. Crossan, *The Historical Jesus: The Life of a Mediterranean Jewish Peasant* (San Francisco: HarperSanFrancisco, 1991). Crossan argues that communal eating (and by implication, the drinking of wine) was at the heart of Jesus' ministry: "His strategy, implicitly for himself and explicitly for his followers, was the combination of free healing and common eatings, a religious and economic egalitarianism that negated alike and at once the hierarchical and patronal normalcies of Jewish religion and Roman power. . . . He was neither broker nor mediator but, somewhat paradoxically, the announcer that neither should exist between humanity and divinity or between humanity and itself. Miracle and parable, healing and eating were calculated to force individuals into unmediated physical and spiritual contact with God and unmediated physical and spiritual contact with one another. He announced, in other words, the brokerless kingdom of God."

6. W. K. C. Guthrie, *The Greeks and Their Gods* (Boston: Beacon Press, 1950), p. 174.

7. Although Reformation leaders such as Luther, Zwingli, Calvin, Brucer, and Cranmer differed on many points, their new conception of faith led them to agree on radically severing the relationship of the Eucharist (Lord's Supper) to the Roman Catholic penitential system. The most obvious reason for this was to undercut the Roman Catholic Church's claim of apostolic succession through which only its bishops and priests were considered to be empowered to perform the Church's saving sacraments. Other factors that led to Protestantism's break with the doctrine of transubstantiation pertained to changing views of the individual's relationship to God, renewed efforts to return Christian practice to the letter of scripture, and increasing intellectual pressures to accommodate Christianity to the rising spirit of secularism (and its tendency to renounce supernaturalistic modes of thinking).

8. Emil Oberholzer, *Delinquent Saints: Disciplinary Action in the Early Congregational Churches of Massachusetts* (New York: Columbia University Press, 1956), p. 152.

9. Reliable discussions of the use of wine in ancient Israel can be found in Roland de Vaux, *Ancient Israel* (New York: McGraw-Hill, 1965), and in the entry on wine in *Encyclopedia Judaica* (Jerusalem: Keter Publishers, 1971). Sources that describe the use of wine in contemporary Jewish life are Rabbi Hayim Halvey Donin's books, *To Be a Jew: A Guide to Jewish Observance in Contemporary Life* (New York: Basic Books, 1977) and *To Pray as a Jew* (New York: Basic Books, 1980). Also helpful is Rabbi Gersion Appel's *The Concise Code of Jewish Law* (New York: Yeshiva University Press, 1977).

10. A more thorough description of the prescriptions governing the use of wine in Jewish religious observances can be found in Charles Snyder, *Alcohol and the Jews: A Cultural Study of Drinking and Sobriety* (Glencoe, IL: Free Press, 1958), pp. 19–34.

11. Robert F. Bales, "The 'Fixation Factor' in Alcohol Addiction: An Hypothesis Derived from a Comparative Study of Irish and Jewish Social Norms," cited in Snyder, *Alcohol and the Jews*, p. 21.

12. Robert Bales, cited in Snyder, *Alcohol and the Jews*, p. 34.

13. See Mary Douglas, *Purity and Danger* (New York: Penguin Books, 1970), and "Pollution," in her *Implicit Meanings* (London: Routledge and Kegan Paul, 1975), pp. 47–59.

14. *The Jewish Dietary Law* (New York: Rabbinical Assembly of America, 1982), p. 73.

15. Appel, *The Concise Code of Jewish Law*, p. 274.

16. Timothy Weber, "The Baptist Tradition," in Ronald L. Numbers and Darrel W. Amundsen, eds., *Caring and Curing: Health and Medicine in the Western Religious Traditions* (New York: Macmillan, 1986), p. 297.

17. See Sydney Ahlstrom's discussion of the "sectarian impulse" in *A Religious History of the American People* (New Haven: Yale University Press, 1972), pp. 472–490; and Winthrop Hudson, *Religion in America* (New York: Charles Scribner's Sons, 1981), pp. 182–205.

18. Selden Bacon, "Alcohol and Complex Society," in David Pittman and Charles Snyder, eds., *Society, Culture, and Drinking Patterns* (New York: John Wiley and Sons, 1962), pp. 78–93.

19. Donald Horton, "The Function of Alcohol in Primitive Societies: A Cross-Cultural Study," *Quarterly Journal for the Study of Alcohol* 4 (1943): 199–230.

20. Bacon, "Alcohol and Complex Society."

21. See William R. Perkins and Barthnius L. Lick, *History of the Amana Society* (1891; reprint, New York: Arno Press, 1975); and Bertha Shambaugh, *Amana That Was and Amana That Is* (Iowa City: Historical Society of Iowa, 1932).

22. George Kraus (as told to E. Mae Fritz), *The Story of an Amana Winemaker* (Iowa City, IA: Penfield Press, 1984), p. 45.

23. Mary Douglas, "On Deciphering a Meal," in *Implicit Meanings*, p. 260.

24. Ibid.

25. Of further interest is the use of wine by the Harmony Society led by George Rapp. First settling in Harmony, Pennsylvania, Rapp eventually led his followers to New Harmony in the Wabash Valley of Indiana. There, as in Pennsylvania, the

groups constructed large wine cellars and produced what was reputed to be excellent wine. See my *Religion and Wine*, pp. 37–38.

26. *Doctrine and Covenants,* Section 32, 2.

27. Ibid., Section 27, 3–4. Many Latter-day Saints interpret the word "new" to mean unfermented grape juice.

28. Ibid., Section 27, 5.

29. Ibid., Section 89, 5–6.

30. Joseph Smith, *History of the Church of Jesus Christ of Latter-Day Saints, Period 1, History of Joseph Smith, the Prophet, By Himself,* 5 vols. (Salt Lake City: Deseret, 1954), 2: 369.

31. Ibid., p. 378.

32. Ibid., p. 446.

33. LaMar Petersen, *Hearts Made Glad: The Charges of Intemperance Against Joseph Smith the Mormon Prophet* (Salt Lake City: n.p., 1975), p. 167.

34. Ibid., p. 84.

35. Oliver Huntington, cited in Petersen, *Hearts Made Glad,* p. 156.

36. Diary entries of Apr. 23 and Apr. 29, 1846, by Samuel Richards, cited in Petersen, *Hearts Made Glad,* p. 200.

37. Brigham Young, cited in Leonard Arrington, "An Economic Interpretation of the Word of Wisdom," *Brigham Young University Studies* (1959): 46. LaMar Petersen cites the diary entry of John D. Lee, who visited Brigham Young on May 15, 1867: "On the following day I went to see him in his Mansion where I spent near 1/2 day—verry agreeable indeed. He had a Decanter of Splendid Wine brought in of his own make & said, I want to treat Bro. Lee to as Good an article, I think, as can be bought in Dixie. The wine indeed was a Superior article. He said that he had some 300 gallons & treated about 2000$ worth of Liqueurs yearly & continued that we [he] wished that some one would take his wine at 5$ Per gallon & sell it, where upon Pres. D. H. Wells Said that he would take 200 gals. at 6$ a gallon &c. (*Hearts Made Glad,* p. 156).

38. Arrington, "An Economic Interpretation of the Word of Wisdom," p. 47.

39. Leonard Arrington's article provides a convincing argument that the Word of Wisdom functioned to help the Latter-day Saints in Utah achieve economic self-sufficiency. Further interpretation of the cultural setting in which Joseph Smith received the Word of Wisdom can be found in Thomas G. Alexander, *Mormonism in Transition: A History of the Latter-Day Saints, 1890–1930* (Urbana: University of Illinois Press, 1986), pp. 258–271.

40. See R. Laurence Moore, "Insiders and Outsiders in American Historical Narrative and American History," *American Historical Review* 87 (1982): 390–412.

41. See Victor Turner, *The Ritual Process* (Ithaca: Cornell University Press, 1969), pp. 131–140.

42. William James, *The Varieties of Religious Experience* (Cambridge: Harvard University Press, 1985), p. 19. For further discussions of Harris's role in both American religious and psychological thought, see Robert C. Fuller, *Mesmerism and the American Cure of Souls* (Philadelphia: University of Pennsylvania Press, 1982), and Fuller, *Americans and the Unconscious* (New York: Oxford University Press, 1986).

43. Thomas Lake Harris, quoted in R. Laurence Moore, *In Search of White Crows* (New York: Oxford University Press, 1977), p. 12.

44. Ibid., p. 18.

45. Thomas Lake Harris, quoted in Herbert Schneider and George Lawton, *A Prophet and a Pilgrim* (New York: Columbia University Press, 1942), p. 160.

46. Thomas Lake Harris, quoted in Leon Adams, *The Wines of America* (New York: McGraw-Hill, 1990), p. 142.

47. Schneider and Lawton, *A Prophet and a Pilgrim*, p. 167.

48. The following information is contained in a pamphlet published by Summum titled *The First Encounter.*

49. The basic beliefs and practices of Summum are contained in Summum Bonum Amen Ra's *SUMMUM: Sealed Except to the Open Mind* (Salt Lake City: Summum, 1988).

50. From a Summum pamphlet titled *Nectar of the Gods.*

Chapter 5

1. There are several excellent discussions of unchurched religion in the United States. Helpful introductions to this topic are Catherine Albanese's chapter on cultural religion in *America: Religions and Religion* (Belmont, CA: Wadsworth, 1981); and Peter Williams, *Popular Religion in America* (Englewood Cliffs, NJ: Prentice-Hall, 1980). Of further help are Charles H. Lippy's *Being Religious American Style: A History of Popular Religiosity in the United States* (Westport, CT: Greenwood Press, 1994), and his *Modern American Popular Religion: A Critical Assessment and Annotated Bibliography* (Westport, CT: Greenwood Press, 1996). Also of value are the twenty essays in Peter H. Van Ness, ed., *Spirituality and the Secular Quest* (New York: Crossroad, 1996).

2. See Roger Finke and Rodney Stark, *The Churching of America, 1776–1990* (New Brunswick, NJ: Rutgers University Press, 1997), pp. 15–16.

3. See Princeton Religion Research Center and the Gallup Organization, *The Unchurched American* (Princeton: Princeton Religion Research Center, 1978).

4. Wade Clark Roof, *A Generation of Seekers: The Spiritual Journeys of the Baby Boom Generation* (San Francisco: HarperSanFrancisco, 1993). It is interesting to note that Roof found that many "highly active seekers" among the Baby Boomers have at some point in their lives experimented with some form of mind- or mood-altering drugs. According to Roof, drugs opened up ways to expand consciousness. Getting high led to psychic adventure, an exciting freedom from conformity that prompted individuals to explore novel philosophies and religions. Roof offers us the example of Mollie, one of the persons whose spiritual journeys feature prominently in his study. Mollie, who began experimenting with drugs in the sixties, "has been on a spiritual quest ever since. She has explored many of the spiritual and human potential alternatives of the post-sixties period: holistic health, macrobiotics, Zen Buddhism, Native American rituals, New Age in its many versions. She's read a lot about reincarnation and world religions. . . . She's an explorer down many religious paths." It would appear that Mollie, much like William James be-

fore her, traveled a path that led from experimental drug use to spiritual outlooks that might be characterized with such words as pluralism, postmodernism, and religious eclecticism.

5. See the review of these studies in Lippy, *Being Religious American Style,* p. 230.

6. Excellent discussions of recent trends in unchurched spirituality can be found in Robert Ellwood's *Alternative Altars* (Chicago: University of Chicago Press, 1979), Ellwood's *The Fifties Spiritual Marketplace* (New Brunswick, NJ: Rutgers University Press, 1997), and *The Sixties Spiritual Awakening* (New Brunswick, NJ: Rutgers University Press, 1994). My *Americans and the Unconscious* (New York: Oxford University Press, 1986) examines how Americans have turned to both academic and popular psychology for symbols depicting humanity's connection with "deeper" forces and powers. My *Alternative Medicine and American Religious Life* (New York: Oxford University Press, 1989) explores the connection between alternative medicines and unchurched American spirituality.

7. Ellwood, *Alternative Altars,* p. 171.

8. Ellwood, *The Fifties Spiritual Marketplace,* p. 20.

9. A Buddhist legend attributes the origin of tea to the sacred actions of Bodhidharma, the founder of the Zen sect of Buddhism. It is told that Bodhidharma once fell asleep during an extremely long meditation. Disgusted with himself for his own weakness, Bodhidharma tore off his eyelids and flung them to the ground. Where the eyelids fell, tea plants sprang up, thus providing other Buddhist priests with a tool for extending the reach and power of their meditation. See Stephen Braun, *Buzz: The Science and Lore of Alcohol and Caffeine* (New York: Oxford University Press, 1996), p. 110.

10. Bruce Lincoln, "Beverages," in Mircea Eliade, ed., *The Encyclopedia of Religion,* 16 vols. (New York: Macmillan, 1987), 2: 119. A more developed account of the tea ceremony can be found in D. T. Suzuki's *Zen and Japanese Culture* (New York: Pantheon, 1959), pp. 269–314.

11. The Kaldi legend has many variations. This account is based upon the version recounted in Ronald Siegel's *Intoxication: Life in Pursuit of Artificial Paradise* (New York: E. P. Dutton, 1989), pp. 38–39. Siegel's account is of interest in that he draws explicit attention to the ways in which humanity's choice of food and drugs has been greatly influenced by observations of the animal kingdom.

12. Claudia Roden, *Coffee: A Connoisseur's Companion* (New York: Random House, 1994), p. 12.

13. David Joel and Karl Schapira, *The Book of Coffee and Tea* (New York: St. Martin's Griffin, 1975), p. 6. Joel's and Schapira's thirty-page history of coffee is among the most readable and reliable of those appearing in popular trade books.

14. Cited in Roden, *Coffee,* p. 14.

15. Joel and Schapira, *The Book of Coffee and Tea,* p. 15.

16. Roden, *Coffee,* p. 27.

17. Joel and Schapira, *The Book of Coffee and Tea,* p. 15.

18. See Catherine Calvert, *The Essential Guide to Coffee* (New York: Hearst Books, 1994), p. 47.

19. Charles Perry, *The Haight-Ashbury* (New York: Random House, 1984), p. 20.

20. Ibid.

21. Stephen Braun provides summarizes the psychopharmacological effects of caffeine in his *Buzz: The Science and Lore of Alcohol and Caffeine*, pp. 107–193.

22. Dawn Campbell and Janet Smith's *The Coffee Book* (Gretna, CA: Pelican, 1995) includes a poem from an eighteenth-century anonymous writer that celebrates coffee's ability to enhance our mental functioning (p. 21): Coffee works a miracle for those of little wit. With every drop it sharpens the mind and doubles the memory. The most barren of authors is thereby made fertile. Every cup empowers us to gabble without pause, Spouting fable as history. . . .

23. Thomas Frank, "The Marriage of Hip and Square," *Harper's Magazine* (November 1997): 34. See also Frank's *The Conquest of Cool* (Chicago: University of Chicago Press, 1997).

24. Howard Schultz, *Pour Your Heart Into It: How Starbucks Built a Company One Cup at a Time* (New York: Hyperion, 1997). Also, see Ray Oldenbury, *The Great Good Place: cafes, coffee shops, community centers, beauty parlors, general stores, bars, hangouts, and how they get you through the day* (New York: Paragon House, 1989).

25. The Chairman and CEO of Starbucks, Howard Schultz, cites Oldenburg in describing Starbucks as "a Third Place—a comfortable, sociable gathering spot away from home and work, like an extension of the front porch" (*Pour Your Heart Into It*, p. 5). Schultz notes that the decor and music found in Starbucks is intended to provide a "gathering place," a forum for "human interaction."

26. Ibid., p. 107.

27. A more extended discussion of how Alcoholics Anonymous functions as a form of unchurched American spirituality can be found in my *Alternative Medicine and American Religious Life*, pp. 99–103. References to the role of "coffee therapy" in Alcoholics Anonymous can be found in Irving P. Gellman's *The Sober Alcoholic: An Organizational Analysis of Alcoholics Anonymous* (New Haven: College and University Press, 1964).

28. See Howard Becker, *Outsiders: Studies in the Sociology of Deviance* (New York: Free Press, 1963), and "History, Culture, and Subjective Experience: An Exploration of Drug-Induced Experiences," *Journal of Health and Social Behavior* 8 (September 1967): 163–176.

29. From the Indian Hemp Drug Commission Report (1893), cited in Solomon Snyder, *Uses of Marijuana* (New York: Oxford University Press, 1971), p. 20.

30. Ronald K. Siegel, *Intoxication: Life in Pursuit of Artificial Paradise* (New York: E. P. Dutton, 1989), p. 146.

31. See Franz Rosenthal, *The Herb Hashish Versus Medieval Muslim Society* (Leiden: E. J. Brill, 1971).

32. See the discussion of marijuana's medical use by Solomon Snyder, Professor of Psychiatry and Pharmacology at Johns Hopkins University School of Medicine, in his *Uses of Marijuana*.

33. Brief social histories of marijuana use in the United States can be found in Lester Grinspoon, *Marihuana Reconsidered* (Cambridge: Harvard University Press, 1971); Canadian Government's Commission of Inquiry, *The Non-Medical Use of Drugs* (New York: Penguin Books, 1971); and Snyder, *Uses of Marijuana*.

34. Canadian Government's Commission of Inquiry, *The Non-Medical Use of Drugs*, p. 117.

35. Snyder, *Uses of Marijuana*, p. 71.

36. Charles Tart, *On Being Stoned: A Psychological Study of Marijuana Intoxication* (Palo Alto: Science and Behavior Books, 1971).

37. Ibid., p. 212.

38. William Novak, *High Culture: Marijuana in the Lives of Americans* (New York: Alfred A. Knopf, 1980), p. 9.

39. See Robert C. Fuller, "Biographical Origins of Psychological Ideas: Freud's Cocaine Studies," *Journal of Humanistic Psychology* 32 (Summer 1992): 67–86.

40. Novak, *High Culture*, p. 12.

41. Ibid., p. 124.

42. Ibid., p. 155.

43. Tart, *On Being Stoned*. Tart devotes considerable space to considerations of marijuana users' occult experiences. Yet only 1 percent of his subjects reported that they usually experience "vibrations" or "chakra centers." He also devotes an entire chapter to "Meditation and Growth," giving the implicit message that if marijuana smokers went about their business correctly, they should be meditating, seeking Jungian individuation, and having various parapsychological experiences. It is surely the case that many of Tart's subjects at least entertained alternative religious and metaphysical beliefs. The question of causation is entirely unclear.

44. Novak, *High Culture*, p. 154.

45. See Bruce D. Johnson, *Marihuana Users and Drug Subcultures* (New York: John Wiley & Sons, 1973).

46. See Charles Tart's statistical tables on "Religious Affiliation" and "Effects of Background Factors on Spiritual Experiences," in *On Being Stoned*, pp. 43 and 221.

47. An extended discussion of the relationship between MDMA use and New Age spirituality can be found in Jerome Beck and Marsha Rosenbaum, *Pursuit of Ecstasy: The MDMA Experience* (Albany: State University of New York Press, 1994). Quotations come from p. 39.

48. J. Gordon Melton, *Encyclopedia of American Religions*, 3rd ed. (Detroit: Gale Research, 1988), entry number 1240.

49. See Melton, *Encyclopedia of American Religions*, 6th ed. (Detroit: Gale Research, 1999), entry number 1484. According to Melton, the Ethiopian Zion Coptic Church was founded in 1914 by Marcus Garvey and, after initial attempts to transplant it to the United States failed, was reintroduced to Americans in 1970. As Melton explained, "Church members believe in God who is experienced through the smoking of ganja, i.e., marijuana. Smoking marijuana is described as making a burnt sacrifice to the God within. The ceremonies for smoking the ganja utilize a specially made pipe. Coptics smoke ganja in such quantities that they hope it will reorganize their body chemistry around THC, the psycho-active ingredient in the plant, and they will thus survive the end of this world to live in God's new world. . . . Ceremonially smoking ganja is the major sacramental act of church members, and members quote the Bible (Genesis 1:29; Exodus 3:2–4; Psalm 104:14; and Hebrews 6:7) in support of their use of marijuana."

50. Leonard Barrett, *The Rastafarians* (Boston: Beacon Press, 1977), p. 104.

51. A discussion of Rastafarian rituals involving ganja can be found in Barry Chevannes, ed., *Rastafari and Other African-American Worldviews* (London: Macmillan, 1995), pp. 17–18.

52. Barrett, *The Rastafarians*, p. 129.

53. Ibid., p. 130.

54. H. Warner Allen, *The Romance of Wine* (New York: E. P. Dutton, 1932), p. 18.

55. See Victor Turner, *The Ritual Process* (Ithaca: Cornell University Press, 1977).

56. George Saintsbury, *Notes on a Cellar-Book* (New York: Macmillan, 1933), p. xvii.

57. Charles Senn Taylor, "Prolegomena to an Aesthetics of Wine," *Journal of Speculative Philosophy* 2 (1988): 132.

58. William James, *The Varieties of Religious Experience* (Cambridge: Harvard University Press, 1985), p. 307.

59. Ibid.

60. William James, "Subjective Effects of Nitrous Oxide," *Mind* 7 (1882): 186.

Chapter 6

1. Ronald Siegel, *Intoxication: Life in Pursuit of Artificial Paradise* (New York: E. P. Dutton, 1989), p. 10.

2. See Siegel's discussion of the evolutionary rationale for the human propensity to drug-induced intoxication, pp. 210ff.

3. Felicitas Goodman, *Ecstasy, Ritual, and Alternate Reality* (Bloomington: Indiana University Press, 1988).

4. William James, *The Varieties of Religious Experience* (Cambridge: Harvard University Press, 1985), p. 66.

5. Ibid.

6. See Victor Turner, *The Ritual Process* (Ithaca: Cornell University Press, 1969), and *Dramas, Fields, and Metaphors* (Ithaca: Cornell University Press, 1974).

7. Turner, *The Ritual Process*, p. 132.

8. Turner, *Dramas, Fields, and Metaphors*, p. 137.

9. Weston La Barre, *The Peyote Cult* (New York: Archon Books, 1975).

10. Timothy Miller, *Hippies and American Values* (Knoxville: University of Tennessee Press, 1991).

11. See I. M. Lewis's discussion of the "sociology of ecstasy" in his *Ecstatic Religion: An Anthropological Study of Spirit Possession and Shamanism* (Middlesex, England: Penguin Books, 1971). Lewis differentiates between the social functions of ecstasy in reinforcing a society's "official" morality and the uses of ecstasy for indirect protest by alleging supernatural authority for variant moral outlooks.

12. Turner, *The Ritual Process*, p. 97.

13. Ronald Shor, "Hypnosis and the Concept of the Generalized Reality-Orientation," in Charles Tart, ed., *Altered States of Consciousness* (New York: Wiley & Sons, 1969), p. 236.

14. See Roland Fischer's discussion of altered states of consciousness in terms of the ratio of sensory-intake versus sensory-processing activities in the brain. "A Cartography of the Ecstatic and Meditative States," *Science* 174 (November 26, 1971): 897–904. Although Fischer's model minimizes consideration of the cultural and ritual influences on the structuring of consciousness, it does provide a helpful framework for understanding how specific drugs might give rise to specific, state-bound modes of consciousness.

15. Shor, "Hypnosis and the Concept of the Generalized Reality-Orientation," p. 245.

16. See Charles Tart, *States of Consciousness* (New York: E. P. Dutton, 1975); and H. L. Barr and R. J. Langs, *LSD: Personality and Experience* (New York: Wiley & Sons, 1972).

17. Arthur J. Deikman, "Deautomatization and the Mystic Experience," *Psychiatry* 29 (1966): 324–338, reprinted in Tart, ed., *Altered States of Consciousness*, p. 43.

18. Ibid., p. 44.

19. Mircea Eliade, *Shamanism: Archaic Techniques of Ecstasy* (Princeton: Princeton University Press, 1972), p. 401.

20. R. C. Zaehner, *Mysticism: Sacred and Profane* (New York: Oxford University Press, 1961).

21. Bertrand Russell, "Critique of Mysticism," in *Reason and Responsibility* (Belmont, CA: Wadsworth, 1985), p. 88. The quotation was slightly altered to avoid use of gender-specific language.

22. Ibid.

23. James, *The Varieties of Religious Experience*, p. 21.

24. Lewis, *Ecstatic Religion*, p. 34.

25. Ibid., p. 49.

26. G. Reichel-Dolmatoff, *The Shaman and the Jaguar: A Study of Narcotic Drugs Among the Indians of Colombia* (Philadelphia: Temple University Press, 1975), p. 132.

27. Ibid., p. 202.

28. See the essays in Steven Katz, ed., *Mysticism and Philosophical Analysis* (New York: Oxford University Press, 1978); and Steven Katz, ed., *Mysticism and Religious Traditions* (New York: Oxford University Press, 1982). See also Wayne Proudfoot, *Religious Experience* (Berkeley: University of California Press, 1986).

29. Robert Gimello, "Mysticism in Its Contexts," in Katz, ed., *Mysticism and Religious Traditions*, p. 63.

30. Ibid., p. 62.

31. Steven Katz, "Language, Epistemology, and Mysticism," in Katz, ed., *Mysticism and Philosophical Analysis*, p. 59.

32. Ibid., p. 66.

33. The debate between advocates of the "social-contextualist" and "metaphysical" schools of thought can be seen in a lively exchange between Steven Katz and Huston Smith that appeared in the *Journal of the American Academy of Religion.* Smith, attempting to deflect criticism of his theory of mysticism and the perennial philosophy, directly engaged Katz's arguments in an essay titled "Is There a Peren-

nial Philosophy?" *Journal of the American Academy of Religion* 55 (Fall 1987): 553–566. Steven Katz issued a rejoinder titled "On Mysticism," *Journal of the American Academy of Religion* 56 (Winter 1979): 751–757. Jonathan Shear provides an excellent overview of both Smith's and Katz's positions as well as advances his own critique of these positions in his "On Mystical Experiences as Support for the Perennial Philosophy," *Journal of the American Academy of Religion* 62 (Summer 1994): 319–343.

34. Robert K. C. Forman, *The Innate Capacity: Mysticism, Psychology, and Philosophy* (New York: Oxford University Press, 1997), p. viii.

35. See the concluding portion of William James's discussion of mysticism in *The Varieties of Religious Experience*, pp. 335–339.

36. Ibid., p. 55.

37. From R. Rutland, ed., *Papers of George Mason*, cited in Justice Sandra Day O'Connor's dissenting opinion in *City of Boerne v. Flores*, reprinted in *United States Law Week* 65 (June 24, 1997): 4625.

38. From G. Hunt, "James Madison and Religious Liberty," cited in Justice Sandra Day O'Connor's dissenting opinion in *City of Boerne v. Flores*, ibid., p. 4626.

39. See the section of the federal code dealing with "Drugs and Controlled Substances," *25 Am Jur 2d*. Section 171 specifically deals with court interpretations of government authority to regulate drugs, even when they are used for religious purposes.

40. See the lengthier discussion of the temperance and prohibition movements in my *Religion and Wine* (Knoxville: University of Tennessee Press, 1996); J. C. Furnas, *The Life and Times of the Late Demon Rum* (New York: Capricorn Books, 1973); and W. J. Rorabaugh, *The Alcoholic Republic* (New York: Oxford University Press, 1979).

41. See the discussion of the larger social conflicts underlying Prohibition in Norman Clark, *The Dry Years: Prohibition and Social Change in Washington* (Seattle: University of Washington Press, 1965).

42. A discussion of the Progressive Movement and its link to Prohibition can be found in James H. Timberlake, *Prohibition and the Progressive Movement, 1900–1920* (Cambridge: Harvard University Press, 1966).

43. Charles Welch, quoted in William Chazanof, *Welch's Grape Juice* (Syracuse: Syracuse University Press, 1977), p. 1.

44. Quoted in Ruth Teiser and Catherine Harroun, "Volstead Act, Rebirth, and Boom," in Doris Muscatine, Maynard Amerine, and Bob Thompson, eds., *The University of California/Sotheby Book of California Wine* (Berkeley: University of California Press, 1984), p. 54.

45. See the federal statutes on Public Health and Welfare, 42 U.S.C.S. Sec, 1996, N. 1 (1997).

46. A helpful review of the *Smith* case can be found in Jesse H. Chopper's "The Rise and Decline of the Constitutional Protection of Religious Liberty," 70 *Nebraska Law Review* 651 (1991).

47. *Employment Division, Department of Human Resources of Oregon et al. v. Smith et al.* 494 U.S. 879.

48. Ibid., p. 885. Quotation does not include quotation marks from citation of previous courts' rulings.

49. Ibid., p. 888.

50. Ibid., p. 916.

51. Ibid., p. 909.

52. The provisions of the Religious Freedom Restoration Act are succinctly summarized in the opening sections of the report on *City of Boerne v. P. F. Flores, Archbishop of San Antonio,* 65 U.S.L.W. 4597 (U.S. June 24, 1997).

53. The text of opinions rendered in *Boerne v. Flores* can be found in *United States Law Week,* ibid.

54. Ibid., p. 4619.

55. Ibid., p. 4628.

56. James, *Varieties of Religious Experience,* p. 307.

57. Huston Smith, "Do Drugs Have Religious Import?" *Journal of Philosophy* 61 (October 1964): 530.

58. Paul Tillich, quoted in Smith, "Do Drugs Have Religious Import?" p. 530.

59. Smith, "Do Drugs Have Religious Import?" p. 628.

60. William James, unsigned review article, *Atlantic Monthly* 34 (November 1874), p. 628.

61. Goodman, *Ecstasy, Ritual, and Alternate Reality,* p. 41.

BIBLIOGRAPHY

General

Bourguignon, Erika, ed., *Religion, Altered States of Consciousness, and Social Change* (Columbus: Ohio State University Press, 1973).

De Ropp, Robert S., "Psychedelic Drugs" in Mircea Eliade, ed., *The Encyclopedia of Religion* (New York: Collier Macmillan, 1987).

Dobkin de Rios, Marlene, *Hallucinogens: Cross-Cultural Perspectives* (Albuquerque: University of New Mexico Press, 1984).

Eliade, Mircea, *Shamanism: Archaic Techniques of Ecstasy* (Princeton: Princeton University Press, 1972).

Furst, Peter, ed., *The Flesh of the Gods: The Ritual Use of Hallucinogens* (New York: Praeger, 1972).

Goodman, Felicitas, *Ecstasy, Ritual, and Alternate Reality* (Bloomington: Indiana University Press, 1988).

Kiev, Ari, ed., *Magic, Faith, and Healing* (New York: Free Press, 1964).

La Barre, Weston, "Hallucinogens and the Shamanic Origins of Religion" in Peter Furst, ed., *The Flesh of the Gods.*

Lewis, I. M., *Ecstatic Religion* (Middlesex, England: Penguin Press, 1971).

Mandell, Arnold J., "The Neurochemistry of Religious Insight and Ecstasy," in Kathleen Berrin, ed., *Art of the Huichol Indians* (New York: Abrams, 1979).

Prince, Raymond, ed., *Trance and Possession States* (Montreal: R. M. Bucke Memorial Society, 1968).

Schultes, Richard E, and Albert Hofmann, *Plants of the Gods: Origins of Hallucinogenic Use* (New York: McGraw-Hill, 1979).

Siegel, Ronald K., *Intoxication: Life in Pursuit of Artificial Paradise* (New York: E. P. Dutton, 1989).

Smith, Huston. "Do Drugs Have Religious Import?" *Journal of Philosophy* 61 (October 1964): 517–530.

Tart, Charles, *States of Consciousness* (New York: E. P. Dutton, 1975).

Tart, Charles, ed., *Altered States of Consciousness* (New York: John Wiley and Sons, 1969).

Zaehner, R. C., *Mysticism: Sacred and Profane* (New York: Oxford University Press, 1961).

Aberle, David, and Omer Stewart, *Navaho and Ute Peyotism* (Boulder: University of Colorado Press, 1957).

Aberle, David, and Omer Stewart, *Peyotism in the West* (Salt Lake City: University of Utah Press, 1984).

Berrin, Kathleen, *Art of the Huichol Indians* (New York: Abrams, 1979).

Brown, Joseph Epes, ed., *The Sacred Pipe: Black Elk's Account of the Seven Rites of the Oglala Sioux* (Baltimore: Penguin Books, 1971).

Harner, Michael J., ed., *Hallucinogens and Shamanism* (New York: Oxford University Press, 1973).

Howard, James, "The Mescal Bean Cult of the Central and Southern Plains," *American Anthropologist* 59 (1957): 75–87.

Hultkrantz, Ake, *The Religions of the American Indians* (Berkeley: University of California Press, 1967).

Hultkrantz, Ake, "The Shaman and the Medicine-Man," *Social Science and Medicine* 20 (1985): 511–515.

La Barre, Weston, "Native American Beers," *American Anthropologist* 40 (1938): 224–234.

La Barre, Weston, "The Narcotic Complex of the New World," *Diogenes* 48 (1964): 125–138.

La Barre, Weston, *The Peyote Cult* (New York: Anchor Books, 1975).

Linton, Ralph, *Use of Tobacco Among North American Indians* (Chicago: Field Museum of Natural History, 1924).

Meyerhoff, Barbara, *Peyote Hunt: The Sacred Journey of the Huichol Indians* (Ithaca: Cornell University Press, 1974).

Mortimer, W. Golden, *Peru: History of Coca—"The Divine Plant" of the Incas* (New York: J. H. Vail, 1901).

Park, Willard, *Shamanism in Western North America* (Evanston, IL: Northwestern University, 1938).

Powers, William K., *Yuwipi: Vision and Experience in Oglala Ritual* (Lincoln: University of Nebraska Press, 1982).

Radin, Paul, *The Winnebago Tribe* (Lincoln: University of Nebraska Press, 1970).

Reichel-Dolmatoff, G., *The Shaman and the Jaguar: A Study of Narcotic Drugs Among the Indians of Colombia* (Philadelphia: Temple University Press, 1975).

Robicsek, Francis, *The Smoking Gods: Tobacco in Mayan Art, History, and Religion* (Norman: University of Oklahoma Press, 1978).

Schaefer, Stacy B., and Peter T. Furst, eds., *People of the Peyote* (Albuquerque: University of New Mexico Press, 1996).

Schleiffer, Hedwig, ed., *Sacred Narcotic Plants of the New World Indians* (New York: Hafner Press, 1973).

Schultes, Richard E., "An Overview of Hallucinogens in the Western Hemisphere," in Peter Furst, ed., *Flesh of the Gods* (New York: Praeger, 1972).

Shonle, Ruth, "Peyote: The Giver of Visions," *American Anthropologist* 27 (1925): 53–75.

Slotkin, J. S., *The Peyote Religion: A Study in Indian-White Relations* (Glencoe, IL: Free Press, 1956).

Stewart, Omer, *Peyote Religion: A History* (Norman: University of Oklahoma Press, 1987).

Wilbert, Johannes, *Tobacco and Shamanism in South America* (New Haven: Yale University Press, 1983).

Psychedelics and Metaphysical Illumination

Beck, Jerome, and Marsha Rosenbaum, *Pursuit of Ecstasy: The MDMA Experience* (Albany: State University of New York Press, 1994).

Cohen, Sidney, *The Beyond Within: The LSD Story* (New York: Atheneum, 1965).

Dunlap, Jane, *Exploring Inner Space: Personal Experiences Under LSD-25* (New York: Harcourt, Brace, and World, 1961).

Grof, Stanislav, *Realms of the Human Unconscious: Observations from LSD Research* (New York: Viking Press, 1975).

Grof, Stanislav, *Beyond the Brain* (Albany: State University of New York Press, 1985).

Grof, Stanislav, and Joan Halifax, *The Human Encounter with Death* (New York: E. P. Dutton, 1978).

Hofmann, Albert, *LSD: My Problem Child* (New York: McGraw-Hill, 1980).

Huxley, Aldous, *The Doors of Perception* (San Francisco: Harper and Row, 1954).

James, William, "Subjective Effects of Nitrous Oxide," *Mind* 7 (1882): 186–208.

Katz, Martin, and Irene Waskow, "Characterizing the Psychological State Produced by LSD," *Journal of Abnormal Psychology* 73 (1963): 460–469.

Leary, Timothy, "The Religious Experience: Its Production and Interpretation," *Psychedelic Review* 1 (1964): 324–346.

Leary, Timothy, *High Priest* (New York: World Publishing, 1968).

Leary, Timothy, Ralph Metzner, and Richard Alpert, *The Psychedelic Experience: A Manual Based on the Tibetan Book of the Dead* (New York: Citadel Press, 1964).

Masters, R. E. L., and Jean Houston, *The Varieties of Psychedelic Experience* (New York: Holt, Rinehart and Winston, 1966).

Perry, Charles, *The Haight-Ashbury: A History* (New York: Random House, 1984).

Smith, Huston, "Empirical Metaphysics," in Ralph Metzner, ed., *The Ecstatic Adventure* (New York: Macmillan, 1968).

Smith, Huston, *Forgotten Truth: The Common Vision of the World's Religions.* Appendix: "The Psychedelic Evidence" (San Francisco: HarperSanFrancisco, 1992).

Solomon, David, ed., *LSD: The Consciousness Expanding Drug* (New York: G. P. Putnam's Sons, 1964).

Stevens, Jay, *Storming Heaven: LSD and the American Dream* (New York: Harper and Row, 1988).

Watts, Alan, *The Joyous Cosmology* (New York: Vintage Books, 1965).

Wine and the Varieties of American Religious Life

Adams, Leon, *The Wines of America* (New York: McGraw-Hill Book Co., 1973).

Fuller, Robert, "Wine, Symbolic Boundary Setting, and American Religious Communities," *Journal of the American Academy of Religion* 63 (Fall 1995): 497–517.

Fuller, Robert, *Religion and Wine: A Cultural History of Wine Drinking in the United States* (Knoxville: University of Tennessee Press, 1996).

Heath, Dwight, "Anthropological Perspectives on Alcohol: A Historical Review," in Michael Everett, Jack Waddell, and Dwight Heath, eds., *Cross-Cultural Approaches to the Study of Alcohol* (The Hague: Mouton Publishers, 1976).

Hyams, Edward, *Dionysus: A Social History of the Wine Vine* (New York: Macmillan, 1965).

Lender, Mark, and James Martin, *Drinking in America* (New York: Free Press, 1982).

Muscatine, Doris, Maynard Amerine, and Bob Thompson, eds., *The University of California/Sotheby Book of California Wine* (Berkeley: University of California Press/Sotheby, 1984).

Pinney, Thomas, *A History of Wine in America* (Berkeley: University of California Press, 1989).

Pittman, David, and Charles Snyder, eds., *Society, Culture, and Drinking Patterns* (New York: John Wiley and Sons, 1962).

Rorabaugh, W. J., *The Alcoholic Republic* (New York: Oxford University Press, 1979).

Younger, William, *Gods, Men, and Wine* (Cleveland: World Publishing, 1966).

Drugs, Aesthetics, and Unchurched Spirituality

Andrews, George, and Simon Vinkenoog, eds., *The Book of Grass* (New York: Grove Press, 1967).

Braun, Stephen, *Buzz: The Science and Lore of Alcohol and Coffee* (New York: Oxford University Press, 1996).

Chevannes, Barry, ed., *Rastafari and Other African-American Worldviews* (London: Macmillan, 1995).

Fuller, Robert, "Religion and Ritual in American Wine Culture," *Journal of American Culture* (Spring 1993): 39–46.

Joel, David, and Karl Schapira, *The Book of Coffee and Tea* (New York: St. Martin's Griffin, 1975).

Johnson, Bruce, *Marijuana Users and Drug Subcultures* (New York: John Wiley & Sons, 1973).

Lincoln, Bruce, "Beverages," in Mircea Eliade, ed., *Encyclopedia of Religion*, vol. 2: 119–123.

Miller, Timothy, *The Hippies and American Values* (Knoxville: University of Tennessee Press, 1991).

Novak, William, *High Culture: Marijuana in the Lives of Americans* (New York: Alfred A. Knopf, 1980).

Oldenburg, Ray, *The Great Good Place: cafes, coffee shops, community centers, beauty parlors, general stores, bars, hangouts and how they get you through the day* (New York: Paragon Books, 1989).

Roden, Claudia, *Coffee: A Connoisseur's Companion* (New York: Random House, 1994).

Snyder, Solomon, *Uses of Marijuana* (New York: Oxford University Press, 1971).

Tart, Charles, *On Being Stoned: A Psychological Study of Marijuana Intoxication* (Palo Alto: Science and Behavior Books, 1971).

Taylor, Charles Senn, "Prolegomena to an Aesthetics of Wine," *Journal of Speculative Philosophy* 2 (1988): 120–139.

Index

Mije people (Mexico)
mushrooms used by, 31
Milk, 127
Millbrook estate (New York), 71
G. Gordon Liddy's raid on, 70
Leary's work at, 68–69
Miller, Timothy, 82, 162
Mind/body connection
mystery of, 165
Mind-manifesting drugs, 15, 72, 78. *See also*
Psychedelic drugs
and metaphysical illumination, 85
Mission Trail (California)
wine and Catholic priests along, 96
Mitchell, S. Weir, 199n47
Mixtecs
puffballs used by, 5
Mogar, Robert, 72
Mohammed, 72
Morellet, Abbé
Benjamin Franklin's letter on wine to,
205n4
Mormons
wine used by, 108–114, 120, 121, 156, 163,
171, 207n37
Morphine, 53
Mountain Cahuilla (California)
datura used by, 33
Mourning
and visions, 41
Muir, John, 71
Mushrooms, 27, 160, 191
ceremonial use of, 31
psilocybin and psilocin in, 3
sacred, 6
Music, 9
and dropping out, 79
in mescal rituals, 34
Muslims
and coffee, 129–130
and hashish, 140
Myerhoff, Barbara, 40
Mysticism
and constructivism, 173–174
and nature religion, 14
and receptivity, 15
religious authority challenged by, 13
shortcomings of drug-induced, 168
William James on, 56

Naegle, John, 112
Nagasawa, Kanaye, 116
"Narcotic complex"
New World, 25–38
Native American Church
courts and ritual use of peyote, 185,
187
incorporation of, 45
legal protection for peyote ritual of, 193
and peyotism, 30, 38–48, 191, 192

Native American Church of North America, 46
Native American Church of the United States,
45–46
Native American heritage, 17–49
and New World "narcotic complex," 25–38
peyotism and Native American Church,
38–48
pursuit of ecstasy in American Indian
religion, 19–25
Native American religions
difficulties in generalizing about, 19–20
psychoactive plant use in, 4
Native Americans
belief in supernatural power by, 20
and divination, 28, 32
and drug-induced ecstasy, 174
drugs, spiritual power and, 156
drugs and vision quests of, 9
hallucinogenic substances used by, 5–6
healing practices of, 23–24, 28, 32–33, 34,
43
and legal protection of peyote rituals, ix,
184–188
narcotic complex of, 26–27
peyote use by, 10
spirituality of, 15
tobacco used by, viii, 35–38, 160
vision quests by, 11, 21–22, 32, 36, 41
Natural order
God perceived in, 12–16
Nature religion, 12–16, 71, 139, 143, 168, 191
Navajo
datura used by, 33
Near-death experiences, 125
Nebraska
peyotism among Plains Indians of, 41
"Nectars of the gods," 118–119, 127
Neo-American Church, 81
Neurotransmitters, 165, 167
effect of caffeine on, 135
New Age religions, 117
Newland, Constance, 65
New Mexico
peyote use by tribes in, 41
"New Romanticism," 77, 85
New World "narcotic complex," 25–38
New York
coffee drinking in, 132
illicit drug use in, 53
Nicotiana attenuata, 35
Nicotiana rustica, 35
Nicotine, viii
effect of, on nervous system, 167
in native tobaccos, 35
in tobacco, 180
Nitrous oxide, 9, 155
William James's experiences with, 54–55,
57, 86, 192
Noah (Old Testament)
and wine, 92